VOLUNTARY SECTOR IN TRANSITION

Hard times or new opportunities?

Linda Milbourne

First published in Great Britain in 2013 by

Policy Press
University of Bristol
6th Floor
Howard House
Queen's Avenue
Bristol BS8 1SD
UK
t: +44 (0)117 331 4054
f: +44 (0)117 331 4093
tpp-info@bristol.ac.uk
www.policypress.co.uk

North America office:
Policy Press
c/o The University of Chicago Press
1427 East 60th Street
Chicago, IL 60637, USA
t: +1 773 702 7700
f: +1 773-702-9756
sales@press.uchicago.edu
www.press.uchicago.edu

British Library Cataloguing in Publication Data
A catalogue record for this book is available from the British Library.

Library of Congress Cataloging-in-Publication Data
A catalog record for this book has been requested.

ISBN 978 1 84742 723 6 hardcover

Cover design by Policy Press.
Front cover: image kindly supplied by istock.
Printed and bound in Great Britain by TJ International,
Padstow.
Policy Press uses environmentally responsible print partners.

Contents

About the author

Linda Milbourne is a senior lecturer and course director for voluntary, community and youth studies in the School of Social Sciences at Birkbeck, University of London. She has undertaken research and teaching in higher education since 1998, focusing on social policy initiatives related to community-based work. Linda's research has included a variety of projects, spanning concerns in social policy, community and youth studies, management and education but she is particularly interested in the effects of a rapidly changing welfare and funding landscape on small community-based organisations and hard-to-reach groups. Cross-sector relationships, marketisation, accountability, local participation, trust and the tensions of translating policies into practice are key themes in recent research and writing. Among recent studies, Linda has contributed to research on the impacts of public funding cuts and on collaborations and communication between local government and voluntary agencies. She has a particular interest in organisations working with children and young people, and has written for policy, practice and academic audiences on youth policies and young people's disengagement from services. Linda has over 30 years of professional and practical experience in public and voluntary sector organisations, including as a college principal, voluntary sector trustee and active campaigner.

Acknowledgements

This book owes much to the encouragement of others. I would like to express particular thanks to Mike Cushman for intellectual advice and emotional encouragement and for his generous efforts in editing text, without which this book might never have been realised. My thanks also go to academic colleagues at Birkbeck – Ursula Murray, Jan Etienne and David Tross – for contributing to thinking and ideas around the book's themes over the course of its development. I would like to thank postgraduate students on the Voluntary and Community Studies programme at Birkbeck for their enthusiastic discussion of ideas during teaching sessions, which added to my reflections on earlier drafts of material for the book. I am also grateful to other colleagues who provided feedback on papers or presentations and helped to move my ideas forward, especially staff at the Institute for Voluntary Action Research, including Marilyn Taylor and Mike Aiken; and to Phil Hodkinson, Heather Hodkinson and Meg Maguire for invaluable advice on writing.

I am indebted to the young people, staff and management committee members from a wide range of voluntary and community organisations, whose willingness to participate in research made much of the material in this book possible. Their openness, cooperation and continued interest in the outcomes of the research gave me added encouragement to complete the book.

Preface

Much social policy research shares the problem of dating, and of mapping continuities and new directions across periods of time. Over the last quarter century, the voluntary sector in the United Kingdom (UK), along with similarly constructed organisations in other countries, has seen an intensification of changes, as the political ideology surrounding welfare services and their delivery has been transformed. While this book primarily addresses changes in the UK, themes from UK research resonate elsewhere. Similar trends observed in Australia, New Zealand and North America, and more recently, in parts of Europe, make it relevant for readers outside the UK. The concept of a UK voluntary sector has itself undergone fragmentation with the growth of devolved government in Scotland, Wales and Northern Ireland (Danson and Whittam, 2011); and in discussion of recent times, this book focuses mainly on empirical study of the English experience.

There are, of course, significant differences across different countries, not least in the language used to describe the voluntary, third or non-profit sector, and this preface offers a brief clarification for non-UK readers. The UK voluntary sector has had a particular historical set of relationships with the state, including that embedded in UK Charity Laws. This both enables and restricts the organisations entitled to be identified as 'charities' – that is, those registered with the Charity Commission. There are many voluntary and community-based organisations that despite broadly philanthropic aims are not included within this register because of size, turnover or primary, often political, purposes. Throughout the book, the traditional UK term 'voluntary sector' is used to encompass a wider range of organisations than charities only; and the first chapter addresses these questions of terms and definitions further. However, much of the quantitative data that informs research on the size and shape of the UK voluntary sector have been drawn from the charities register. Charities therefore remain an important category within the UK voluntary or non-profit sector since they are the organisations about which most is publicly known but this visibility often obscures the complexity and diversity of other parts of the sector.

This book concerns organisational and policy changes through the period of the New Labour government especially, during which time the voluntary or third sector was aligned with 'Third Way' policies and was given a significant role in tackling the perceived failures of both state and market to address social problems. In 2010, when the Conservative and Liberal Democrat coalition government came to power, there was a marked ideological shift: dependency on state welfare (big government) was blamed for many budget and social ills, and the responsibilisation of individuals, volunteers and civil society groups in *Big Society* were to provide solutions both to social problems and the need to reduce welfare spending. Although changes in government mark shifts in ideology, strategy and discourse, at the organisational level, ambiguity, tensions and contested territory often accompany such changes. These are the common experiences of everyday policy delivery, especially when the pace of change is rapid. Many of the issues currently posing dilemmas and hard times for the UK voluntary sector have wider relevance and also inhabit public agencies: issues around professional and organisational autonomy; values, meanings and approaches around delivering welfare; tensions around managerialism and performativity; competitive contracts; transforming the culture of services; welfare spending; and doing more for less.

These are some of the contexts that frame the research discussed in this book.

Finally, in organising material for this book, the aim has been to draw together interlinking themes that construct an overall narrative while also writing chapters that can stand alone to some degree, as many readers will select aspects that most interest them. For this reason, there is some commentary and explanation that spans chapters, such as in describing the settings for the research studies and reference to case study data that illustrate different themes.

Linda Milbourne
London, 2013

ONE

The voluntary sector: contested or strategic ground?

Why the voluntary sector?

This is a challenging time to write about the voluntary sector (VS) when discussions about public services and the role of civil society are constantly shifting narratives both in the UK and internationally. Cultures and arrangements surrounding the delivery of welfare services are rapidly changing, and while the public sphere has been pared back, voluntary sector organisations (VSOs), closely associated with ideas of civil society, have, until recently, been expanding. However, this too is changing.

Questions about the dismantling of public welfare services, the growing power of markets, the role of civil society and the location of the VS within these changes are central concerns for this book. It examines transitions in voluntary organisations against this context of sweeping changes to the political ideologies and arrangements underpinning social and welfare policy in the UK, in particular, exploring the extent to which voluntary organisations can remain autonomous *and* survive in the face of multiple challenges.

Over some 20 years, transformation in public services has generated a significant body of literature but, despite the visible impacts on other sectors, study of changes in the VS is still a limited, if recently growing, field of academic research. Yet during this period, the UK VS has grown rapidly, more than doubling its income, with the biggest growth in state-funded service delivery. These transitions, together with speculation about future roles for voluntary and community organisations, and their relationships with both the state and the private sector, have renewed public and academic interest in the VS, making the content of this book timely.

Over several decades, the legacy of New Public Management and associated arrangements for service delivery have pervaded political thought, alongside an economic approach privileging markets, outsourcing services to non-statutory providers and reducing public welfare spending. In parallel, the striking failures of the market together with disillusionment in state mechanisms to generate the promised solutions to social problems have produced new emphases on community and voluntary action. Civic engagement, active citizenship, community endeavour and mutualism have all been promoted as offering locally based solutions both to challenging social problems and financial deficits. The VS is identified as closely allied to these various agendas, and political discourse has seen a recent shift in emphasis from choice and agency in publicly funded services to wider collective responsibility for their delivery. As politicians work to displace dependence on big government by embedding a new hegemonic concept of *Big Society*, in which civil society – individuals and organisations – alongside private companies are charged with a major role, questions arise around the degree of continuity or change between New Labour and coalition government priorities. The extent to which both previous and current policy agendas are seen to extend the governable terrain of the state to previously more autonomous organisations is a significant question throughout this book. If voluntary organisations are to maintain independent goals and actions, rather than the inclusive and mimetic strategies of more recent years, greater resistance and new alliances may be needed.

Shifts in political ideology and associated policy and organisational arrangements, including the pervasive effects of competitive funding and managerial cultures on VS identities and activities, thus form the backcloth for a number of the concerns that this book explores. The empirical studies from which later chapters draw were conducted during the New Labour regime but as Chapter Two argues, the changing history of state–VS relationships over time offers salutary insights for the present and potentially the future.

In the contradictory worlds of decreased public service delivery, increased regulation, community empowerment and recent VS growth, questions of VS autonomy, differential power and trust between agencies and across sectors emerge as concerns. Equally, as public funding declines, organisational resilience and survival are growing anxieties and the emphasis on entrepreneurialism has spread. The chapters explore a range of examples from empirical research to consider VS changes, raising issues of relevance to wider policy debates. Among these, the book identifies a growing disparity in fortunes emerging between large and smaller organisations, with some of the smallest becoming casualties of economic recession. Chapters also question whether, as small community-based providers experience declining resources for services and growing constraints imposed by funders, some under-represented groups are becoming further marginalised. In examining patterns emerging from the empirical material, concepts of 'power' and 'resistance', 'trust', 'risk' and 'resilience', and theories concerned with governmentality and institutional change, are used to frame discussion of the policies, structures and agency at play in changes.

Reflecting earlier debates on the VS in Britain (Knight, 1993), a recurrent theme through the chapters is VS independence: the book questions whether a sector that Beveridge (1948) argued to retain alongside new state welfare services in the 1950s for its innovative influence, is becoming subsumed into state goals and purposes, losing its independence and distinctive approaches. This leads to a second question of whether resistance and alternatives to dominant models of organisation and arrangements are either feasible or desirable. The third question arising from recent changes is the extent to which future choices are limited to either separation from the state and its purposes or incorporation into the cultures and arrangements of dominant organisations and the market. The book therefore considers whether it is possible or relevant still to continue to define a distinctive VS (distinct, that is, from public or private sectors) in the dual contexts of its internal diversity and a multiplicity of new organisational forms, networks and partnerships.

In the UK, the current construction of the VS owes much to shifts in political ideology and social welfare policies over the last century. While it is tempting to conflate ideas of a voluntary (or third) sector with the New Labour government's Third Way ideology since 1997 – an alternative to state and market – the history of welfare relationships between state and VSs is a long one and its transitions are instructive for understanding both present and future directions. As political and financial changes affect public and voluntary organisations, understanding these transitions and the extent to which we can imagine the continuance of a distinct and autonomous VS and the role of ideology within this are therefore significant ongoing themes in the book. Do the characteristics attributed to distinguish a voluntary, non-profit or non-government sector in earlier debates (Billis, 1989; Knight, 1993; Salamon and Anheier, 1997) remain valid despite recent changes, and to what extent have VS independence and distinctive ideological foundations been compromised? In examining these questions, the book considers not only hard times and new opportunities but also the shifting shapes, values and feasibility of a distinct VS.

This chapter now considers the diverse meanings and forms of the UK VS before briefly discussing material in later chapters.

Contested meanings and terms: voluntary, non-profit, charity or third sector?

Referring to *a* or *the* VS presupposes a definable entity, which as research suggests, may be increasingly open to challenge, as boundaries between sectors become blurred, hybrid organisations become commonplace (Billis, 2010) and political ideology has now shifted to downplay VS distinctiveness. Despite growing international interest in non-profit, community-based and voluntary solutions, Salamon and Anheier (1997) have acknowledged the difficulties of defining a coherent voluntary or non-profit sector outside countries such as the UK and the United States. Definitions of the VS have frequently been based on a 'negative default notion' (Alcock, 2010a, p 7) – a sector situated outside the state or market. However, negatives (non-government, non-profit) offer limited insight into what the sector is or does, or how individuals or organisations within the sector understand their identity.

A number of commentators have preferred to develop definitions from examining the key nature of voluntary organisations and activities (Salamon and Anheier, 1997; Halfpenny and Reid, 2002); or their common or distinctive features (Billis, 1989; Perri 6, 1991; Knight, 1993; Kendall and Knapp, 1994). A distinguishing feature clearly concerns financial support: the proportion of income that comes from voluntary or philanthropic funding. For registered charity organisations[1] figures indicate that some 40% comes from membership or donated sources (NCVO, 2010), a proportion that is currently rising. Other significant features include self-governing structures and the use of volunteers, especially voluntary management boards. Independence from other bodies, however, has been a recurrent characteristic (Knight, 1993); and there is an ongoing debate about whether voluntary organisations can necessarily be associated with values linked to socially worthwhile purposes and the public good (Billis, 2010; Nevile, 2010). This latter discussion is significant in understanding organisational identities, meanings and purposes and is also reflected in the stakeholders to whom organisations regard themselves as accountable. However, the diversity of organisations – large and small, service providers, locality or interest-based, campaigning groups and members' clubs, to name just a few dimensions – demonstrates the divergence of purposes and accountabilities, challenging easy assumptions about organisational values.

As Knight's (1993) study concludes, voluntary agencies in the UK fulfil diverse functions, which range from intermediaries (support and infrastructure bodies); to broadly philanthropic service activities;

to self-help and mutual aid groups; to groups campaigning for social change; and to those creating new projects. Levels of organisational formality also vary widely, as also levels of independence from external constraints; use of volunteers; and association with different fields of service activity, as Salamon and Anheier's (1997) extensive typology of international organisations demonstrates.

The diversity of organisations, and associated terminology, together with the different perspectives and interests of researchers, policy makers and practitioners, have therefore resulted in little consensus in definitions or naming. In effect, characteristics previously attributed to a particular sector, be that voluntary, public or private, may be visible across organisations in each sector; and divergent characteristics within sectors, previously defined with greater assurance, are also emerging (Newman and Clarke, 2009). However, examining different kinds of cross-sector relationships, in particular those between the state and the VS, have been somewhat absent from these debates, yet have had a significant bearing on the evolution of organisational forms and features in the VS's past and present. These are discussed further in later chapters.

In introducing the ideas for this book, therefore, I acknowledge the difficulty of using terms around voluntary and community sectors, third and non-profit sectors (to name a few commonly used terms), since in summarising material it is all too easy to refer to a 'sector' as if it were homogeneous. Questions of terms and definitions are not new but a brief discussion here serves as a helpful starting point in clarifying the scope of the book.

Terminology

The question of defining and naming a sector is disputed ground, with debates swayed by cultural and political legacies, ideological differences and arising from different national contexts. However, terms signify meanings and Alcock (2010a) highlights the contested field, even in UK terminology, of 'voluntary', 'community' and 'third' sectors, which has been substantially influenced by policy trajectories. UK policy documents shifted terminology from VS and voluntary and community sectors during the 1990s, to use of third sector, paralleling New Labour's Third Way; while the terms non-governmental and non-profit organisations have more frequent use internationally. The New Labour government adopted the term 'third sector' during its latter years (OTS, 2007), to embrace a much wider range of organisations than previously assumed within the voluntary and community sector, including social enterprise and hybrid organisations, cooperatives, mutual aid and other civil society organisations. This parallels the European context where the latter organisations and groups have traditionally formed a key part of non-governmental associative life (Evers and Laville, 2004). The coalition government has adopted the wider term of 'civil society', rebranding the Office for the Third Sector as the Office for Civil Society, assigning it a key role in promoting strategies associated with the Big Society (Cabinet Office, 2010b).

The policy-driven dominance of terms in the UK has generated some resistance, and research has sought to be more specific in defining the kinds of organisations discussed. For example, the use of 'third sector' has been criticised for obscuring the distinctive contribution of small community groups (Richardson, 2008) and (in parallel with debates on the earlier use of 'third world') for its association with derogatory notions of third class and deficit (Chambers, 1997). This book mainly adopts the broad terms 'voluntary sector' (VS) and 'voluntary and community organisation' (VSO), which have widespread use in the UK. They also differentiate VSOs from other parts of wider civil society, increasingly under political discussion, in which individuals and informal groups may play a greater part. The scope of civil society associations and activities is significantly broader than the core of VSOs, although again definitions are contested (Evers, 2010), but this book largely excludes this additional ground of trades unions, cooperatives and mutual financial institutions, which historically have been a part of the UK VS.

The diversity of organisations across the VS makes adopting a broad term for discussion inevitable and the book also distinguishes between VSOs generally, and smaller community-based organisations on which much of the empirical data introduced in later chapters are based.

Diversity

In mapping the history of the VS, Taylor and Kendall (1996, p 58) discuss its 'breathtaking diversity', a diversity that is no less apparent in exploring recent trends. Divergent features and experiences linked to size, structural and legal definitions and trading activities highlight obvious differences; while association with different silos of welfare services (social care, health, housing, education) clearly affect activities and protocols in different ways. Voluntary organisations also diverge in their primary purposes: some provide services; some advocacy; some are self-help, membership or campaigning organisations; and others operate primarily as community anchors or infrastructure organisations. Others still are self-funding enterprises with a social purpose. Many fulfil more than one, even all of these functions, defeating attempts to typecast those with limited independent finance, as against others whose goals 'remain unfettered by contracting arrangements' (Knight, 1993, p 297). The differences identified here are broad but even where purposes appear similar, such as in advice agencies, underlying values and the characteristics of stakeholder communities or user groups may differ greatly.

Voluntary organisations delivering welfare services are frequently associated with specific welfare fields whose influence in terms of policy changes, professional practice and regulatory frameworks has often been as significant as systemic changes affecting the sector, such as outsourcing and increased regulation (Kendall, 2003). Over two decades, a tide of policies and interventions has permeated provision in different service fields, such as housing, education, healthcare and social care, affecting the nature of public service delivery, and these have been well documented elsewhere (Clarke et al, 2000a; Hills et al, 2007) but their subsequent effects on voluntary organisations, examined further in Chapter Two, have received more limited attention.

Arguably, large and merged VS agencies – for example, large housing associations or care home providers – have become distinct from other parts of the VS in values, culture and modes of operation (Mullins, 2010). Similarly, services focused on children, young people and vulnerable adults, where regulating risk has become an overriding concern, have allied some VS providers more closely with parallel public and private agencies. However, it is also common for community-based providers to work more holistically (Milbourne, 2005; Hoggett et al, 2009), that is, offering services that cross different welfare fields. Consequently, while discourse specific to discrete welfare fields has exerted powerful influence, many voluntary organisations have concurrently shared problems and experiences with groups in different service fields. These include: concerns about short-termism and organisational survival; funding bids and performance targets; loss of autonomy; and pressures to change modes of operation in relating to the state and the market (6 and Kendall, 1997; Harris, 2001a; Moxham and Boaden, 2007; Andersson, 2011).

Size, nevertheless, has become a growing factor in distinguishing organisations' experiences and is reflected across different welfare fields. Comparing registered UK charities in 2010, there were marked differences in income: of an estimated 171,000 registered VSOs, the largest 3% received over 75% of the income, while the 91,000 smallest (micro[2]) organisations received less than 1% of the total £35.5 billion income (NCVO, 2010). If all small and medium sized organisations are included in these figures, some 97% of organisations received less than 25% of the total income to the VS.

Alongside significant overall growth in the charity sector up to 2009, the gap between the incomes of the largest and smallest organisations also increased year on year from 1995 but this picture is complicated by the changing fates of the largest organisations, with formations, dissolutions and mergers shifting the winners and losers among them (Backus and Clifford, 2010). There is also a disparity in charitable donations, with both individual and corporate giving increasingly focused on the largest voluntary organisations (Breeze, 2010). Nevertheless, state-funded contracts have been mainly responsible for driving growth (Wilding, 2010), with the largest voluntary organisations depending significantly on this income. In a context where sources of donated income are now declining, and outsourcing via ever-larger contracts is growing, the largest organisations are likely to continue to benefit disproportionately from income to the sector and the accompanying financial viability. Clearly, as dependence on state funding is challenged after several years of reduced public spending, this picture may change, not least as the private sector gains a larger share of public service contracts; and more numerous social entrepreneurs evolve.

The growing disparity in experiences between large, often national, VSOs and smaller, community-based organisations emerges as a recurrent theme from research discussed in later chapters. Among a wider range of civil society organisations, including the hundreds of membership organisations, cooperatives, self-help and campaigning groups, a recent Carnegie Trust (2010) report also notes similar disparities, in particular, a weakening of smaller civil society groups compared to large ones.

The size and scope of the VS are also contested since these depend on definitions, inclusions and exclusions and limited available data. The registered charity sector, with some 170,000 organisations, makes up a small fraction of the estimated 900,000 civil society organisations (Carnegie Trust, 2010); and both these figures exclude thousands of informal or web-based groups, engaging in associative activities but often hidden 'under the radar' (Scott, 2009). While the VS in terms of registered charities and formal organisations grew markedly in terms of size and income over some 10 years, with recession, this began to reverse after 2008 (NCVO, 2010), there was also a decline in funding from donations and membership fees. The Charity Commission (Carr, 2009) shows the disappearance of some 15,000 organisations in 2009 against some 7,000 new or merged organisations established but the evidence emerging over 2010 and 2011 (NCIA, 2011) indicated far more casualties. The question of casualties and survivors is taken up in Chapter Seven.

Much of the publicly available data miss organisations and associative activities that fall outside the remit of the Register of Charities. There are therefore significant gaps in research and policy awareness around small and campaigning organisations (McCabe and Phillimore, 2009), and as the Community Sector Coalition (Scott, 2009) has emphasised, much information on the VS misses the volume and heterogeneous nature of under-the-radar activity, which different community infrastructure organisations estimate as some 600,000 or more organisations and groups. Also excluded from the data discussed above are organisations and societies that have played a historically significant role in the development of welfare, including mutual financial institutions, credit unions, trades unions, benevolent and friendly societies, cooperatives and universities, and a growing number of social enterprises emerging.

The current book concentrates on organisations that are a part of the registered charity sector but also includes a number of small community-based organisations that fall outside this public register. The wider reach of civil society gives rise to a much broader discussion around civicness and civility related to the development of active citizenship, which is largely beyond the scope of this book. Like Evers (2010), I am therefore challenging the necessary alignment of the VS with civil society, implicit in other literature and explicit in recent policy and political debate, which has tended to elide building a good or Big Society with the roles of voluntary organisations.

Shifting ideology and values

While the triad of state, market (for-profit sector) and civil society (inclusive of VSOs) provides a simple tool for distinguishing the different features, values and principles associated with organisations in each sector, most definitions acknowledge intersecting and porous boundaries (Billis and Harris, 1996; Billis, 2010). In these overlapping segments, organisational characteristics and values may well be influenced by the cultures and practices of more powerful sectors or agencies (Harris, M., 2010), creating challenges for organisational identity. Evers and Laville (2004) argue for differentiating the formally organised VS from other parts of civil society identified as more fluid and less open to such influence, and this mirrors Billis' (1989) distinction of organisational spheres (public, voluntary and private) from a fourth sphere focused on the personal world, or the informal groupings of civil society.

The VS can be regarded as distinct from the state by its independence; from the market by its non-profit principles; and from 'community' and informal spheres of civil society by its more formal organisation. Evers and Laville (2004), nevertheless, highlight fields of tension where the different sectors or spheres intersect, pointing to areas of potential inter-sectoral influence and hybridity in overlapping segments. However, typologies inevitably suggest ideal types whereas differences in features and values, for example, between a community-based organisation and an informal community group (more closely allied to the personal world) may be less clear. Additionally, these fields of tension reveal a complexity of cross-sector players involved, such as in partnership working, discussed further in Chapter Six. Similarly, as Billis (2010) argues, the multiple possibilities for influence and overlap between sectors both complicate relationships between organisational actors and impact on ideological and sector differences.

While acknowledging blurred boundaries, Kendall (2003) highlights the values embedded within organisational cultures as ways in which sectors have traditionally been distinguished, with the state associated with formality and regulation; the market with competition and entrepreneurship; and the VS with less formal arrangements, altruism and mutualism. The visible shift in language over a century from charities, to voluntary organisations, the voluntary *and* community sector and, more recently, the third sector, has solidified the idea, if not the reality, of a unified sector, effectively extending the scope of agencies included in the governable terrain of the state (Carmel and Harlock, 2008). The creation of the Office of the Third Sector in 2006 and its subsequent strategies and influential discourse illustrate this extension of influence, although 6 and Kendall's (1997) analysis of earlier government policies from the Wolfenden Report (Wolfenden, 1978) to the Deakin Report (Deakin, 1996) highlights ways in which political ideology has been instrumental in shaping the VS over time. However, the more recent conceptual construction of a third sector including organisations, such as social enterprises, mutuals and cooperatives, not previously assumed within concepts of the VS had a clear impact on the profile and identities of voluntary organisations within public policy during the New Labour regime (OTS, 2007). Now that political labelling has changed again, encompassing the wider sphere of civil society and individual actions (OCS, 2010), the domain of influence for government-driven ideology and policy is perceptibly extended; but paradoxically, the message is about reduced government influence and local devolution of power (McCall, 2011).

This discussion implies not only a convergence of values within the organised VS, as promoted by New Labour over the last decade, but also the promotion of a new hegemonic discourse around voluntary action and civil engagement, intended to make inroads into personal as well as organisational worlds. Implying a convergence of values among voluntary organisations and civil society actors in assuming greater local responsibility for service deficits, however, masks enormous diversity and conflicts of interest; and recent studies suggest that encroachment into the traditional terrain of community organising and its autonomous purposes may be generating resistance (Benson, 2010). While Alcock (2010a, p 15) identifies the strategic importance of a VS alliance and the 'shared benefits to be accrued from a unified voluntary sector policy discourse' in terms of continued funding and investment, following the rebranded community discourse of the coalition government, VS infrastructure and the sector's privileged position in service delivery have been dismantled, deconstructing and fragmenting the concept of a cohesive VS. Voluntary sector importance was initially assured (Maude, 2010) but the reality of severe budget reductions affecting all kinds of organisations suggests that the promised interim assistance is 'too little and too late' (Slocock, 2012, p 70).

In both the New Labour and coalition government regimes, hegemony and consensual ideology have played a strong part in discourse and strategic directions. Kendall (2010) argues that pressures towards homogeneity, exacerbated by growth and developments, have generated a lack of clarity around VS values and ideology for some time, creating a decontested policy space, partly driven by funding needs and linked to powerful organisational cultures. Larger organisations that have targeted growth as a primary objective may exhibit ambiguity in values, with a drift away from previously more clearly defined goals (Carnegie Trust, 2010). This reflects ongoing debates around the potential for mission drift, as compelling pressures from more powerful sectors or agencies come into play (Billis and Harris, 1996; Cairns et al, 2006; Macmillan, 2010). However, where consequent tensions and conflict are suppressed and ignored, consensus is often coerced and necessarily fragile, potentially resulting in splits and factional identities (Hoggett, 2004). As greater pressures are exerted on the spaces that individuals and organisations previously identified as independent of the state, a significant question for later chapters is therefore the kind of modification, resistance and challenges to new pressures that may emerge, and the potential for recreating contested policy spaces.

The increased separation of interests between smaller and larger VS organisations highlights one aspect of this contested space, with susceptibility to different ideological pressures creating probable ground for compliance or resistance. The ability to influence policy is the overriding goal for campaigning organisations, and while many larger organisations have the resources to claim a place at the policy table and are more likely to share organisational discourse and cultures (and debate alternatives) in ways more comfortable for policy makers and funders, this place may instead have been used for competitive advantage for service growth (Pfeffer, 2003). In any case, size and available resources have effectively produced a disparity of experience, leading to insiders and outsiders within the VS: those few able to influence policy debates and service criteria and the many others who experience marginalisation (Milbourne, 2009a). While being an insider is seductive, it can also lead to loss of independence, as first activities and gradually values and identities are compromised. Remaining an outsider, as subsequent chapters illustrate, may enable greater freedoms but also threaten institutional survival.

While the discussion of size argues ideological differences resulting from growth and the gradual incursion of a range of external cultures and practices – an outcome of institutional isomorphism (DiMaggio and Powell, 1983) – other research describes growing differences in the sector as driven by underlying or pre-existing ideology. In a recent study of UK charity shops, Yong et al (2010) suggest that non-profits are split between those that strongly adhere to ideas of philanthropic missions and cooperative, social and ethical values, and those identified as untrustworthy partners by the first group, associated with opportunistic behaviours and commercially led practices. Despite parallel needs to compete for trade and funding, and therefore to engage in entrepreneurial activities, the authors argue that among the first group of non-profits, the importance of avoiding ruthless, corporate practices and of maintaining social legitimacy and ethical standards is fundamental in underpinning organisational meanings. Thus, there is a key distinction here between a socially legitimate VS, engaged in trading for financial survival, and organisations that are seen to have sold their souls to market practices.

In the example above, altruism and philanthropy are distinguished from opportunism and heartless entrepreneurialism. Kendall (2010), however, differentiates a third group of VSOs committed to social change, identifying three broad ideological factions linked to different policy strands: entrepreneurial; community oriented; and those identified with democratic renewal, empowerment and activist agendas. The first group describes organisations embracing dominant, market-driven ideology, concerned with innovation and with demonstrating worth as service providers. The second comprises groups engaged in community development and civil renewal activities, linked to policy discourse around social inclusion and community cohesion, allied to a vision based on consensus and social and social order. The third includes groups committed to social and collective actions associated with change, and although they can be linked to policies promoting democratic renewal, active engagement and local empowerment, crucially their vision acknowledges conflict and competing interests.

In recent Big Society strategies, the second and third groups are hardly distinguished, and locally designed service provision is somewhat elided with voluntary action and local enterprise. This fusion of purposes and values is significant, as the third category above appears distinct in advocating autonomous actions, promoting alternatives rather than accommodating values, principles and arrangements defined within a mainstream consensus. Thus, recent attempts to extend the reach of government strategies to wider civil society can be construed as curbing VS autonomy, with locally designed services and community organisers supported only in so far as they appear to accede to state projects. The extent to which actions are circumscribed by values and arrangements promoted through state, market or other dominant agencies, therefore affects VS autonomy and its potential for resisting hegemonic approaches.

As several authors argue (Evers and Laville, 2004; Paton, 2009; Alcock and Kendall, 2011), demarcations of sectors and organisations, and associated identities and values, are inevitably products of different layers of policy, of political and historical legacies and of social and academic constructs. Activities and values change over time and in line with contemporary concerns. For example, associative forms of mutual aid, healthcare and financial support needed in the late 19th century were superseded by the growth of public services, and subsequently, as awareness of welfare failures and increased poverty grew, by diverse campaigning and community development groups in the late 1960s. Similarly, recognition of state and market failures through the late 20th century saw the growth of social exclusion and community regeneration projects in the early 21st century, while recent economic recession has led to a resurgence of proposals for community-led, self-help and volunteer projects in political discourse. However, the nature of change is inevitably contested since historical, cultural and ideological legacies generate resistance to new, externally driven, definitions, and social change movements may also exploit the openings within shifting spaces, while also being subject to their influence and constraints.

Alcock's (2010a) argument that one reason for limited resistance to policies seeking to homogenise the voluntary and community sector is the strategic and financial advantage in compliance with the appearance of unity, appears no longer warranted when sector resources are being severely reduced and it has lost its privileged place in public policy and service delivery. While Carmel and Harlock (2008) have argued that the apparently consensual nature of recent developments and the mainstreaming of the VS have largely been driven by politicians and policy makers whose purposes it serves, this book challenges the argument that this is the only terrain. It also explores the spaces beyond obvious sites for policy intervention and control, spaces where alternatives and different approaches have been constructed and sustained. While pervasive ideologies and arrangements steer the actions and choices of apparently autonomous organisations and individuals into serving the interests of powerful institutions (Rose, 1999), there are also examples of processes being disrupted and resisted by 'subversive citizens', changing the intended shape of services and outcomes (Barnes and Prior, 2009). As Lever (2011) argues, study of governmentality offers important insights into how community projects are driven and moulded by powerful political forces (Foucault, 1977) but its application often fails to take account of the individuals and organisations involved, through whose agency unpredictable outcomes and resistances also emerge.

This need to explore below the surface (Stacey and Griffin, 2005) at the micro level alongside broad trends to make sense of VS difference and divisions emphasises the case for including 'small stories' and illustrative examples from empirical research, through which to examine diverse values, approaches and identities among VSOs. Through the data introduced in later chapters, this book also addresses another absence from much research on the VS: the limited voice given to practitioners, service users and community stakeholders – those engaged in compliance, compromise and resistance, and voluntary action of different kinds.

Framing the discussion

This chapter has discussed the diversity of features in the VS and the contested nature of definitions, seeking to locate recent changes in the context of the changing policy and political environment. In the light of the limits of VS research, clarifying some of this ground is an important starting point.

The book contains eight further chapters, representing distinct but connected themes and stories drawn from research exploring changes in the VS. The chapters are framed by, and also develop, debates drawn from contemporary social and organisational theory. Some of these, for example, modernisation and public service re-engineering, localism, collaboration and governance, have been discussed more widely (Newman, 2000; Huxham and Vangen, 2004; Ellison and Ellison, 2006; Davies, 2011) but with limited application to VSOs. Initially, Chapter Two draws on these debates to consider the changing face of UK welfare over several decades, from a VS perspective. It identifies continuities and changes in recent government regimes and their effects on the VS, discussing the benefits and drawbacks of different transitions. The chapter also introduces theoretical explanations for ways in which VS changes have occurred and which later chapters build on through discussion of the empirical data. This chapter's historical perspective places recent changes in state–VS relationships in the context of the sector's adaption to different roles over time, also comparing these with recent trends identified internationally.

An important concern of this book has been finding a balance between academic research and the everyday concerns of VS actors in experiencing and dealing with changes. Policy changes often lead to unanticipated consequences even when local actors do not set out to be subversive (Barnes and Prior, 2009); and one of the tasks for researchers is to recover the standpoints of those who enact, experience and confront policy and interrogate the reasons for their perspectives. Changes in the policy and organisational environment have to be understood as part of a complex web of sometimes contradictory directions, where unpredictable social interactions can affect their interpretation and outcomes (Ball, 1997). In contrast to the rhetoric of policy documents, everyday policy delivery is not systematic but characterised by 'tinkering' and 'bricolage' (Ciborra, 2002, p 47). Policies present problems that have to be resolved in context but as new political ideologies shift the terrain of understanding, meanings become contested and actions sometimes constrained, increasing locally experienced dilemmas. As Ball (1997, p 270) points out, 'the range of options may be narrowed ... or particular goals or outcomes set', but this still demands a response of actors within the everyday context, which involves choices and 'creative social action of some kind'. This action may involve compliance, adaption, compromise or resistance or a combination of these in different circumstances. It is this juxtaposition of insights into everyday dilemmas and actions set against changing policy and political contexts that the book seeks to examine.

The book overall draws on local area-based studies and individual organisational cases from several urban areas to examine local experiences of a VS in transition and the everyday responses and actions adopted in these changing policy spaces. Chapter Three describes the different studies that provide examples and cases for subsequent chapters, explaining the methodological approach and some difficulties of researching the VS. While the focus is on smaller, community-based organisations, mainly situated in socioeconomically deprived urban localities in England, the inclusion of data from a few larger regional and nationally based agencies illustrates different perspectives. One study, for example, involves several small VSOs providing education services to young people out of school, which has been ongoing research since 1999 and has involved tracking the effects of different policy changes on their organisational environments, user groups and activities, up to the present. Chapter Three also describes several other studies in other areas, whose data inform the themes of later chapters.

The timing for writing this book means that the fieldwork for the empirical studies was mainly completed during the New Labour administration but chapters reflect on continuities under the coalition government, and include some more recent examples. Most examples concern organisations that both provide a service and also support some kind of advocacy role; and the extent to which the latter role has been sustained is the subject of Chapter Eight. Many examples involve services for children and young people, and this has allowed for comparison across geographic areas. It has also prompted some reflection on the numbers of VSOs that have developed in this field and their prospects for survival.

The chapters that follow draw on and develop different theoretical ideas to examine the empirical cases. Debates about the changing nature of society and the public sphere (Beck, 1992; Newman and Clarke, 2009) offer insights into shifts in values and dominant modes of organisational operation in all sectors, with implications for service delivery, for relationships with stakeholders and for professional and voluntary roles. In a world detached from traditional roles and expectations, consumer choice, short-term enterprise and changing career profiles sit unhappily with the value-driven work narratives and longer-term social commitment, often attributed to work and workers in VS agencies (Hoggett et al, 2009). Small voluntary agencies often construct strong communities of practice and a strong ethos of belonging for user groups who may experience marginalisation elsewhere (Milbourne, 2005). These may well be jeopardised with growing pressures to compete for funds and to adopt professionalised and managerial practices.

Chapters Four to Eight consider the implications of different aspects of this changing social and organisational environment for the VS, for organisational identities and for practitioners and users, questioning the extent to which autonomous spaces are being constricted. Chapter Four focuses on the dilemmas posed by competition and the market-driven culture that has gradually invaded VS service provision since the initial outsourcing of public services from the early 1990s. While the stated aims of more recent commissioning and procurement include the creation of better and more responsive, local services, this chapter questions whether market-driven arrangements and increasingly large contracts are achieving or can achieve these proposed outcomes. Are they instead creating a shadow state (Wolch, 1990) divested of its normal welfare accountabilities? The chapter discusses flaws in the justification for markets, illustrating difficulties that emerge, especially in poor areas, in ensuring fair access and equitable provision, when democratic mechanisms for planning public services and providers are displaced.

Much emphasis has been placed on capacity building to create a level playing field for small providers (Harris and Schlappa, 2008) but the power exercised by large agencies also highlights the barriers for small VSOs and more marginal users in influencing the shape of services. A growing polarisation between large and small VSOs is apparent, and organisations keen to win contracts may also be pressured into significant compromises (Cairns et al, 2006). The examination of power in these processes also highlights the ways in which trust relationships within and across sectors are undermined by competitive frameworks, generating far from intelligent commissioning practices.

Chapter Five explores questions of power and trust further, using trust as a valuable lens through which to examine the effects of an increasingly burdensome performance culture on VSOs: on activities and values, and ultimately on independence. A distinctive characteristic attributed to VSOs in earlier decades was their accountability to member and user communities (Kendall and Knapp, 1996) but as Power (1999) argues, the growth and dominance of the audit culture has profoundly reshaped the organisational environment. The chapter explores ways in which VSOs have been drawn into these wider changes, illustrating through examples how activities, increasingly directed towards the delivery of measurable performance targets, can all too easily reduce flexibility and creativity in frontline work. The chapter highlights contradictions between tightly specified and monitored services and the desire for innovative approaches, contrasting the controls that serve to manage risk for funders but constrain developmental approaches. It argues for a need to explore alternatives to the current dominance of measurable performance, which may increase apparent risks but are likely to decrease threats to long-term quality.

Levels of trust and confidence in cross-sector relationships, the differential power between organisations (both within and across sectors), the exercise of control and the nature of discourse and communications underpinning arrangements are discussions that traverse different chapters. Chapter Six examines ways in which welfare activities have increasingly been planned and delivered through collaborative work across agencies and sectors, underpinned by new forms of governance. Over two decades, there has been a shift in public policy from welfare state hierarchies towards networks and partnership working (Rummery, 2006), with an emphasis on joined-up working, localism and community-focused approaches to addressing social problems.

Research has identified barriers to collaborative work (Milbourne et al, 2003; Huxham and Vangen, 2004) and also factors contributing to positive outcomes (Glasby and Dickinson, 2008). However, theories of institutional isomorphism (DiMaggio and Powell, 1983) highlight the power of dominant organisational arrangements to permeate those of smaller agencies, supporting the argument that the recognisable habitus (Bourdieu, 1999) of many VSOs is shifting away from values and features described in earlier literature. As Aiken (2010) argues, this isomorphic shift may involve both mimetic and coercive isomorphism: VSOs may purposely adopt strategies that they assume will be advantageous; or they may be coerced through financial necessity. Examples of cross-sector collaboration illustrate the diverse influences on the VS now in play and demonstrate ways that the 'softer' pressures of collaborative working have been as significant in affecting VS autonomy and drawing the VS into governable terrain (Carmel and Harlock, 2008) as more coercive forms of change in terms of finance and monitoring, offering further insights into governmentality (Rose, 1999) at work.

Observations on VSOs are diverse, varying from praise for community champions and volunteers (Toynbee, 2011), to criticism for failure to adapt to 21st-century needs or to grasp its opportunities (Prasad, 2011). The latter is also implied in recent policies (Macmillan, 2011a). How to survive best in difficult times is therefore ridden with contradictions. Chapter Seven addresses survival and draws on ideas of resilience to consider how organisations have been able to navigate the diverse changes and increased risks of the late 20th and early 21st centuries. It examines not only internal assets and approaches that may increase chances of thriving and surviving but also external discourse and interventions affecting survival. The chapter also highlights casualties from economic downturn, comparing case studies of different VSOs to explore the potential benefits and risks of entrepreneurial approaches and those that maintain greater independence in terms of distinctive organisational purpose and meanings (Weick, 1995).

Research related to VSOs has tended to diverge in focus between service provision, campaigning organisations and community development work. However, many VSOs have a history of service delivery *and* advocacy, and have often sought to engage user groups in campaigns as a part of their developmental work. Chapter Eight explores changing perceptions of advocacy work in representing individuals, groups and causes. It identifies the tension between funding dependency and advocating change, highlighting ways that the use of insider tactics is becoming increasingly common (Mosley, 2011). As Brent (2004, p 213) argued, 'community is constantly invoked as an answer'; however, community organisations attempting to assert influence by challenging public policy often experience marginalisation, unless they adopt the dominant rules of play (Clegg, 1989). This gives rise to questions about VS independence and space, not only to operate differently, but also to pursue alternatives critical of the state and hegemonic ideologies. Additionally, the promotion by both recent governments of greater participation from local people in defining and designing services and projects illustrates ways in which community action is being subsumed into government purposes, echoing earlier chapters.

The final chapter draws together the analysis and discussion from earlier chapters, considering the shape of a future VS and the extent to which relationships with the private sector rather than the state are becoming more significant. It considers the rapid changes to the public sphere and the perversity and false promises of different government policies in the ways that different parts of the VS have been positioned so that those previously gaining advantages through compliance are now seeing themselves excluded from contracts secured by corporate providers. It questions the power or interest that different kinds of VSOs may have in rowing against the tide to maintain independence and to make spaces for more progressive change, highlighting the need for the VS to form new alliances if it is to survive in the future.

In a climate of relentless change and seriously hard times for many VSOs, the chapter also considers the shifting balances of power between sectors and the operation of governmentality in increasing fragmentation among diverse VSOs, restricting spheres of activity. While the business sector is gaining a privileged position in service delivery, the integral role of the state in engineering this environment should not be discounted. Overall, the chapter identifies the need to reconstruct an independent narrative for the VS, which, unlike the distinctive roles attributed to VSOs over the New Labour years (and in previous eras), may mean no longer being able to act both within *and* against the state (Holloway, 2005). Reduced state funding could work to enhance autonomy, and the chapter explores spaces for counter-agency, alternative developments and opportunities for challenge, which could draw more effectively on VS roots in advocating social justice. The chapter concludes that the terrain continues to be both negotiated and contested and that values and visions for the future remain in flux, leaving open the question of whether the tigers of the VS are slowly being subsumed into a more domesticated species or even becoming extinct.

Notes

[1] Here 'charity' is used specifically to define organisations registered with the Charity Commission, which enables a range of financial and tax benefits. The Register of Charities is a key source of information about voluntary sector organisations in England and Wales but only includes a small fraction (some 20%) of the estimated 900,000 civil society organisations (Carnegie Trust, 2010).

[2] Using definitions from the National Council for Voluntary Organisations (NCVO, 2010), micro organisations are those with income under £10,000 while small organisations are those with income under £100,000. Mean incomes for medium-sized organisations are around £330,000; for large organisations, nearly £3 million; and for some 438 major organisations, some £36.5 million. The last figure represents about 44% of the total income to the UK charity sector. Since 2010 there has been a significant decline in income affecting smaller organisations disproportionately.

TWO

The changing face of welfare and roles of voluntary organisations

Introduction

This chapter traces key changes and continuities in public policy and political ideology, mapping influences on voluntary sector (VS) change in the United Kingdom (UK) over a century. It concentrates on more recent developments and inevitably can only do limited justice to the complexity of factors involved. The chapter also introduces theoretical frameworks through which issues raised here and in later chapters can be better understood.

Some changes, for example, modernisation and public service re-engineering, the rolling back of the state, managerialism, localism and partnership work, have been widely debated (Newman, 2000; Huxham and Vangen, 2004; Ellison and Ellison, 2006) but their impacts on the VS have seen limited discussion. Although research on voluntary sector organisations (VSOs) is growing, changes, including ways in which the state has extended its reach by greater intervention in the arrangements of apparently autonomous organisations and individuals – governmentality (Foucault, 1977) – have been little applied to understanding VS transitions. New institutional theory (DiMaggio and Powell, 1991) also sheds light on the power and influential roles of large funding agencies in determining cultures and arrangements encompassing the operating environment of VSOs. This chapter considers insights offered through these and other conceptual frameworks, alongside a historical analysis of policy transitions affecting changing VS autonomy.

Over some 25 years, the organisation of welfare has increasingly depended on a mixed economy and a plurality of forms of delivery (Harris, M., 2010), and three broad features characterise the transformation of public policy and services following the demise of the post-1948 welfare settlement, which are discussed in this and successive chapters. The first, on which Chapter Four concentrates, is an ideological commitment to the superiority of the market as a model for improving efficiency and effectiveness in public services.

The second, discussed in Chapter Five, is the establishment of New Public Management cultures (Clarke and Newman, 1997), involving increasingly centralised strategy and policy objectives and associated 'command and control' mechanisms of accountability (Brown and Calnan, 2010). Third, the subject of Chapter Six, are network models of governance (Barnes and Prior, 2009) involving partnerships and localism: planning, managing and delivering public services through local coordinating bodies, cross-sector and collaborative forms of working. These three parallel sets of arrangements have been significant features of the previous Labour administration, and are also evident among current government strategies. There are, of course, marked differences of emphasis, discussed later in the chapter.

Recent research has begun to consider ways in which these features have been instrumental in harnessing VSOs into delivering government priorities, including 'improved public services, community empowerment and building social capital' (Baines et al, 2011, p 337). The extension of government into terrain previously occupied by more autonomous organisations, workers and volunteers is an identifiable trend (Carmel and Harlock, 2008) but is also contested, since it potentially overlooks the counter-agency of individuals and organisations subverting or inadvertently deflecting these developments. The extent to which close relationships with the state have historically also entailed restrictions affecting VS independence, comparable with the more recent state–VS conditions, is an underlying question for the chapter.

Initially, the chapter introduces conceptual frameworks, which are applied later in the chapter to explain effects of wider policy and organisational changes on the VS. As subsequent chapters develop, it is evident that some of these frameworks offer valuable insights for understanding empirical examples, while others have more limitations. State–VS relationships have a long and varied history, which is also helpful for illuminating contemporary relationships, as well as the diverse elements of VS activity (Kendall and Knapp, 1996); and the next part of the chapter briefly considers this historical context. The chapter then turns to more recent years, examining the effects of markets, managerialism and increased regulation on reshaping the VS and the varied forms of cross-sector relationships involved. When New Labour came to power in 1997, the voluntary sector was assigned a higher profile in government policy than it had experienced since before the massive expansion of state welfare services in the 1950s. The third main part of this chapter considers the costs and benefits of this renewed importance as VSOs were drawn into delivering a growing range of services and initiatives, especially those intended to tackle social exclusion and, subsequently, community engagement.

Since the change of government in 2010, a rapidly changing UK policy environment has ensued, emphasising both community engagement and entrepreneurialism (OCS, 2010), while imposing severe reductions on public spending and eroding the state's responsibility for welfare. In concluding, the chapter questions the extent to which recent social policy and organisational changes are producing an apt environment in which VSOs can continue to maintain their social values and legitimacy in service provision, and represent a distinctive and independent force in society. Are they instead being incorporated as agents of the state to manage risks to social order, with the state increasingly relinquishing its own responsibilities for welfare and injustices?

Policy, research and theorising the voluntary sector

There has been a tendency for research to examine British social welfare policy primarily in terms of statutory services, treating the VS as an addendum (Jones et al, 1983). Yet, welfare provision has always relied on a combination of public, private and VS agencies, alongside individual voluntary action. The VS in Britain has a long history of providing humanitarian social welfare, where, until the late 19th century, the state's role was essentially confined to poor relief.

Despite their relative absence from academic literature, VSOs have played an important role in social action in British history: in developing and providing health and welfare services and mutual aid; in campaigning and advocacy; and in influencing welfare values and policies (Kendall and Knapp, 1996). They have also been characterised as reactive do-gooders, perpetuating existing ideologies and patterns of privilege (Brenton, 1985) and as a means to exert social control over poor and potentially disruptive groups in society (Taylor and Kendall, 1996). Underlying such contradictory readings is the enormous diversity of organisations and purposes identified in the previous chapter, which, from pre-industrial times, have been grouped together because of their legal independence from the state and broadly philanthropic aims (Harris, B., 2010).

While ambiguities and contradictions highlight the heterogeneous nature of the VS, some common ground in research, in policy and 'street-level' practice (Lipsky, 1980) points to a VS closely associated with, but distinct from, both state and market that is integral to a 'mixed economy of welfare in which a plurality of organisational forms coexists' (Alcock, 2010a, p 10). This broad description has both historical and recent applicability but the rationale for the development of the VS at various times has been conceptualised as a response to both state and market failures to adequately address social welfare problems (Billis and Harris, 1996). Theory that points to the comparative advantages of the VS under certain conditions, especially in working outside mainstream services and with marginal groups of people (Billis and Glennerster, 1998), also explains the reasons for different VS activities being maintained independently as complementary and supplementary to state services.

Examining recent history, Kendall (2003) identifies three stages of VS development, with a shift from the enormous growth of charity organisations in the first half of the 20th century, to a gradual consolidation of distinct and complementary roles for public services and VSOs after the post-war welfare settlement, subsequently reaffirmed in the 1978 Wolfenden Report (Wolfenden, 1978). The third stage evolved from the 1997 New Labour government's proactive mainstreaming of the VS (Kendall, 2010), integral to its Third Way policy agenda, which prompted questions about compromised independence (Cairns, 2009). There is now a fourth phase of realignment as the state retreats from welfare responsibility; state and VS infrastructures are dismantled; large service delivery contracts shift towards a corporate market; and the emphasis on voluntarism and localism grows.

Many of these transitions raise questions about the ongoing role of the VS, its ability to remain autonomous and distinctive and retain social and philanthropic values against diverse pressures for change, and considerable fragmentation is visible, in particular between large national and international VSOs and small locally based organisations (Alcock, 2010a). Underlying these questions is a need for better understanding of recent developments, and while VS research has focused attention on defining the sector and its rationale for existence in different circumstances, it has sometimes fallen short of drawing on a wider range of social and organisational theory.

A Weberian organisational analysis would suggest that mutual and voluntary movements inevitably degenerate, gradually relinquishing social values in favour of growth, formal organisation and for-profit motives (Morgan, 1988). Resource dependency theory (Pfeffer, 2003) parallels aspects of this analysis and assumes that external pressures to survive successfully necessarily produce organisations that seek to maximise their advantages through growth and increased income. In other words, all organisations are essentially competitive, driven by growth and survival needs. While this explains the actions of some VSOs heavily influenced by contractualism, it fails to explain VSOs that have remained resolutely altruistic or the many VSOs that appear torn between social missions and financial viability.

The concept of 'institutional isomorphism' in new institutional theory (DiMaggio and Powell, 1991) has been applied more widely in VS research and offers a more nuanced analysis. It identifies strong tendencies for smaller, less powerful organisations to take on the features and arrangements of larger, more dominant organisations. DiMaggio and Powell (1991, p 67) point to the likelihood of organisations mimicking 'high-status' agencies in similar fields of operation. This mimetic isomorphism may initially be simply rhetorical or expedient; or it may be used instrumentally to secure advantage (Aiken, 2010). Equally, isomorphism may be coercive, such as when small VSOs are under concerted pressure to adopt formal contracts and the financial, management and monitoring practices typically associated with larger agencies, since survival may depend on compliance. As such arrangements slowly become accepted ways of doing things among VS service providers, there is a gradual transformation of the organisational environment, as individual VSOs comply with a dominant culture and practices that have thus become normative, in turn exerting further pressure on resisters. Where cross-agency working and boundary-crossing professionals are also prevalent, hybridity extends shared expectations, discourse and arrangements fostering normative isomorphism.

Power embedded in dominant organisational cultures and arrangements determines the contextual rules of play (Clegg, 1989) and also underpins these isomorphic tendencies. In a variety of inter-organisational settings this legitimises and controls the discourse, models and approaches of more powerful actors and organisations and devalues alternatives, highlighting the power of government in cross-sector relationships. Differential power in contractual relationships is overt and often positional (Lukes, 1974) and contracts are increasingly controlled through detailed specification and regulation: 'rituals of verification' (Power, 1997), which not uncommonly lead to gaming. Examining differential levels of power and participation and ways that these generate inclusions and exclusions therefore provides valuable insight into organisational relationships.

While networks and partnership settings are apparently more open, there is also a tendency for hierarchical power to pervade more fluid governance spaces (Davies, 2011), undermining cooperative working and trust-based relationships. Extending ideas of Foucauldian governmentality offers a valuable lens through which to examine the steer that partnerships, networks and related discourse and information systems exert on expectations of organisational behaviours. In collaborative and cross-agency work, the way things are done is ostensibly consensually defined, yet powerful underlying forces are at work, which shape communicative action and limit individual agency and alternative approaches (Rose, 1999). Examining how recent forms of governance have shaped cultures and practices around the VS adds to an understanding of normative isomorphic forces and the processes that promote both VS conformity and willing engagement in changes (Carmel and Harlock, 2008). Recent pressures on VSOs to adopt entrepreneurial models (OCS, 2010) highlight a more conscious steer from a government seeking to utilise nudge theory (Thaler and Sunstein, 2008) to influence the behaviours, not only of organisations but also of individual citizens (Ellison, 2011).

A decade or more of VS growth and participation in diverse cross-sector infrastructure, planning and consultation bodies, together with multiple delivery roles, suggests increased strength and influence. However, as state services and responsibilities are progressively transferred to non-state institutions, it raises questions about the construction of a shadow state (Wolch, 1990). Conceptually, this offers a helpful lens through which to assess the implications of recent changes in welfare work, and as Wolch emphasises, in such transitions, democratic accountability weakens, as the state withdraws and the public sphere declines.

This brief conceptual discussion will be developed in later parts of the chapter to help analyse the effects of VS changes, also framing subsequent empirical discussion. The chapter now considers the extent to which conditionality and directive interventions featured in earlier state–VS relationships and the VS has protected autonomy and adapted to external demands over time.

Historical perspectives on voluntary sector independence

The 19th and early 20th centuries

Historically, state provision of welfare was marked by its limitations and its distinction between the deserving and undeserving poor, a distinction perpetuated in state and charitable services well into the 20th century (Midgley, 1995). With reduced welfare spending and an ideological shift away from state responsibility, this distinction is again becoming visible. From the 16th to the 19th century, the balance of state resources were directed towards punitive or coercive mechanisms, leaving humanitarian aid to the Church, the rich and a growing number of charitable associations (Davis Smith, 1995). There was a slow transition towards secularisation and formalisation of philanthropic action (Owen, 1964), as the 18th and early 19th centuries witnessed significant changes in British society, economically, politically and ideologically. Industrialisation moved work away from homes and families away from the protective patronage of aristocratic estates. Charitable organisations grew in number but were often influenced by puritanical religious beliefs, with activities focused on improving moral welfare among lower classes (Thompson, 1980). Nevertheless, some organisations pursued humanitarian reform, establishing medical dispensaries, town poverty missions and sponsored education projects (Prochaska, 1988). As Knight (1993, p x) describes, industrialisation saw a growth in profit motives but also 'a new concern for people'; and urbanisation contributed to the emergence of working–class organisations, such as trades unions, mutual aid and friendly societies (Kendall and Knapp, 1996), beginning a distinction between philanthropic, humanitarian and self–help organisations (Aiken, 2010).

Charitable societies grew throughout the 19th century, with considerable influence over social welfare; but the state's residual role meant an overall failure to respond adequately to widespread poverty and chronic social needs (Titmuss, 1974). The spread of suburban housing and better transport increasingly separated professional classes from the urban poor, withdrawing voluntary resources from poor neighbourhoods. The settlement movement developed from this context, with groups deliberately returning to poor urban neighbourhoods to establish community and education programmes (Beveridge, 1948). From 1884 to the end of 19th century, 30 settlements were created, with some surviving to the present as strong community anchor organisations. The settlement movement signalled a new liberalism in VSOs, advancing innovative models of welfare delivery and support for mutual aid groups. Other progressive VSOs campaigned to improve urban health and housing conditions and remodel education (Shotton, 1993). By the turn of the century, however, Booth (1892) and Rowntree's (1901) work highlighted rising and unaddressed levels of unemployment and poverty.

With the exception of publicly supported voluntary schools and hospitals, the majority of VSOs remained independent of state regulation and funding until the early 20th century (Taylor, 1995). The harsh social and economic impacts of the Boer and First World Wars prompted increased state intervention in social welfare, with the 1905 Liberal government instituting reforms, and slowly increasing public services.

Voluntary action was seen to have limits and VSOs feared displacement; but the state funded charities to deliver welfare activities on its behalf (Beveridge, 1948), foreshadowing later outsourcing. Smaller mutual aid societies declined as social insurance schemes became established but the role of VSOs overall strengthened, especially where they were willing to adapt to services needed by the state (Knight, 1993).

The inter-war period saw further transitions in state–VS relationships, as the VS became part of a growing safety-net of welfare, following the 1930s economic depression. Unemployment clubs, workers' and youth education classes developed (Shotton, 1993), extending services to otherwise neglected groups, and the establishment of campaigning organisations, including the National Council for Civil Liberties and others with international links, reflected the expanding roles of some VSOs in relation to marginalised groups and injustices. A new coordinating body, the National Council for Social Service,[3] established in 1919 to provide a VS advice and liaison network and to channel government development funds, signalled growing VS importance in welfare provision (Harris, B., 2010). Cross-sector relationships appeared closer but often concealed underlying mistrust, with local government representatives continuing to regard voluntary organisations as lacking professionalism, and VSOs wary of becoming state subsidiaries – mistrust also reflected more recently (Smerdon, 2009).

Post-war to the late 1970s

The Second World War created emergency needs and social dislocations, generating further state-resourced growth in VS services; often a more egalitarian ethos in services; and new organisations, including Citizens Advice Bureaux and the Women's Voluntary Service (Leat, 1995). Legislation between 1944 and 1948 radically changed the profile of social welfare provision, introducing universal rights to secondary education and healthcare, and creating a systematic safety-net of state benefits for unemployed, sick and older people (Beveridge, 1948). For the first time, the state was dominant in welfare provision, reducing dependency on voluntarism. Beveridge, nevertheless, confirmed the importance of VSOs in developing innovative work alongside state services, drawing on personal experience of the settlement movement; and new services also increased expectations. Many local authorities therefore continued to fund VSOs to address unmet needs. Growth in public services reduced charitable giving (Davis Smith et al, 1995) but rather than a period of decline or subsidiarity (Knight, 1993), the VS both adapted and engaged in alternative independent developments.

At a national level, the Charities Act 1960 confirmed the VS's continued importance, while at grassroots level, small self-help and community projects flourished during the 1960s and 1970s (Taylor, 1995), with a combination of public funds and growth in community-based action (Taylor and Lansley, 1992; Leat, 1995). This resurgence of community developments, which coincided with emerging social justice and anti-poverty movements worldwide, reflected the failure of the post-war welfare state to eliminate widespread social problems. Organisations, including the Child Poverty Action Group and Shelter, were established; and many local campaign and advocacy organisations and alternative service models grew from 1970s social movements in conscious reaction to both perceived state bureaucracy and the growth of private enterprise (Challis et al, 1988). Some advice centres assumed more overtly political identities as welfare rights centres, and criticisms of state welfare and controls over social and political life permeated theoretical and practical debates (Armistead, 1974; Wright, 1989). These developments demonstrated a significant cultural transition from the VS's earlier philanthropic associations (Kendall and Knapp, 1996) and distinctive independence in missions.

National and local governments continued to expand public services, notably with the creation of local social service departments catering for all ages (Brenton, 1985), and encouraged cooperative service relationships with some VSOs, leading to innovative work on social inequalities across sectors (Jones et al, 1983). In the 1970s, public sector professionals had a fair degree of local autonomy (Goldberg and Griffiths, 1977; CSSAS, 1978); and state-resourced VSOs experienced few real constraints (Deakin, 1994). However, growing diversity among VSOs meant that new models emerged, while more traditional philanthropic approaches also continued (Taylor, 1995).

Economic growth, coupled with government concerns about poverty and disorder in urban areas, drew increased resources into community development and education priority areas (Glennerster, 1995), creating considerable VS growth in urban projects (Mayo, 1975) and a 'new wave of community ... organisations' (Kendall and Knapp, 1996, p 57). In representing local interest groups, these VSOs offered a marked contrast to the perceived bureaucratisation and one-size-fits-all of public services, and sometimes patronising attitudes of large, regional and national VS agencies (Harrison, 1987).

Despite growth and a changed emphasis, the VS had a relatively low profile in social welfare compared to the state during this period. While the 1978 Wolfenden Report affirmed VS strengths in delivering cost-effective, responsive and pioneering work (Wolfenden, 1978), it did little to challenge the status quo. Instead, it confirmed the broad welfare consensus in place since the 1950s, including the important supplementary and complementary roles of VSOs (Harris, B., 2010). The Wolfenden Report therefore neglected criticisms from the political Left, arguing for an enhanced role for VSOs to promote more flexible service models (Harrison, 1987; Taylor and Kendall, 1996). Similarly, the report ignored criticisms from the New Right, directed at inefficient and ineffective state services and advancing private sector involvement (Jones et al, 1983). However, government interest in the VS revived, not least because of low service costs, as it faced economic austerity. As reduced spending and a new era of accountability encroached on public services in the late 1970s, the positions rejected by the Wolfenden Report were progressively reversed (Glennerster, 1995).

The three Ms: markets, monitoring and managerialism

From 1979 onwards, massive changes permeated welfare services, as the incoming Conservative government mounted an ideological attack on profligacy in public services. Local authority-administered welfare services were criticised for poor responsiveness, inefficiency, fragmentation and duplication; and blamed for contributing to the severity of the economic crisis (Glennerster, 1995) – a somewhat familiar refrain in 2012. Contemporary reductions in public services are justified by rhetoric around budget deficits but there are also parallels with the past in the emphasis on decreasing dependency on state welfare. In the 1980s, these changes produced an increase in central government controls and upward accountability in local services (Pollitt, 1993).

From the late 1970s onwards, conservative governments drew on criticisms of welfare systems, including high costs and lack of accountability, to institute new models of public sector management. These were intended to counter the perceived problems of welfare professionals with unwarranted autonomy and vested interests; and ineffective local government service management (Glennerster, 1997). Instead of centralised bureau-professionalism, competitive markets were advocated as a means to increase efficiency, premised on public choice theory (Boyne, 1998) and promoting new discourses of quality and customer focus (Butcher, 1995; Ferlie et al, 1996). Following compulsory competitive tendering legislation, by the mid-1990s, key services, including in housing (Mullins and Riseborough, 2001) and subsequently social care (Kendall and Knapp, 2001), were being outsourced to non-state providers. Outsourcing and contractualism, together with the spread of New Public Management cultures and performance monitoring, were significant features in the shifting public sector environment that faced VSOs.

The rationale for extending the role of VSOs in these developing service markets was the failure of state provision. Costs and efficiency were also strong justifications, especially where the limited size or marginal nature of provision was neither cost-effective for the state nor attractive for private sector providers. Private sector management practices had significant influence on UK public sector transitions during the 1980s and 1990s (Le Grand, 2003), but until recently, public sector arrangements have had the most direct effects on VS changes, especially through the purchase of services (Harris and Rochester, 2001). Until the late 1990s, most VSOs receiving public resources were grant-funded through local government departments, extending up to the mid-2000s for small VSOs in some areas. These grant-based arrangements underpinned cross-sector relationships in many service fields, with some VSOs also receiving local support in kind, including officer and staff support, rent-free spaces and access to professional training, considerably supplementing their resources (Leat, 1995). However, pressures on local government funds gradually reduced these benefits, and successive governments have advanced a series of schemes involving loans, purchase of community assets, bursaries and social investments (Cabinet Office, 2009, 2011), to promote VS ownership and self-sufficiency.

Outsourcing in public services began a process of re-engineering welfare services, which diversified providers and recast the roles of public sector managers, while reducing the autonomy of frontline professionals (Harris and Rochester, 2001). Many new contracts emphasised criteria related to efficiency, quality and consumer choice, and displaced priorities concerned with equity and social justice (Pollitt, 1993; Butcher, 1995). This shift highlighted the disparate values and approaches of providers from different sectors, and led to anxieties among VSOs about the extent to which competing for services would mean reshaping their activities (Kumar, 1997). Overall, financial support from the state to the VS increased through the 1980s and 1990s (Harris et al, 2001), but with changing initiatives, redirected funds and public spending cuts, there were also losses, especially among small VSOs (Mabbott, 1993). As Chapter One indicated, overall VS growth has often concealed winners and losers.

The introduction of markets into welfare services marked an ideological shift away from the post-war welfare settlement, and was accompanied by a realignment of relationships between central and local government, aimed to curb the autonomy of both powerful local governments and welfare professionals. The VS offered a flexible and cost-effective means through which central government could limit local government monopoly over welfare provision. However, outsourcing propelled many VSOs into more regulated relationships with the state, and highlighted conflicts between funding needs and organisational independence (Scott et al, 2000), in many cases, damaging trust relationships built up locally across sectors. In parallel, funding for core activities, unrelated to specific service outputs or special projects, was gradually eroded, raising questions about broader advice and advocacy roles. The effects of these '3 Ms' in changing VS work are considered further in later chapters.

Growing pressure to demonstrate efficiency and specified performance outcomes meant that over a number of years, local government officers, and in turn VSOs, have increasingly focused attention on upward accountability, often reshaping activities to meet specifications associated with funding. Since the mid-1990s, the spread of information and communication technologies has allowed the numerical measures used to monitor performance to proliferate, and instead of VSOs being accountable primarily to users or local stakeholders, funders' criteria and targets have become increasingly dominant (Harris, M., 2010). As contractualism, increased levels of audit and New Public Management cultures encroached on VSOs from the late 1990s, critics began to question whether these more formal and regulated approaches would stifle the more flexible service environment and more innovative approaches that had hitherto distinguished the VS (Locke et al, 2001; Scott and Russell, 2001). The extent to which VSOs have been able to make sense of their purposes and values (Weick, 1995) and consciously address mimetic and coercive isomorphic pressures to change has affected their abilities to avoid unintended mission drift (Cairns et al, 2006). Arguably, the benefits of VS changes were largely one-way, and despite closer links with the state in some respects, few VSOs saw gains, such as greater influence over service needs or monitoring criteria (Kendall, 2003). Not all VSOs faced with accommodating or rejecting externally driven changes, however, were able to adapt and retain their core purposes and activities.

Despite some research on VS experiences of these changes (Lewis, 1996, 2005; Scott and Russell, 2001), much empirical work, both in the UK and internationally, is relatively recent, documenting a more complex picture from the late 1990s onwards, when the VS began to gain a higher profile (Proulx and Denis-Savard, 2007; Baines et al,

2011). A pervasive reshaping of goals, activities and values has ensued – cultural shifts, which have resulted both from increased involvement in national and local policy debates and from pragmatic accommodation of funding criteria (Harris, M., 2010). These transitions can be understood as a consequence of normative isomorphism, as the cultures of managerialism associated with public sector arrangements (examined further below) became more widespread and permeated VS practices.

Managerialism: reconfiguring service values and accountability?

The gradual re-engineering of the organisational environment surrounding welfare services, including marketisation and the adoption of New Public Management, fundamentally altered organisational roles and relationships in public services, shifting the emphasis of public sector activities towards management and monitoring and away from direct delivery, distancing many public sector professionals from service users (Le Grand, 2003). The transitions in values, increased controls and privileging of rational planning and managerial judgements over those of welfare professionals, which pervaded public services, have been examined elsewhere (Clarke and Newman, 1997). Clarke et al (2000a), in particular, map the far-reaching consequences of reforming the state's role in welfare delivery to a regime dominated by managerialism, for redefining public sector roles and consequent relationships with other sectors.

An outcome of the gradual dispersal of service delivery has been the increasing number of non-state organisations being drawn in to deliver, or fill gaps in, public services (Baines et al, 2011) – currently an escalating process. Paradoxically, dispersal extends centrally controlled frameworks to a wider range of agencies and projects, enabling the spread of governmental powers, ensured through policy and monitoring frameworks (Newman, 2000). While such changes have most affected VSOs providing services, sometimes blurring boundaries between large VSOs and public agencies (Lewis, 2008), they have also permeated cultures of community projects and other less service-driven arrangements (Taylor, 2011a).

Many smaller VSOs have succumbed to pressures to conform to pervasive organisational arrangements, taking on features of more powerful agencies, as conceived in new institutional theory (DiMaggio and Powell, 1983). VSOs have been drawn into delivering initiatives, devised by central government and directed and monitored through local government agencies; and as VSOs have increased their share of publicly funded activities, managerial controls have permeated their previously, less formal organisational environments (Taylor, 2001; Baines et al, 2011). However, concepts of 'control' and the 'right to manage' implied in dominant managerial cultures and associated arrangements have often undermined the kinds of flexible approaches developed by community-based organisations to reach groups of people outside mainstream services (Milbourne, 2009a). This juxtaposition of contradictory approaches in many recent initiatives – locally responsive and managerial – highlights tensions and challenges that small VSOs face, which are explored further in later chapters.

The wider range of organisations benefiting from public funding inevitably extended formal accountability requirements but also increased governmental controls over service management. A series of regulatory frameworks established in the mid-1990s was intended to counter criticisms about the lack of accountability in a market model of service delivery, reliant on consumer choice (Deakin, 2001). This question of democratic accountability has re-emerged as a pressing concern, with the contemporary escalation in the marketisation of services. However, there is a tension between the need for public accountability and ways in which audit shapes and constrains service activities (Power, 1994), and often little attempt to develop intelligent middle ground. Increased regulation associated with competitive contracts and growing performance measurement, over the last two decades, has progressively extended formal management procedures and data requirements in VSOs, diverting resources from frontline work and requiring additional capacity and skills among workers and governance boards (Harris, 2001b). In many VSOs, such changes represent coercive isomorphic pressures since compliance is secured because of fears of jeopardising funding (Milbourne, 2009a). Many other organisations have also accommodated changes willingly, internalising the desirability of fitting into dominant cultures, as a means to gaining legitimacy or competitive advantage (Suchman, 1995), conforming to resource dependency theory.

Managerialism, then, has appeals: it represents a way of imposing a rational order on the chaos of changing systems, ambiguous arrangements and their often irrational rule systems (Peters, 1993; Clarke and Newman, 1997). It also offers an apparently professional approach to managing the 'messy and muddled, yet vibrant' sorts of organisations often generated in the VS (Harris et al, 2001, p 13). For both public and VS professionals, managerialism therefore provides strategies for coping with the complexities of reflexive modernisation (Giddens, 1999)[4] – the uncertainties and painful choices of a less traditionally ordered and boundaried society. It offers structures for managing risk and individually stressful roles, when faced with seemingly intractable welfare problems, and thereby a defensible narrative for decision making.

Processes of centralisation, coupled with dispersed delivery, represent dominant trends and tendencies in the way organisations have been shaped and managed from the late 1990s onwards. However, the development of these trends in both the public and voluntary sectors has been uneven and often contested (Clarke and Newman, 1997; Scott and Russell, 2001; Barnes et al, 2007). While the characteristics of public service changes can be widely recognised in discourses of improved quality and performance, public choice and customer orientation (Le Grand, 2003), the foundations for realising organisational reforms have been complex and often tenuous. Not surprisingly, then, instabilities and role confusions, dissent and disputed values, have emerged from consequent transitions in the VS (Billis, 2010; Nevile, 2010; Alcock and Kendall, 2011), producing questions about legitimate modes of operation for VSOs, the interests served by changes and their effects on VS autonomy (Cairns, 2009). These changes have also exacerbated asymmetries of power between different players and sectors: state, business, VSOs, community stakeholders and service users.

Summarising inter-organisational changes

In an attempt to encapsulate some key configurations and changes over the last 25 years, Table 1 offers a typology of VS–state relationships. The gradual shift from grant aid to competitively allocated contracts is outlined by levels 2 and 3, and has been accompanied by a corresponding loss of core funding (level 1), which has also had a negative impact on advocacy activities (level 6) and the support offered through infrastructure organisations.

These transitions have been ongoing through the early 21st century, while in parallel, a plethora of projects and joint local planning bodies based on cross-sector networks and partnership working (levels 4 and 5) have become established – both short and long term. There has been a transition in structural emphasis from hierarchical government power – whether through allocation of grant-funding or contracts – to network governance in these relationships over the last decade. However, the hierarchical nature of contractual relationships has continued in parallel, and as Davies (2011) argues, hierarchies have a tendency to trump apparently more open and egalitarian arrangements, effectively reasserting governmental powers.

Table 1:Types of voluntary sector–state relationships

Level	Relationship	Description
1	Core funding	Public funding for core activities of VSO (unspecified services) (almost none/much infrastructure support lost)
2	Grant aid	Public funding, some joint public/VSO development of services (minimal)
3	Contracted service	Public contract funding for specified VSO service provision – now widely open to private providers – displacing VSOs as direct contractors
4	Joint planning	Local boards/groups plan services and decide criteria for services (advising/informing commissioners)
5	Joint delivery	Provision through cross-agency work/partnerships with shared responsibility (increasingly shifting to sub-contracting)
6	Advocacy	Advocacy by VSOs – funded by public bodies (almost none), charitable fundraising, membership, volunteers

Source: Adapted from Milbourne and Cushman (2010)

Like any typology, the categories are indicative, not exhaustive or definitive; types of interactions are not neatly ordered chronologically, since most (except core funding and grant aid, which are now minimal) are ongoing but are increasingly subject to change, overlap and fusion. The same pairing of a VSO and public body may be simultaneously engaged in several of these relationships. Consequently, relationships that are constructive at one level, for example, when a public agency has involved a VSO in identifying local service needs, can be disrupted by interactions at another, when competitive contracts are introduced. Recent encouragement of private sector organisations into these inter-organisational settings (discussed later) has added to the complexity of models.

New Labour: the voluntary sector and the Third Way

For 10 years or more, Conservative governments promoted an unfounded picture of increasing wealth and overall economic growth, denying government responsibility for poverty and social problems (Walker and Walker, 1997). This myth was also used to legitimate a neoliberal market ideology, encouraging the belief in individual opportunity and meritocracy, and negating the need for earlier equalities policies and special projects – except those required to maintain public order. Opening public services to market competition reduced state welfare delivery and increased the share delivered by other providers and when New Labour came to power in 1997, it continued this pluralist approach (Deakin, 2001).

However, there were two major differences: New Labour acknowledged the growing polarisation between rich and poor, which had significantly worsened over the previous two decades (Gordon et al, 2000); and it publicly recognised the distinctive expertise of the VS. It is from this context that the empirical work discussed in subsequent chapters is drawn. Strategy documents were swiftly published, highlighting the extent of social problems to be addressed (DSS, 1998), but New Labour echoed the previous government's view that overall economic growth would filter down to enhance opportunities for those at the bottom of society (Brown, 1997). However, it highlighted a 'Third Way' as an alternative to both state and market failures to resolve challenging social problems (Giddens, 1998), in which the third or VS would have a key role.

By identifying the space occupied by the VS and civil society as offering alternative solutions, New Labour disassociated itself ideologically from previous Labour statism and from Conservative dependence on neoliberal markets. Thus, New Labour combined targets to alleviate poverty and social exclusion with a Third Way ideology and pluralist, market-driven means in welfare interventions, which applauded community-based efforts. New Labour ideology and policies therefore offered the VS a new and appealing concept of its role in relation to the state and social welfare. The Third Way was associated with community, mutuality and moral responsibility (Le Grand, 1998). Its powers were located in civil society and specifically, the VS, in territory between the controlling arm of the state and an amoral free market based on individual self-interest (Rose, 1999).

The role identified for the state under the coalition government is now markedly different but the Big Society discourse contains a remarkable echo of the community, mutuality and moral responsibility promoted in Third Way strategy; and Blond's (2010) commentary on how 'broken Britain' should be 'fixed' similarly stresses the need for the remoralisation of markets.

Under New Labour, the variety of relationships between local government funders and VS service providers not only expanded but also became considerably more complex, encompassing hierarchical roles alongside cross-sector partnership and joint agency work, as described above. A new emphasis on cross-sector collaboration (SEU, 2001) evolved and purportedly addressed asymmetries in power and influence between sectors by promising greater inclusiveness of VS groups in designing strategies. The Third Way agenda emphasised the VS's expertise in tackling social problems, from which state agencies could learn, linking welfare problems with alternative and innovative means to their solution (Mulgan, 1998). As in earlier periods, there were benefits and drawbacks for the VS in gaining this recognition: greater influence in developments versus a level of incorporation – a discussion explored further through examples in later chapters.

Raising the profile of the VS involved New Labour in launching a national compact between the VS and central government (Home Office, 1998), upgrading the government unit concerned with the VS and initiating a charity tax review (Anheier and Kendall, 2002). Packaging state–VS relationships as a compact increased the sector's political status and repositioned it as a key player in mainstream public policy, rather than continuing to cast it as the recipient of piecemeal changes arising from different policy fields (Kendall, 2000). The national compact recommended the adoption of similar principles locally; however, negotiating meaningful local compacts consistently proved more problematic than establishing national guidelines (Zimmeck, 2010). Compacts were designed to build and sustain effective partnership arrangements between local governments and the local VS (Deakin, 2001) and to underpin positive contractual relationships, supporting fairer practices, good communications and mutual obligations (Kendall, 2003). However, studies have since found considerable variation in local practice and compacts have proved to be weak mechanisms to promote these goals (Zimmeck, 2010).

While compacts can be identified as symbolic policies of intent, recognising the importance of VSOs, they have allowed governments to institutionalise and regulate relationships with the VS, largely ignoring its diversity and the numerous community-based organisations below the radar of most research information (McCabe and Phillimore, 2009). Casey et al's (2010, p 76) research on comparable compact principles in other countries reaches similar conclusions, acknowledging that these agreements are often 'empty gestures'. Later UK initiatives involving local strategic and community partnerships generated some positive practical outcomes from local compacts (Craig et al, 2005; IVAR, 2008; Compact Voice, 2009). Nevertheless, codes of good practice that are not legally binding have been widely criticised for 'lacking teeth' without legislative power (Casey et al, 2010) and have done little to alleviate mistrust as state agencies continue to determine the rules of play (Taylor, 2001). Although experiences vary (IDeA, 2008), research suggests that many small local providers have experienced increased formality and control in funding relationships rather than the improved communications and contracting practices sought, with compacts serving merely as a 'handsome façade' with little foundation (Zimmeck, 2010, p 131).

Kendall (2010) argues, however, that compacts were always created primarily as an ideological tool, intended to signal the importance of closer relationships with the state for a diverse range of VSOs, where greater specificity would have negated this inclusiveness. He nevertheless traces contrasting ideological strands embraced by compact discourse, identifying statism (command and control), market choice (neoliberalism) and community renewal (communitarianism) as all present in an apparently consensual and inclusive rhetoric. While Alcock (2010a) highlights the strategic importance to the VS of compacts and vertical policies in constructing this apparent unity, others have emphasised the drawbacks of an artificial union, which masks differences and conceals resistance to what Kendall (2010) identifies as energetic mainstreaming.

This ideology of consensus and inclusiveness involves both normative and coercive isomorphic pressures on VSOs to conform to dominant arrangements. If these are accepted without resistance or highly visible preservation of alternatives, the VS effectively becomes an agent or civilising force for government in advancing hegemonic practices. This is governmentality at work (Foucault, 1977), and as Rose (1999) describes, apparently self-determined agency is insidiously moulded by pervasive arrangements, networks and communications, which serve the social and economic interests of powerful institutions. Yet theorising processes of governmentality at macro levels, as Barnes and Prior (2009) and Lever (2011) highlight, may overlook micro-level resistance and the unwitting actions of individuals and small organisations that subvert and deflect outcomes from their intended paths.

Modernisation: continuity or change?

Ideologically, the rationale for market competition, state regulation and independent Third Way solutions were promoted concurrently as elements of public service modernisation (Kendall, 2010), with a shift in emphasis towards localism and community participation during the latter New Labour years. New Labour pursued both the hollowing out of state delivery of welfare services that the previous Conservative government had begun and a political ideology more inclined to assume responsibility for addressing welfare failures. Many strands of New Public Management thinking were incorporated into New Labour's policies, however, and accountability frameworks in publicly funded services increased (Newman, 2000).The problems of contract culture and increased monitoring facingVSOs not only persisted but also intensified, with significant impacts onVS activities (Lewis, 2005; Moxham and Boaden, 2007; Harris, M., 2010).

New Labour continued to adhere to an economic agenda premised on market competition and utilised the weakened power of the local state and trades unions and consequently greater controls gained by central government to effect further changes in public services (Clarke et al, 2000a). It argued the need to modernise local government, to meet the changing demands of a modern society and global economy (DETR, 1999), rationalising the strategies proposed to improve services as addressing new priorities and previously neglected needs (Geddes et al, 2000).This was the ideological framework for BestValue service reviews, and with a shifting discourse, has been a rationale for ongoing public sector changes for over a decade, to the extent that modernisation has become its own justification.

BestValue generated further transfer of welfare services from public to independent providers, and while outsourcing under Best Value combined criteria of effectiveness and efficiency, cost reduction nevertheless played its part (Fergusson, 2000). Choosing provision based on diverse criteria potentially favouredVS providers because of their comparative advantages over other sectors, in value for money and reaching otherwise excluded groups of people (Billis and Glennerster, 1998). However, the use of 'open' competition (DETR, 1999, para 16) generated ambiguity, andVSOs were simultaneously encouraged to collaborate in consultative exercises about local service needs *and* to compete for funding, although consultations more often included larger VSOs (Harris, 2001a; Milbourne, 2009a). These potentially contradictory roles have continued through the recent years of local planning partnerships and local authority commissioning, adding to factors destabilising relationships between VS and local government workers, and between larger and smallerVSOs (Milbourne and Murray, 2011).

The BestValue review processes introduced other problems forVSOs (Mullins and Riseborough, 2001) because of the detailed benchmarking and performance measures required to demonstrate services needs, and compare quality and competitiveness against other provision (UNISON, 2000). Small VSOs faced a bewildering variety of new requirements for which they had limited capacity, skills or resources (Rochester, 2001).

Qualitative and quantitative performance measures were considered for varied projects and services but, in practice, numerical data reporting has been consistently privileged over narrative reporting and process-based indicators, and despite criticisms, continued to dominate the last decade (Shaw and Allen, 2006). Selection of certain outcomes for report, rather than others, results in disproportionate value attributed to measurable aspects (Power, 1999), narrowing goals and activities and marginalising less quantifiable factors, such as staff commitment, the quality of interventions (Brown and Calnan, 2010) or the value added by volunteers (Rochester, 2001). Therefore, VSOs required to demonstrate their worth to gain or retain funding have found themselves increasingly drawn into shaping their activities to meet specified contract criteria, and quantifiable targets and outcomes (Milbourne and Murray, 2011). As Chapter Five discusses, this often sits uneasily with the flexible and developmental work for which VSOs have been sought and valued, creating tensions within organisations and at organisational boundaries.

Underlying this discussion is an ambiguity in what counts as legitimate organisational knowledge and approaches: the values, norms, information and arrangements regarded as appropriate (Suchman, 1995). New Labour recognised the VSOs' expertise in reaching groups of people who had historically been marginalised but increasingly created a service marketplace where financial and economic legitimacy and performance measurement were dominant, despite its underlying aims of significantly improving social welfare. As Bennett (2011) highlights, social and market legitimacy belong to different institutional settings but the state has increasingly created rules and criteria around outsourcing services, which have, until recently, demanded both social and market expertise, encouraging more entrepreneurial skills in the VS.

Overall, modernisation drew VSOs into increasingly formal systems of engagement with public agencies, encouraging a shift towards funders' cultures and ways of doing things (Hoggett, 2004) and away from those of community stakeholders (Buckingham, 2009). The power inscribed in the managerial cultures of large (public) funding bodies conducts these isomorphic tendencies (DiMaggio and Powell, 1983) extending dominant arrangements but paradoxically, undermining the alternatives for which VSOs have been sought, also marginalising diverse community concerns (Mills, 2009).

Partnerships, collaboration and community

Over the last decade, while markets continued to underpin political ideology and core funding strategies, there was a marked policy shift towards network and partnership working, localism and community-level solutions to problems (Ellison and Ellison, 2006; Rummery, 2006). Numerous inter-agency initiatives, based on network governance theories (Thompson, 2003), involved community representatives in planning and delivery partnerships alongside private and public sector agencies (see Table 2.1). However, the collaborative cross-sector work implied has often been at odds with the structurally embedded power in parallel contractual relationships. Equally, mistrust and vested interests often permeate apparently collaborative work (Kimberlee, 2001) since the competitive nature of mechanisms for service funding have increasingly privileged larger organisations (O'Brien, 2006) and those adopting the dominant rules of play (Clegg, 1989). The language of collaboration and partnership apparently offers VSOs a more equal role as insider in discussions. However, many small VSOs have experienced their involvement as outsiders in a process in which unequal positioning prevails, 'with statutory partners unwilling to share power in any meaningful way' (Taylor, 2001, p 97).

While the VS gained particular prominence in policy, as an alternative to state and market solutions to social problems, the underlying transition in public sector roles pervaded new partnership initiatives and inter-agency relationships, extending dominant ways of doing things to the VS through powerful hierarchies pervading new governance networks. Through the last decade, constantly shifting policy and priorities generated opportunities for many new VS projects but also curtailed and redirected others, with initiative funding diverting resources towards specific government priorities (Kendall, 2000). Many developments sought innovative approaches but depended on agreement to deliver prescribed activities and outcomes, restricting flexible responses to unanticipated needs (Milbourne, 2009a). While the concept of 'partnership work' was not new, under New Labour it proliferated (Taylor, 2001), encouraging greater cross-over and hybridity of organisational arrangements. By extending the reach of governable terrain beyond traditional welfare service delivery, partnership developments opened the way to increased influence over community-based activities.

The permeation of powerful hierarchical relationships into apparently more fluid forms of governance supports Davies' (2011, p 3) analysis that 'networked' governance closely resembles the 'modernist' systems that it was designed to supplant, often re-instituting 'technocratic managerialism' and exclusivity, and displacing the potential for creativity and trust. Networked governance can therefore be construed as an active neoliberal project promoting entrepreneurialism while minimising overt state intervention. However, even in retreating, the state maintains an integral role in asserting hegemonic goals (Gramsci, 1971); hence, forces of governmentality remain pervasive in the balance of collaborative work played out between different cross-sector actors.

Partnership working has also been associated with the community turn in public policy (Rummery, 2006). In promoting active and responsible citizenship and wider civil society engagement – elements that also feature strongly in coalition government strategies (OCS, 2010) – this community turn can be understood as enlisting VSOs and civil society as part of a civilising force for government (Rose, 1999). This trend has not been restricted to UK policy but mirrors reliance on non-statutory, community development agencies internationally (Hoggett et al, 2009), as different national governments seek solutions to socioeconomic problems, with declining resources.

In recent UK policies, community-based organisations have been charged with engaging local groups and individuals in strategies aimed at enabling wider participation in, and influence over, local decision making and services (Newman and Clarke, 2009; OCS, 2010), and to bridge divides between diverse local groups (Harris and Young, 2010). While community organisations are encouraged to participate as 'partners' in defining local needs, the structurally embedded power discussed above, which has legitimised certain activities and arrangements and marginalised others, generates mistrust in collaborative relationships. Thus, the promise of more egalitarian relationships, and VS hopes of enhanced influence through new models of governance, have proved elusive (Zimmeck, 2010).

Policy ideals around community-based collaboration are repeatedly construed in consensual ways that render competing publics invisible (Brent, 2009). However, communities of people and those delineated by geography both exclude and include, and 'community' as a concept is problematic, evading definition (Brent, 2004). Yet 'community-based' strategies have been at the heart of policies for improving services, advancing aspirations of local influence over the bureaucratic state. As local government roles contract further under the current coalition administration, significant questions arise about future democratic accountability and the loss of public agencies as local arbiters in checking unmediated power, highlighting the duality of governmental powers in fashioning outcomes but also providing safeguards.

Continuities and challenges among coalition policies

The continuity of discourse between the New Labour and coalition governments in relation to increasing reliance on locally designed projects and services is striking. However, the goals underpinning the coalition's ideology related to shrinking the state and associated infrastructure demonstrate a marked departure. This provokes questions about whether a shadow state is under construction enacted through various mechanisms in civil society (Wolch, 1990) but the decline in local democratic accountability mechanisms and infrastructure bodies supporting VS groups offers little evidence of this. What is emerging instead, as the public sphere contracts, is greater reliance on ad-hoc voluntary actions, combined with progressive privatisation of public service provision (Murray, 2012, p 43) in a somewhat unregulated market.

Debates on VS development have tended to neglect underlying ideology (Kendall, 2010), but as earlier discussion identifies, the ideological and practical worth of VSOs have been clearly signalled in different political agendas (Kendall, 2010; Maude, 2010), with selected VS actors invited to contribute to strategy. Recent political programmes and priorities have emphasised the potential of self-help communities, civic and civil action, and the shift from government towards more fluid governance (Evers and Zimmer, 2010), promising much to VSOs willing to embrace changes (OCS, 2010). The lines of continuity from New Labour to coalition strategies are evident in partnership initiatives, and in the focus on volunteering, active citizenship, mutuals and local ownership. Ideologically, local empowerment strategies associated with Big Society rhetoric are based on a consensual, pragmatic and purposely 'depoliticised' politics (McCall, 2011), reminiscent of New Labour's approach.

However, the discourse around the VS has shifted a level: demarcation lines between public, private and voluntary sectors are increasingly blurred; and voluntarism and philanthropy are crucial elements of the Big Society, alongside localism and community initiatives (Alcock, 2010b; Taylor, 2011b). In parallel, the rhetorical emphasis on entrepreneurialism, which displaces social values and community expertise, refers to multiple opportunities that can be 'seized' for those willing to adopt an entrepreneurial spirit, new skills and a more business-like approach (OCS, 2010, pp 6-8). That VSOs will need to adapt to new organisational models, involving greater efficiency and less dependence on the state, indicates, as Macmillan (2011a) suggests, a deficit model of current VSOs, negating existing strengths and expertise and their significant role in delivering 'public' welfare services for over a decade. Similar incongruities are endemic in rhetoric around localism and the Big Society, and reflect different ideological strands underpinning current conservatism dominating government policies, and which Ellison (2011) distinguishes as compassionate, Burkean and pragmatic.

While ostensibly, compassionate conservatism most resembles previous New Labour strategy, demonstrating a concern for social justice, it also highlights the apparent breakdown of wider British society, drawing on Blond (2010) and ideas from the Centre for Social Justice. Competition and markets are assumed components of economic strategy, although Blond (2010) recommends a more moral operation of the market. The compassionate model and the Burkean 'little platoons' are both visible in Big Society rhetoric but like Burke's philosophy, this second strand of recent conservatism lays strong emphasis on the successful operation of civil society free from state constraints, allying it more closely with traditional conservatism. The moderation of free market ideology with associative frameworks also allows traditional values around family, kinship and locality to be associated with mutuality, self-help and voluntarism, which then emerge as rational strategies for contemporary times (Willetts, 2008).

Together, community-based and compassionate elements of conservatism provide a rationale for the Big Society, leaving free market ideology unquestioned; but it is the 'Behavioural Insight Team' underpinned by nudge theory (Thaler and Sunstein, 2008) that offers a means to achieve these aspirations by strategies designed to manoeuvre behaviours. Ellison (2011) identifies this as pragmatic conservatism, which similarly has been used to rationalise vastly reducing state welfare spending to address budget deficits, and to advance privatisation of public services to improve efficiency and effectiveness.

In combination, these seemingly contradictory ideologies and strategies – neoliberal market ideology, local co-production and citizen empowerment – underpin the moral case for change: to reduce the socially damaging effects of welfare dependency. Its more 'compassionate' features have also enabled recent conservatism to disassociate itself from less caring Conservative Parties of the past, although worsening social conditions are calling the caring nature of government into question. Critics of New Labour's command and control statism have, however, welcomed the promised local flexibility and decline in top-down regulation but signs so far do not bode well, with prospects for local creativity and design of services encountering significant barriers (Butler, 2011). As Taylor (2011b, p 259) identifies, when service markets are freed from state accountability, the trend towards scaling up means that instead of small VSOs developing opportunities locally, the 'corporate battalions' are likely to win out, with little 'sacred but the bottom line'. There is already evidence that

VSO service providers are being excluded from recent contracts, except as subcontractors (Benjamin, 2011; Marsden, 2011); and few signs of remoralising the market to curb the monopolistic practices and corporate privileges that Ellison (2011) argues work to the disadvantage of the poorest in society, exacerbating inequalities.

Procurement decisions are increasingly using financial criteria and business reputation to allocate giant contracts, ostensibly to judge anticipated performance and reduce risks (Bennett, 2011); and local service experience and expertise are being sidelined (see, for example, DWP, 2010). Effectively, market values and reputation are supplanting social values and local knowledge as indicators of organisational legitimacy (Suchman, 1995). While large VSOs and social enterprises have sought to enhance their business capacity and reputation, financial thresholds have precluded the majority of smaller VSOs from bidding. The inclusion in recent contracts of Payment by Results for achievement of long-term targets raises the bar significantly, since few smaller VSOs have sufficient reserves to cover, often, a year's income for delivering services.

The continuities of approach between the coalition government and New Labour cannot be separated from other recent changes, including widespread spending cuts, a reduced public sector and a state retreating from direct responsibility for social welfare. During the New Labour era, many VSOs, especially those that expanded as service providers, became reliant on public funding; and unprecedented public sector budget cuts are often disproportionately affecting VSOs (Kane and Allen, 2011) and those least able to voice their concerns (Slocock, 2012), with some local government areas indicating reductions of some 60% to 70% to VS contracts. Backus and Clifford's (2010) research demonstrates that VSOs most dependent on public resources are more numerous in socioeconomically deprived areas, often serving socially excluded user groups, suggesting an inequity in losses as resources are withdrawn. In New Labour's mixed economy of welfare, arguably, the expectation was that the VS would continue to make a prominent contribution to outsourced services (Cabinet Office, 2009). However, underlying many of the coalition's changes are assumptions about the superiority of the market and business models; and that solutions to economic problems lie in private sector (not VS) growth. In parallel, solutions to social problems are assumed to follow from reducing dependency on the state, and greater individual and community responsibility.

There is ample evidence of geographic inequalities in voluntary and civic action, and of a greater prevalence of voluntary action in more affluent areas (Rochester et al, 2010; Clifford, 2011). If responsibility for addressing loss of publicly funded services and for unmet social needs is to reside with individuals and communities, this unequal distribution will exacerbate inequalities. Cuts in services and incomes inevitably reinforce social exclusion, and poorer people and areas are further disadvantaged, without additional resources to establish new forms of participation, undoubtedly increasing, rather than redressing Coote (2011), existing social disparities. While many community-based organisations are losing significant resources (Slocock, 2012), local demands on them have grown, as also pressures to evolve new models associated with the community organisers' programme. The latter, however, provides only time-limited funding for a few hundred community organisers country-wide. Taylor (2011b, p 262) argues that while rebalancing 'power between state and communities, providers and service users' may be desirable, it should not mean an absence of services and facilities if people cannot be self-sufficient. The loss of longstanding and locally valued VS provision, while new, unfamiliar providers sweep up funded services, is similarly counterproductive.

Unprecedented change for the future

This chapter has mapped transitions in the role and prominence of an independent VS in the mixed economy of British welfare delivery for over a century, drawing on concepts from social and organisational theory to examine the effects of changing policy ideology. As the chapter illustrates, VSOs have experienced far-reaching changes over some 25 years following the dismantling of the post-war welfare settlement, with VS growth, adaption and survival closely tied to transitions in the public sector. However, a question that Harris (2001a) posed over a decade ago is equally relevant now: to what extent have VSOs influenced the shape of changes they have assumed? Financial survival has generated coercive pressures but some VS actors have also copied or willingly engaged in the discourse and modes of operation of more powerful agencies, drawn by promises of growth, influence and recognition.

Many recent challenges for VSOs seem set to continue and intensify. Recent reductions in public sector spending, a policy agenda increasingly reliant on community-based and civil society solutions and further transfer of public services to corporate providers are all in train. The Big Society signalled an important role for VSOs but the Big Society banner has rapidly lost prominence among questions about ambiguity. For many VSOs, there are tensions about the extent of their involvement in funded services, prompting questions about future resources and the extent to which they will need to broker relationships with business in order to survive. Similarly, policy distinctions between the organised VS and broader civil society are increasingly blurred, and give rise to questions about its distinctive contribution, as VSOs are repositioned either within corporate supply chains or in community organising or voluntary welfare safety-nets.

Whatever the opportunities for increased community action, 'hard times' for VSOs are clearly emerging from a turbulent environment (Evers and Zimmer, 2010). Plunging income, increased competition for resources and overwhelming demand for advice and services are generating stress and casualties among small VSOs (Kane and Allen, 2011; IVAR, 2012). Continuing to be creative in this tough environment is a challenge explored in later chapters and may demand a re-evaluation of future VS roles.

This chapter examined broad policies and trends, seeking to understand some of the powerful influences that have defined organisational norms, approaches and behaviours at macro levels. These ideologically driven reforms have reshaped systems, organisations and ways of organising and the chapter inevitably misses the variations at micro levels, where individual VSOs may accommodate some changes while deflecting or subverting others. Thus, VS agency, resistance, resilience and compliance are among themes that subsequent chapters explore in considering detailed experiences of change among local VSOs in three key arenas of markets, performance and collaboration. The space for challenge and independence to maintain alternatives to incorporation into dominant arrangements are critical concerns among these themes, as are the ways in which tensions, synergies and conflicts are played out.

Notes
[3] Renamed the National Council for Voluntary Organisations in 1980.

[4] Reflexive modernisation (Giddens, 1999), as distinct from simple modernisation, refers to the conditions of a modern, high-risk society (Beck, 1992), which force people back onto their individualised resources, requiring them to question and pass judgement on their past, present and future, offering few certainties and constant change in Giddens' 'runaway world'. Processes of individualised questioning and judgement are heavily influenced by a range of ideological influences dominant in modern society, which also have to be navigated.

THREE

Researching the voluntary sector

Difficulties of researching the voluntary sector

Earlier chapters considered difficulties in defining the voluntary sector (VS) and examined historical and contemporary changes within a discussion of social policy and social and organisational theory. This chapter sets the scene for subsequent chapters by outlining the different empirical studies that they draw on. Much research involves a complex interweaving of theoretical reflection, practical decisions and ethical considerations; and the work described here is no different. Without rehearsing epistemological and methodological debates at length, this chapter offers a background for the empirical studies, explaining how they have been designed and framed, assumptions underlying the approach to research and some dilemmas encountered.

From Chapter One, it is already evident that researching the VS is not simple for three fairly concrete reasons. First, it is a relatively young field of research located variously with several academic disciplines, each drawing on different traditions of research and related methods. Second, despite growing VS research, the sector's scope and definitions are contested (Alcock, 2010a), and an estimated 75% or more of small or micro organisations potentially exist 'below the radar' of good research information (McCabe and Phillimore, 2009). This highlights, third, the diversity of organisations and purposes potentially encompassed in the VS and extending into civil society; and whereas, for example, social policy research will tend to focus on one welfare field, be it health, housing, education or social care, the VS not only operates across many service fields, but also combines other roles, such as community advice, mutual aid groups, membership associations and campaigning.

The studies discussed in this book largely focus on VS providers of children and young people's services but also draw on some wider examples. While most voluntary sector organisations (VSOs) included provide services, some are also membership organisations, encouraging self-help activities and fulfil broader community resource functions, including advocacy. A rapidly changing environment both from a policy and an organisational perspective adds to difficulties in undertaking research in this sector. This is common to much research in social policy, and it is to address this challenge that earlier chapters have adopted a historical perspective, so that where empirical data have been gathered over a shorter period, overall continuities and disparities are more visible.

Research interest in the role of the VS has grown markedly, in parallel with the sector's heightened profile in alternative welfare solutions and strategies intended to improve community engagement. The relative lack of research information on VSOs has been widely recognised (Macmillan, 2010), with some recent developments in research capacity receiving government support. These developments, together with a higher policy profile for the VS and civil society, have highlighted the limited specialist literature available, and within that, a relative lack of empirically based research on recent changes. Broad but incomplete data are available on registered charities and civil society organisations (Carnegie Trust, 2010; NCVO, 2010; Mohan, 2011) but offer sparse information on small community-based and micro organisations, including small services providers. As Scott (2009, p 5) points out, much information misses the large numbers and 'heterogeneous nature of under the radar activities', which contribute to the VS. In part, seeking to redress this gap, the focus of subsequent chapters is on small VSOs, although not all are under the radar, that is, outside the Register of Charities. However, in a limited number of chapters, addressing the diversity of VS activity is not a realistic task, and the following pages outline the scope and settings of the studies discussed.

The research in this book reflects situated experiences of changing social policies and related organisational cultures. How we define social and organisational problems – the lens through which we view them – crucially affects how they are, or are not, researched and addressed. Yet the modern conventions of social welfare policies have focused largely on evaluating 'what works' through quantitative measurement of specified outcomes, using proxy indicators, as if they had real worth as social phenomena rather than being recognised as socially constructed criteria. These conventions obscure the underlying ideology that constructs what is defined, and what aspects are researched, understood and selected for action. The consequence is that processes and contested meanings are suppressed, together with significant underlying questions around structural and institutional causes for problems (Milbourne, 2002a); and the privileging of dominant (often statistically derived) approaches to research and evaluation largely conceal the extent to which policies control, regulate or engender resistance. As Lister (2010) underlines, social policy deals with aspects of society involving highly contested concepts, including social needs, citizenship, social justice, exclusion and the somewhat less fashionable terms of equality and equity. These can all be defined and addressed in different ways according to underlying politics and worldviews.

Research, therefore, has an important role in exploring beneath the surface (Stacey and Griffin, 2005) of macro policies and organisational trends, and this book uses cases and qualitative study to gain insights into the micro processes and lived experiences of change in practical settings. At the same time, larger social forces influence the actors involved in these everyday settings, and it has also been important to locate the research subjects with wider social contexts and meanings so as not to lose 'the bigger picture' (Maguire and Ball, 1994, p 8). In this sense, the research is committed to uncovering patterns of local events and linking them with broader patterns of social change, recognising the interwoven nature of structures, governmental strategies and agency in accounting for local experiences and outcomes (Barnes and Prior, 2009). How practitioners are affected by structural and institutional conditions, and how they interpret their voluntary sector habitus (Bourdieu, 1977), actions, inactions and resistances, are therefore integral parts of this research process.

The research also takes on as a part of its purpose a social responsibility for revealing aspects of apparent justice and injustice, reflecting on how these might be enacted differently. The research settings include some groups of people who were relatively powerless and I was committed to avoiding two areas of criticism often levelled at researchers (Hammersley, 1992): producing findings that would be irrelevant to those being studied; and exploiting my potential power as a researcher to limit the problems studied to those determined by social science or policy makers, rather than issues that the research participants experienced as important. This meant, for example, that I needed to question dominant ideology about what counted as success, such as in reporting performance indicators (see Chapter Five), contrasted with a VSO's celebration of achievements; and also what counted as knowledge in the research process that would lead to understandings of human society (Habermas, 1990).

Rationale for the research

The empirical data discussed in this book were gathered at a time of considerable transition during the New Labour years in office, which saw a plethora of policy initiatives concerned with the VS and work with young people. The studies set out to uncover information where there were clearly gaps in empirical work, identifying qualitative methods and a focus on case studies based in specific localities and organisations as the most appropriate means to do this. For example, as Smith and Pekkanen (2012) point out in relation to advocacy, the wide range of behaviours that could be understood as advocacy is not conducive to measurement. Similarly, understanding the everyday experiences of small organisations and their actors is unlikely to be revealed through quantitative methods. The research for this book overall has aimed to study continuities and changes in depth over time by drawing together and comparing the data from different qualitative studies. Despite the transformation in public services discussed in Chapter Two, resulting in a significant body of literature, study of the detailed effects of recent changes in VSOs is still limited, especially the shifting fates of smaller organisations (Baines et al, 2011); and the examples in later chapters aim to address such gaps in empirical work. The growing work from the Third Sector Research Centre's 'Real Times' longitudinal studies due to be completed in 2013 will provide valuable research in this context.

Much VS research until recently has lacked empirical grounding or focused on trends drawn from wide-scale surveys, which inevitably miss detail and small organisations outside the remit of broad databases, such as the Register of Charities. For this reason, much information on the United Kingdom (UK) VS has involved larger agencies or has focused on fields of social care (Kendall and Knapp, 2001) or housing (Mullins and Riseborough, 2001; Mullins, 2010), where outsourcing occurred earlier and more data have been accessible. Limited work has traced organisational changes through detailed local cases or in VSOs working with young people.

Work on multi-purpose and advocacy organisations (Cairns et al, 2010a), on community bridge building organisations (Harris and Young, 2010), on homelessness activities (Buckingham, 2009) and faith-based groups (Cairns et al, 2007; Rochester and Torry, 2010) are among recent studies that have begun to redress the limited information on the more detailed picture. Evers and Zimmer (2010) also highlight cases of social services, sports and culture organisations, mapping commonalities and differences across parts of Europe. In addition, the Real Times longitudinal case studies (Macmillan, 2011b), the differential experiences of urban and rural VSOs, of different countries in the UK (Danson and Whittam, 2011) and of VSOs working with different interest groups (Mills, 2009; Montagné-Villette et al, 2011) are making valuable recent additions to literature available.

While locality-based and comparative studies are growing, there is, nevertheless, a lack of research that involves views from service users; or

that addresses questions around the extent to which VSO alterna'
provide effective services (Macmillan, 2010); or how their impac'
be assessed (Baker et al, 2011). Underlying these questions, of course, is
a bigger issue around the overall effects of outsourcing public services
on service quality and the experiences of users (Ellison, 2011). While
the impact of service changes more widely is an important ongoing
question, it is the effects of such changes on VS services and their related
community roles that are the focus for research here.

Voluntary sector independence has been identified as a central
question for this book and is closely related to understanding how
features and approaches in the VS are valued and ways in which this
is changing. Again, concerns around independence have had limited
academic debate but are reflected in recent work focused on cross-
sector hybridity (Billis, 2010). The Baring Foundation, after its initial
work on the independence of voluntary action from government
(Smerdon, 2009), has recently highlighted the importance of renewing
discussion in this area.

Situating the research: diversity and work with young people

In summarising broad trends and directions in the VS, it is all too easy
to refer to the VS sector as if it was homogeneous, while in practice, as
Chapter One highlights, there is a remarkable diversity of organisations,
including divergent experiences linked to size, core purposes and
characteristics of stakeholder communities. The question of diversity
among VSOs emphasises the case for qualitative research methods,
which gather in-depth data and detailed examples from case studies,
which highlight both common experiences and differences. The focus
is mainly on small organisations in multi-ethnic, inner-city English
areas, whose activities mainly involve service provision; but in certain
chapters – for example, highlighting service procurement (Chapter
Four), models of accountability (Chapter Five), collaborative working
(Chapter Six) and survival (Chapter Seven) – some examples from
research with larger organisations are also discussed. As examples in
later chapters show, many organisations are multi-purpose, and a more
flexible and holistic approach to services means that their activities
often cross traditional professional or service boundaries.

Some work suggests that studying specific or like fields of activity
may facilitate the research task in such a diverse sector (Evers and
Zimmer, 2010) and can help to distinguish VS features and identities
among growing organisational hybridity (Brandsen et al, 2005). The

focus in later chapters, then, largely on VSOs working with children and young people, is potentially helpful, since there is considerable diversity otherwise in size and types of activity. Many of these VSOs have experienced similar changes, including: greatly increased regulation; requirements to professionalise; the need to bid for commissioned services; and associated performance reporting.

Arguably, such changes are common to vertical policies affecting all VS service providers but the nature of policy, regulations and professional requirements experienced in children and young people's services comprise particular features arising from horizontal policies in this field. Among a range of priorities, the following have had particular impacts: child protection; young people's rights; improving educational and health outcomes; integrating children and young people's services; youth volunteering schemes; pressures for greater accountability in informal youth work (Frost and Stein, 2009).

The emphases during the late 20th and early 21st centuries on reducing child poverty, on young people's rights and participation and on the expansion of childcare and young people's projects led to growth and renewed interest in youth and community initiatives, which had declined and lost funding during the 1980s and early 1990s. While the last decade also saw public and private providers involved in these services, community childcare, related early years' programmes, such as Sure Start, and youth participation and volunteer projects have increasingly been outsourced to the VS and small social enterprises (Milbourne, 2009b). Such projects, designed to address poor services in socioeconomically deprived areas and to engage disaffected young people and families (DfES, 2007), recognised VS expertise in reaching marginal user groups. Private providers have engaged in childcare, nursery and after-school services, especially in more affluent areas but few contracts for youth services or youth-led projects in deprived areas have attracted private sector bids until recently; and many projects were developed in parallel with other community provision, whether in neighbourhood or faith-based centres, or focused on issues, such as young people's health or sports projects.

Locating children and young people as vulnerable or objects of charity has long been a concern in critical policy thinking (Milbourne, 2009b), and illustrates a parallel limitation in the traditions of philanthropy. Despite the desire for independence identified among many VSOs (Smerdon, 2009), the policy shift during the New Labour years from philanthropic action to empowering young people reinforces a parallel interest in studying organisations in this field. The chapters also refer to related service fields; and questions about the extent to which service users are involved in defining aims and activities in VS services have wider relevance for examining directions in contemporary changes.

Work with children and young people in relatively deprived urban areas, in the same way that Buckingham (2011) describes of homelessness services, highlights a need for the kinds of social commitments and values often seen as attributes of the VS and regarded as central to successful services in such localities. These include: the ability to attract hard-to-reach user groups; flexible and holistic approaches; and a history of engaging and empowering community service users.

As Chapter Two confirms, VSOs are increasingly being asked to deliver a range of projects that demand, not only these strengths, but also the ability to be enterprising and survive in adverse environments. However, it is often not until the experience of policy implementation is studied in specific localities that the problematic and unanticipated consequences of policy assumptions are revealed, which bring into question their effectiveness (Milbourne et al, 2003). If VS characteristics are deemed important for successful policy delivery in both welfare services and community engagement, uncovering the ways that these strengths and desirable features are affected by changes is crucial to understanding VS effectiveness in the future.

Research approach and design

Discussion of policy changes is often treated as if they exist in a contextual vacuum in terms of time periods, division from the people and places affected and the historical and ongoing campaigns that have influenced thinking about their implementation (Milbourne et al, 2003). Thus, the problematic separation of research from practice has been an issue that these studies have aimed to address. In identifying the research questions and locations, in designing the research and negotiating with participants, the practical as well as academic value of the research has been important, so that the knowledge created has the potential for informing future policy and offering reflection for participants on past and future actions. While feedback from the research informed review and reflection in a number of organisations, the pragmatic concerns of many VSO participants, especially time constraints, led the design away from action research (Argyris, 1999; Whyte, 1991) even though the participatory nature of the initial design of some of the studies might logically have suggested this.

The studies highlighted in later chapters are located within English multi-ethnic urban areas and sought to address some of the gaps in research discussed above, specifically, the nature of changes experienced byVSOs and the extent to which these have affected their abilities to act independently of the state.What has been lost and gained in the gradual recasting of relationships between the state and the VS? Has funding dependency resulted in a re-engineering of VS purposes and activities? To what extent are compliance, compromise and resistance visible? While each of the studies began with a slightly different emphasis, a common purpose in reviewing and analysing the data amassed for this book was to examine how shifts in policy, together with the wealth of new initiatives, were affecting values, ethos, practices and autonomous goals inVSOs, many of which had gained successful local reputations for addressing challenging social problems.

Adopting qualitative methods, the studies set out to investigate lived experiences of changes in the social world and to explore the meanings behind actions, patterns of behaviour and experiences (Bryman, 2001). The questions identified at the outset were broad and exploratory in most cases, assuming a generative approach (Strauss and Corbin, 1998) in order to respond flexibly to themes that emerged from the data collection. Questions arising from the practical worlds and problems of organisations, their members and users were considered together with debates arising from a review of research across several disciplines. As is evident from Chapter Two, three broad and overlapping discourses have informed the analysis for the book: the first concerned with social policy and the changing environment of welfare; the second with organisational theory; and the third with social theories, which seek to explain and understand what underlies changing social and organisational phenomena.

My approach to coding and analysing the data included in subsequent chapters also assumes a critical examination of material gathered, and extends beyond simply reflecting back and describing qualitative data (Wolcott, 1994). It aims to draw out implications, link to wider social perspectives and contribute to critical discussion on social policy, organisational theory and practice, employing,'different data collection tools and analytic techniques' (Harvey, 1990, p 197) to reveal and make sense of changing social and institutional structures in specific localities and ways in which they may be beneficial or oppressive.

Much of the research uses a case study approach, except inWharton, where information was collected from almost all VS providers of children and young people's services in the area; and in Marsham, where cases were selected using purposive sampling, after an initial mapping exercise of local youth provision. The case studies allowed me to explore the perceptions of different groups of people in and around the VSOs studied: staff, management committee (MC) members, volunteers and young people; professionals from agencies liaising with the VSOs; and local government counterparts. This helped to explore how the organisations operated on a daily basis and their relationships with the local state; and contributed to examining organisational changes over different time periods, when subsequently comparing data across different studies. As Stake (2000) emphasises, case studies are particularly valuable in revealing benefits, shortcomings, contradictions and unanticipated consequences of policy experienced in everyday practice, which are often hidden in broader surveys and statistical research. Adopting a range of methods, including interviews, observations and discussion groups, enabled the collection of in-depth perspectives from a variety of participants via different means over time. While cases can uncover the detailed experiences of individuals and organisations, together they can reveal broader insights, in this case, about policies and practices among small VSOs in transition.

Comparative analysis of data gathered from different sources was used both within and across the studies and helped to improve integrity and depth of findings (Glaser, 1992). Similarly, involving a range of participants in most studies (rather than simply key informants) provided ways to strengthen the research findings. The studies together included some 125 practitioners, 70 service users, 30 volunteers, 20 trustees and 20 local government officers and service managers; and in presenting examples in subsequent chapters I have aimed to represent a range of voices. While some studies involved limited time periods, the comparison with others that spanned longer periods added considerably to insights on the effects of changes.

A case study approach may well uncover flaws in the purposes and construction of policies, opening them to criticism. Consequently, some policy makers have chosen to discount case study findings for lack of generalisability (Hodkinson and Hodkinson, 2002). However, detailed studies reveal important patterns that can be compared with other contexts (Kincheloe and McLaren, 2000), and concepts derived can be tested (in the Popperian sense) and developed as new studies emerge. While the settings from which the data are drawn remain important, the process of making sense of detailed circumstances has contributed to generating new ideas and extending existing theories in this book.

A summary of the studies

There are three locality-based studies, undertaken in different English inner-city local authority areas, from which organisational cases and examples are drawn – largely small, community-based organisations.

These areas all have diverse multi-ethnic populations with a wide diversity of home languages spoken and relatively high indices of social deprivation (Price Waterhouse, 2005; ONS, 2009). While much of the data were gathered using face-to-face methods, a range of documents contributed to the studies. These included: strategy documents; meeting records; publicity and reporting information; current and historical literature on VSOs' work; local commissioning plans and plans for young people's services; contract specifications.

Interviews, including with young people, were tape recorded with permission. Some group activities observed were noted, not recorded, in response to participants' preferences. Detailed field notes, as well as transcripts, therefore contributed to the data analysed.

The studies focused on some VSOs that have been running for nearly 30 years and others that closed after a similar time. Many respondents felt that their organisations had existed in the shadows before the late 1990s, when their work began to feature in national policy developments related to social exclusion and disengaged young people, and policy documents increasingly recognised VS expertise (Home Office, 1998; SEU, 1999; DfES, 2004; DCLG, 2006a). In parallel, the studies included a plethora of small organisations that grew from such policy initiatives, including small community groups that benefited from new funding during the New Labour years in areas such as: after-school learning and holiday schemes; family education and parenting initiatives; provision for refugees and asylum seekers; and youth engagement schemes.

Considering how roles, values and professional practices have been mediated by relationships with state agencies has therefore been a key issue pervading this research.

Rushley

One of the three locality-based studies involved in-depth case studies of three small urban VSOs providing education and advice services for young people disaffected from school in Rushley.[5] Rushley is a large inner-city area with relatively high deprivation within a larger metropolitan area, and some neighbourhoods are among those identified as having significant social problems, with school truancy and exclusion figures much higher proportionately than in many other areas (Milbourne, 2002b). I have followed the fates of these VSOs since 1999, tracking the effects of different policy changes and transitions in public services up to 2011.

These studies have involved some 150 people – staff, volunteers, young people, governing body members, local authority officers and political members, and different community stakeholders in interviews, observations, discussion and focus groups. The initial study, supported by the Economic and Social Research Council, set out to examine the ways in which the VSOs were addressing aspects of social exclusion in a changing organisational and policy climate and the alternatives that they offered young people, through education and access to other social institutions. Against the backcloth of changes described in Chapter Two, the study investigated how pressures to formalise management and activities through detailed specification in service contracts, impinged on the work of these three organisations, examining accommodations, resistances, compromises and survival. As there is little research involving the views of young people outside mainstream services, I also explored how young people viewed and valued the organisations.

The three VSOs – Crossroads, Horizons and The Place – are small and well established, each with nearly 30 years' history of providing education for disaffected young people locally. Such young people were often at the end of a long line of school exclusions or social welfare referrals, or subject to youth justice orders. Each VSO has several paid staff, a number of part-time volunteers and a voluntary MC. Each year, the projects (together) have catered for some 50 young people between 14 and 16 years old whose needs have been poorly met by statutory provision. The VSOs have often taken a critical stance towards mainstream education and its infrastructure, at times challenging these through advocacy and political campaigns. The Place also developed a growing provision for older age groups. At the start of the research these were the only VSOs in this local authority area to provide full-time education for young people out of school. A few other projects offered part-time and drop-in provision but only one of these has subsequently survived.

Wharton

The second study, in Wharton, also a large, urban local authority area, involved a wide range of provision for children and young people, including health, education, early years and youth projects. The area has a diverse, multi-ethnic population, including significant numbers of recent refugees, and has benefited from initiatives intended to address social exclusion, including those targeting areas with poor track records in educational and health outcomes in the area. New organisations and cross-sector partnerships emerged as a result, alongside longstanding

VSOs, including many organisations with a successful local reputation for providing services to young people and families.

The study, undertaken in 2006–07, was commissioned by the local authority and set out to explore ways in which the mainstreaming of service procurement, intended to rationalise and improve local service arrangements, was experienced in community-based organisations. It considered relationships between community and public organisations, and participants were asked about involvement in discussions on future services and their views on planning, monitoring and decision-making processes. It involved some 50 interviews with key informants in VSOs, and additional interviews included representatives of the local voluntary action council, local government commissioning officers and key service managers, including those for early years, youth, Connexions and teenage pregnancy services, Sure Start, the Children's Fund and neighbourhood renewal. These last three services involved time-limited funding streams, highlighting immediate concerns that dominated responses from some participants. While the broad questions were agreed with the sponsor at the outset, interviews were semi-structured and elicited a wide range of information and views.

The study was limited to one local authority area and took place over a relatively short time span, which had the advantage of providing a snapshot of participants' perceptions at a particular stage of the funding and monitoring cycles but there was limited opportunity to re-interview participants or to gather data systematically through other means, such as observing meetings or service activities. The local government in Wharton had received a national Beacon status for a number of local initiatives, including the consultation and involvement of local people and youth in decisions about service planning.

Marsham

The third study, carried out from 2008 to 2010, focused on informal youth provision. Initially it involved a mapping exercise of VS youth provision to establish the range and types of projects in the area, and subsequently eight community-based projects were studied in more detail. These were selected using purposive sampling to include a geographic spread of projects across different neighbourhoods and a variety of project activities. The study aimed to explore activities related to youth and community engagement and how changing relationships with local government exerted influence on projects' goals and activities, including youth participation and youth-led initiatives. For the latter reason, the sample also selected VSOs whose aims included reference to involving young people in planning or decision making.

As in Rushley, the Marsham research involved interviews, observations and discussion groups with some 35 young people and nine workers, and in parallel, interviews with local government managers responsible for special projects, commissioning and liaison with VS youth services. Interviews were semi-structured and most were tape-recorded, while discussions groups with young people and observations of meetings, including for example the Youth Council meetings, relied on field notes.

In statistical surveys (DETR, 2000; ONS, 2009), neighbourhoods in Marsham have consistently appeared among areas with the highest levels of social deprivation in the UK. As in Rushley and Wharton, longstanding VSOs and newer organisations, including recently established social enterprises, have engaged in a range of new community initiatives. Marsham also has a diverse, multi-ethnic population, including significant numbers of refugees and asylum seekers, and over a hundred languages are spoken. An earlier study in Marsham, undertaken during 2000-01 (Milbourne, 2002a), involving community-based projects among hard-to-reach groups, also provided a context and comparative information on the changing environment and experiences.

Other areas

While the focus in these three area-based studies is on smaller, community-based organisations in socioeconomically deprived urban localities, the inclusion of larger regional and nationally based agencies provides additional data, illustrating a wider range of perceptions. As Chapter Two described, the growth of the VS, together with increasingly large contracts through which services are being devolved from the state, appears to have intensified fragmentation and differences within the VS. From 2008 to 2011, I undertook a series of small case studies, interviewing key informants in 12 organisations. My research focus was more comparative, and I collected data from infrastructure organisations and some larger voluntary organisations. The VSOs were more geographically spread across different English urban areas and involved both large and small organisations, two national VSOs with regional bases and a few VSOs delivering a wider range of services within social care. The focus of questions was around the effects of policy and organisational changes and recession, and issues around collaboration, cross-sector and cross-agency relationships.

In the chapters that follow, key themes are highlighted and frame the data illustrated. These themes are chosen, not only for their significance in policy debates and literature discussed in the last chapter, but also because they emerged repeatedly as salient issues from the empirical studies. The themes are closely associated with changing relationships between the state and the VS during this period of rapid changes, and provide insights on central questions for this book around VS independence and the extent of compromise.

Since some of the studies above started out with a different focus, only some of their findings are reflected in material here. In later (and ongoing) studies, concern with growing disparities between the experiences and activities of larger and smaller VSOs, and the effects of wider economic constraints on development and survival, have figured strongly; whereas in studies focused on projects working with young people, findings related to changes in provision for young people have also been prominent (Milbourne, 2009b).

As IVAR's (2011) meta-analysis of collaborative work in the VS emphasises, bringing together the findings from different studies, undertaken initially with different aims, poses challenges, practically and methodologically. However, two themes were common to all the studies: exploring the everyday experiences of members of VSOs of changing state–VS relationships; and seeking to understand consequent effects on VSOs' purposes, values and activities. Moreover, comparing studies that span different timeframes and cases from different geographical areas has added considerably to insights into the effects of changes on VSOs over a period of time. Analysis of data gathered from diverse sources has therefore been used as a deliberate strategy to improve the integrity and depth of findings (Glaser, 1992) and has broadened the scope for generalisation to theory (Yin, 1994). Drawing on studies where data have been amassed over a significant period also provides the advantage of a longitudinal perspective, generating better insights into changes over time, where the more recent snapshots of different organisations offer valuable comparative data sources and a greater breadth of examples.

Framing knowledge about the social world

There is no common paradigm for research in the voluntary sector or wider social policy studies but a diversity of sometimes contested approaches (Denzin and Lincoln, 2000), differences that often result from fundamental questions concerning the nature of our knowledge about the social world and the purposes that research should serve

(Hammersley, 1998). Qualitative research, as Denzin and Lincoln (2000) identify, is characterised by tensions and contradictions and how these are resolved in the research process is shaped by philosophical beliefs about the social world. The inter-disciplinary nature of research in this field and its relative youth mean that methods and underlying epistemology are inevitably varied and contested, and like any research field, relate to the researcher's basic assumptions concerning the nature of the social world. Whether we acknowledge these or not, as Sparkes (1989, p 133) argues, beliefs about 'reality, truth, humans and socio-cultural relations infuse all aspects of the investigative process'.

My approach to research (and these studies) is based on recognition of the complexity of the social world: that it is not readily measured and is constructed in significant ways through people's actions and interpretations (Berger and Luckmann, 1971). Diverse realities rather than one set of facts exist, and therefore it is important to acknowledge the researcher's participation in the process and in rendering the findings (Moustakas, 1990). The difficulty of measuring complex social phenomena argues for research that can gather rich data (which is reflected in findings discussed in later chapters); but the tools and methods through which it is conducted are no less rigorous. In a context where quantification conventionally dominates the research expectations of policy makers in social welfare fields, the integrity of the qualitative research process is all the more important (Blau, 2011).

My research strategies are derived from a grounded theory perspective (Glaser and Strauss, 1967; Strauss and Corbin, 1998), which supports the development of theory from analysis of the data, together with an iterative process between data and existing research. However, my orientation to the research is distinct from the positivist paradigm evident in aspects of Glaser and Strauss's work (Glaser and Strauss, 1967; Strauss and Corbin, 1990, 1998) which suggests an objective status for the data, implying a feasible neutrality for the researcher. It is evident from the preceding discussion that research data are not phenomena divorced from contexts and people that ascribe them meanings; nor is the researcher detached from this process but is involved in communications that gather and analyse data, and jointly create their meanings (Seale, 2004). As Charmaz (2000) argues, data are simultaneously subjective and objective; and research findings are therefore an interactive product of the researcher's and participant's perspectives and the data gathered.

The frameworks of grounded theory provide an approach to design, data collection, analysis and generation of theory that supports rigour in the research process. However, neither technical expertise nor application of criteria can ensure truth or objectivity in presenting findings. In Rushley, three different interpretations of a student's explanation for her absence illustrate how the social context from which data are derived is crucial in providing and understanding meanings and their significance. She explained: "I just couldn't make it yesterday – too much – mum, Jake, no dosh and that." She identified insurmountable barriers to attendance because of home and money problems but the education welfare officer, responsible for attendance policies, questioned whether she had valid reasons for absence since they fell outside 'approved' categories of absence. A staff member at Horizons, with more personal information about the student, understood the context differently again. Each person had a different knowledge of the situation, known from a different perspective: personal, professional or as intermediary; and the researcher's role in any analysis of meanings is to give recognition to the distinct agglomerates of knowledge that may belong to different social contexts (Berger and Luckmann, 1971).

Credibility and validity

Despite and perhaps because of our best efforts as researchers to observe, record, code, categorise, reflect and interrogate experience, data concerned with human actions and the meanings derived from them can only be known through their reconstructions since objective reality can never be wholly captured (Smith and Deemer, 2000). In forming the accounts presented in later chapters, I have therefore employed and been guided by a range of research strategies, moral judgements and unremitting reflection. Groups and individuals may present different interpretations of events and such contradictions offer valuable insights; but it does not follow that all possible interpretations are equally valid. The researcher has a social responsibility to draw on as many tools and strategies at their disposal as possible, and to analyse and interpret the data collected as fully and as best they can.

Adopting varied methods was therefore important in developing integrity in the findings from the studies and contributed to developing an in-depth understanding of the themes that I subsequently compiled for this book. Themes derived from qualitative coding provided important signposts for interpretation, and the process of being continually reflexive about how I developed the material helped me to strengthen and cross-check the analysis. The differences I uncovered led me to puzzle about the reliability of making unreserved deductions from what participants said, especially as they had diverse levels of skill in articulation. This underlined for me the importance of observation material and other field notes and of constant comparative analysis, which helped to generate insights into abstract categories (Glaser and Strauss, 1967). Even where the research commissioned was primarily based on interviews, as in Wharton, observations and related field notes contributed to data and analysis. Comparison of data from several sources and compiled through different methods and testing emerging analysis against other data and existing theory were important parts of the process of developing findings and theory building, adding complexity, depth and therefore credibility (Flick, 1998) to the writing in later chapters.

Dilemmas and ethics in researching the voluntary sector

All the studies were subject to some level of negotiation with research participants. In Wharton, despite questions and topics agreed with the local authority sponsor, participants were interested in using the research as a means to voice their views on a wider range of issues. The longer-term nature of the Rushley case studies meant that the VSOs could be involved in the research design and development and discussion of findings. Similarly, in Marsham, both workers and young people were keen to discuss the research findings, although in practice, changeover of personnel and short-term funding meant that some projects closed before this could happen. Providing feedback, and enabling participants to shape, and share authority in, the research process, is not without problems. If young people are critical of workers or practices, it may be hard to protect anonymity in a small organisation, risking harm rather than good resulting from the research. Similarly, where young people or members of VSOs were critical of local government practices, as was the case in Rushley, Wharton and Marsham, feedback requested by service managers or local government officers had to be handled with caution.

This last point highlights ethical dilemmas facing critical social research of this kind. As Fine et al (2000) suggest, the age of value-free inquiry for human disciplines is over and social researchers have to address the conduct of human relationships in all parts of the research process. In several studies my interviews and observations included young people, and I had a particular duty of care (Gilligan, 1983). While appropriate ethical codes and approvals underpinned all the studies and informed my conduct, each study raised specific dilemmas, some of which posed questions that needed to be resolved in context.

In setting out to examine the effects of policies in specific localities, findings may be critical of powerful institutions and funding bodies; and because of their situatedness, may also appear to criticise the actions of individuals or specific agencies. Some of the Rushley data, for example, revealed local authority officers' opinions of VSO MC members, such as one Rushley education officer describing them as "living in the past, out of touch with real issues". Such views illustrated the negative perceptions of some officers about the three VSOs and helped to explain polarisations in communications and negotiations. Punch (1994, p 94) argues that even though 'there is no consensus or unanimity on what is public and private', researchers have a duty to reveal problems in the public arena. This, however, poses dilemmas around what is public and relies on protecting individuals and organisations through use of pseudonyms. Clearly, anonymity and confidentiality are integral to good research conduct but are also essential for protecting privacy and avoiding harm inadvertently. This is hard for case studies within one locality, where details about the area, organisations, histories and characteristics, which support context and analysis, may lead to recognition.

An example from Wharton illustrates further the kinds of dilemmas that can arise. There, local government officers were keen to know which organisations had been particularly negative about relationships with their monitoring officers with the aim of improving those officers' practices. However, the research, undertaken by independent researchers, was able to elicit this critical information precisely because of researchers' separation from key local government personnel (and funders). The rules of conduct agreed could not be varied part way through to change the nature of feedback, and indeed, participants might not have shared this information because of fears around future funding without assurances of anonymity. Nevertheless, local government officers had sponsored the research partly to improve relationships with the VS.

Such issues highlight a need for trust in research relationships to enhance information sharing. However, while codes of practice often encourage a range of written permissions, Bunge (1996, p 230) points out that these may represent 'a mode of behaviour for the powerful, those who write the contracts', and as such, may not be appropriate to developing good research relationships, and this was a frequent experience in research with community-based organisations. A willingness to recognise moral obligation underpinned by the demands of social linkage rather than by abstract statements (Christians, 2000) was more helpful for building good research relationships in these settings.

Thus, I approached these studies with a broad social ethic, which took seriously the lives and experiences of research subjects. This is a model that seems more compatible with a VS ethos than one grounded only in existing codes of ethics, which tends to obscure the differential levels of power and participation conventionally embedded in the research process. Like Cushman and McLean (2008), I would argue for the adoption of moral principles that include an acknowledgement of subjects' empowerment and challenge paradigms that sustain existing inequalities. While this kind of approach grounded in the social and cultural complexity of the research settings undoubtedly generates a more complex set of demands on researchers, Root (1993) contends that it also creates better conditions for reflexive research and building critical theory. These are certainly aims that I carried into the research and writing processes.

Story without an end

There is no easy point in a research process at which to withdraw from gathering and analysing data; and the material for this book is no exception. Many of the VSOs who contributed data to these studies are continuing in a turbulent environment, although a few, as one featured in Chapter Seven, have not survived. The VSOs' stories, like kaleidoscopes, offer a constantly shifting perspective, while I have halted temporarily to organise this analysis and writing. Recent political changes caused me to hesitate and draw back from completion because the stories are already resuming different forms. Studying the VS in depth over time has demanded a comparison of snapshots and moving times within longer studies and the observation of critical moments and events.

Concepts have continued to evolve and develop, and it has been hard to complete the analysis because organisations and their cross-sector relationships have experienced continual shifts. Changes are a persistent way of life for VSOs, as is, evident from Chapter Two. The ways that individuals within and outside the VSOs studied have interpreted changes also continue to evolve, with corresponding potential for development of research. While further time in the field would undoubtedly affect the ways in which I have assembled the material in the following chapters, all studies and texts have their limits, and tracking the next phase of changes in VS–state relationships (and VS–business relationships) will generate future volumes.

The chapters that follow draw extensively on empirical data from the studies described above, and employ insights from these to extend conceptual frameworks, exploring social and organisational phenomena that underlie the changes illustrated. Examples discussed have been organised thematically, drawing out some common threads of experience, despite the diversity of organisations involved. Doing justice to the range and complexity of data amassed is clearly difficult, and some aspects of the research have been explored elsewhere (Milbourne, 2009b; Milbourne and Cushman, 2012).

Note

[5] All names of people and places are pseudonyms.

FOUR

Dilemmas of market ideology: the impact of growing competition in two urban areas

Introduction

Three broad features identified in Chapter Two characterise the transitions in public services over some 25 years following the post-1948 welfare settlement, and form the focus of discussion for this and successive chapters. The first, on which this chapter concentrates, is an ideological commitment to the superiority of the market as a model for improving efficiency and effectiveness in public services. The second, closely linked to outsourcing, concerns the spread of New Public Management arrangements, involving increasingly centralised policy objectives and associated regimes of accountability in parallel with devolved services and responsibilities. The third feature, examined in Chapter Six, involves new governance models with projects and services planned, managed and delivered through cross-sector partnerships.

Underpinning changes in arrangements are major shifts in the ideology surrounding the public sector and the management of welfare services, coupled with a process of devolving services to non-state agencies. This has destabilised traditional structures and accountabilities, and local means of exerting power and influence. While outsourcing began during the previous Conservative government and was extended during the New Labour administration, the emphasis on competition and free markets together with the prominence of localism and devolving state responsibilities have intensified under the coalition government (McCall, 2011).

These changes have generated far-reaching consequences for different sectors over some 20 years, in particular encouraging significant shifts in emphasis for some voluntary sector organisations (VSOs), including rapid growth in service provision and substantial increases in paid workers. The voluntary sector (VS) has been subject to a process of organisational and ideological re-engineering alongside other sectors, but the effects of this have been slower to emerge in research. As

Newman and Clarke (2009) identify in the public sector, the process has been complex and the new terrain contested, not only accommodated. This is the case also for the VS. New Labour's valuing of the third sector in its Third Way agenda and intentionally inclusive national and local compacts, together with an ongoing dialogue with national VS bodies, continued to promise improvements, curtailing criticism from some quarters (Kendall, 2010). However, many pledges were not borne out in practice. This interchange of discourse has continued in the coalition government's discussion of Big Society plans and the role for civil society and the VS. Disillusionment quickly took root (Marsden, 2011), however, as broken promises over inclusion in new mega-contracts materialised, alongside harsh funding cuts and reduced influence over this new environment.

This chapter focuses on both compliance and resistance among VSOs in relation to outsourcing arrangements. It questions the extent to which markets have contributed to the colonisation of what were previously perceived as the 'ungoverned' and autonomous spaces of VS activities (Rochester et al, 2010). The chapter draws on the experiences of small, VS service providers during two key periods of transition, as initial outsourcing and, subsequently, local area commissioning were introduced. Both studies, described more fully in Chapter Three, were based in relatively poor urban neighbourhoods in England and drew on perceptions of service users and community stakeholders, as well as VSO workers and local government officers.

With a growing political emphasis on the superiority of the private sector and market mechanisms for achieving economic advantages and service improvements (Cabinet Office, 2010c), coupled in discourse with the need for stringent budget reductions, the devolution of public services and public sector responsibility has advanced rapidly. As earlier chapters identified, size has become a signal that differentiates local from regional and national organisations; and growth and diversification of services have moved some VSOs away from earlier community-based goals. Recent years have also seen a trend towards capacity building, with one element being encouraging small VSOs to collaborate and merge to enable them to access and manage increasingly large and complex contracts. While growth promises financial security, and therefore the ability to sustain provision for users, the pressures towards expansion and merger benefit funders and contractors most by minimising transaction costs in larger contracts. However, some small VSOs have resisted changes that propel growth in services at the expense of distancing them from user groups and stakeholder accountability (Harris and Young, 2010).

Earlier research considered some effects of earlier phases of outsourcing public services on VS activities (Harris and Rochester, 2001) but the expansion of the contract culture and the growing VS role in the mixed economy of welfare during the New Labour years make comparative study of more recent examples valuable. Since 2006, the funding strategies of both New Labour and coalition administrations have increasingly privileged larger VSOs and corporate providers (Audit Commission, 2007; Marsden, 2011), despite the rhetoric emphasising community-based and civil society solutions to service and economic problems (OTS, 2007; OCS, 2010). However, progressively larger contracts and the introduction of Payment by Results present insurmountable barriers for small VS providers. In exploring the effects of a growing political commitment to marketisation of services, this chapter considers some of the dilemmas for VSOs between remaining responsive to local stakeholders and competing for service funding.

Re-engineering cross-sector relationships: for better or for worse?

The changes that instilled market forces into public service provision permanently disrupted prevailing cultures of relationships between the VS and the local state, replacing less formal, often trust-based relationships with formal contractual relationships. For VSOs, meeting the new terms and arrangements of competitive contracts diverted considerable resources away from user groups (Locke et al, 2001), unsettling previous balances of power and resources between local government officers, VS representatives and their service users.

This asymmetry of power has been played out in various ways. While VSOs expected greater funding and organisational stability to follow from formal service contracts, stability was, and has continued to be, undermined by short-term projects and policy changes (Milbourne, 2009a). Scott and Russell's (2001) study in the social care sector highlights some of the problems of marketisation, including the ways in which competitive cultures have encouraged VSOs to favour funders' priorities over their own goals in order to gain and retain contracts and potentially to increase provision, supporting Pfeffer's (2003) resource dependency theory. The tighter specification of service activities, increased regulation and performance measurement defined in contracts began to erode VS flexibility and reshape the activities of many services (Buckingham, 2009), also discouraging volunteers (Rochester, 2001). Trust built up through closer state–VS relationships in the decade before outsourcing was established was also damaged by unrealistic contract demands.

As contract culture and NPM encroached on VSOs in the late 1990s, critics began to question whether these more formal contractual relationships were compatible with responding to local needs or whether they would stifle the flexible environment and more innovative approaches that had hitherto distinguished the VS (Locke et al, 2001). As noted, VSOs had initially identified contractual relationships as signalling greater recognition of their work and a more stable and secure basis for funding (NCVO, 1997), but growing research on the impacts of service contracts (Scott and Russell, 2001; Lewis, 2005; Buckingham, 2009) has pointed to negative consequences alongside certain gains, such as considerable growth of income to the sector, especially among small numbers of large organisations (NCVO, 2010).

Many young people's projects, examples of which are discussed later in this chapter, remained outside the net of compulsory tenders for some time, and it was not until the late 1990s that service contracts began to permeate these fields. This was due partly to the nature of provision, involving significant numbers of disparate and mainly small-scale providers (Kendall, 2000). With New Labour's emphasis on services for children and young people, early years and out-of-school hours' projects, and diverse youth provision, including schemes to attract young people not in education, employment or training (NEET), saw considerable expansion – often associated with VSOs. This contrasted markedly with a period of attrition in youth and play services during the 1980s and early 1990s. That picture has now reversed, however, with local government budgets revealing significant cuts to provision regarded as 'non-statutory' or non-essential, the withdrawal of youth development grants and widespread reports of youth projects facing closure (Newburn, 2012).

Accessing local service contracts and bidding for projects funded through national initiatives have been complex, multi-department procedures (Milbourne, 2009a). As a result, service providers have had to engage with numerous agencies whether seeking information, submitting bids or reporting. To counter some of these problems, commissioning procedures, introduced from 2006, were intended to produce more responsive and coordinated local services, planned on an area basis, with more secure, longer-term funding for providers (Home Office, 2004). It was argued that the new arrangements would mitigate inequalities in socially deprived areas by local authorities planning coherent solutions alongside community partners, and by supporting collaboration across traditional service and sector boundaries

(DCLG, 2006a). Local Area Agreements were intended to 'mainstream' contracting arrangements so that services would be planned and commissioned cross-departmentally by local government agencies and local and nationally defined priorities and targets would be combined to develop an outcomes-based model of planning and procuring services. In practice, as Powell and Dowling (2006) argue, the 'top-down' nature of central and local government requirements have confused and weakened the purposes of local strategic partnership bodies, despite their apparent remit for prioritising needs for local services 'bottom up', drawing on local knowledge and expertise.

Area-based commissioning arrangements were intended to address longstanding criticisms (Harries et al, 1998; Geddes et al, 2000) that a surfeit of initiatives and short-term project funding was damaging, undermining the continuity of developments that could make a difference in poor areas. However, local area commissioning offered little to address other negative factors highlighted, including: competitive bidding for funds; inflexibility in statutory organisations; and the dominance of quantifiable performance measures (Kimberlee, 2002; Milbourne et al, 2003).

Empirical studies on recent commissioning are limited but suggest: poor local communications on the rationale for changes; experiences of change imposed 'top down'; and disregard for community expertise (Milbourne, 2009a; Acheson, 2010; Benson, 2010).

Not surprisingly, grant funding to VSOs declined as changes introducing more restricted funding locked into contracts and commissioned services developed. Despite aims to simplify funding streams in local areas, the National Audit Office (2007) reported the enormous complexity of government funding regimes for single charities. Echoing these concerns, regional research (Martikke, 2008) has highlighted the need for better information, advice and support from public bodies if small, local VSOs are to sustain their ability to deliver services as arrangements change.

Macmillan (2010, p 26) argues that research on commissioning is a rapidly growing 'work in progress', with considerable local variation evident in the extent to which VSOs have been involved in identifying needs or planning services. Several studies have pointed to the increased administrative burdens, the hidden costs and complex bureaucracy of contracting (OCVA, 2008; Milbourne, 2009a); and Buckingham (2009, p 245) illustrates the added overhead costs resulting from competitive tendering, producing 'frustrations about the reduced proportion of human and financial resources available for working directly with clients'. While ostensibly funding processes became more transparent and contracts were generally longer term, insecurities about funding did not reduce with commissioning (Cunningham and James, 2009). The pressures to compete have also increased internal organisational tensions, with considerable anxiety focused around the outcome of bids, especially for smaller VSOs (Cairns et al, 2006). Inter-organisationally, competitive bidding has created barriers to sharing skills and resources; and the costs in time and efforts, as contracts increase in size, have proved daunting. From a purchaser perspective, a lack of VS capacity for new work was relatively easily overcome through funded workforce development schemes but Packwood (2007) highlights the ways in which changing policies and short-term funding streams have consistently damaged the stability needed for growth.

A series of government reports (Home Office, 2004; DCLG, 2006a; OTS, 2007) highlighted the need to support small VSOs, to resource community providers properly and for local public agencies to operate fair practice in contracting relationships; but research suggests that these recommendations have not been widely grounded in practice (Zimmeck, 2010). Moreover, none of these documents questions the appropriateness of a competitive approach to allocating contracts in the context of small community-based organisations whose user groups have little market influence, and any support for such organisations recommended recently (OCS, 2010) similarly discounts inherent contradictions.

The latter years of New Labour saw a visible shift in policy, which acknowledged some of the difficulties experienced by VSOs, as integral to commissioning and procurement processes (Macmillan, 2010). Alongside capacity-building schemes, intended to 'level the playing field', guidelines stressed principles of good commissioning (OTS, 2006) and 'intelligent commissioning', recognising poor public sector understanding of VS providers. Complementary schemes, including the Compact Champions and refreshed Compact programmes, were intended to disseminate and promote good practice, encouraging developments in cross-sector work (Casey et al, 2010). While there was some improvement in communication and apparent valuing of VSOs, information on initiatives tended to reach those with the best prior knowledge (IDeA, 2009).

Despite some of the recognised advantages of the VS over other providers (OTS, 2007), including its ability to engage hard-to-reach users and its flexible approaches, many VSOs felt that these attributes were undervalued by local commissioners. VSOs continued to be unsuccessful in gaining contracts because of poor-quality bids and a failure to employ the changing language, agendas and requirements of purchasers (Tanner, 2007). VSOs' abilities to provide value for money because of lower labour costs than many other providers and support from volunteers have been acknowledged but are rarely cited as reasons for contracting VSOs (Bennett, 2008). Many VSOs failed to secure contracts on a full-cost recovery basis, either because of inexperience or because they encountered resistance (Audit Commission, 2007; Packwood, 2007), and this suggests a level of underfunding in services or VS subsidy to provision. The longer-term implications of poorly resourced services are that the underlying fabric and infrastructure starts to crumble, leading to a downward spiral in service quality, factors that are starting to emerge in new corporate delivery contracts.

The last decade saw significant policy developments directed towards expanding VS roles in service delivery to the extent that it raised questions about the emergence of a shadow state (Hogg and Baines, 2011). However, the impact of outsourcing provision on service quality, which has been a major aspiration of successive governments, is unclear. The combination of policy changes related to the VS and marketisation in public services moved VSOs firmly into the 'mainstream' as service providers (Kendall, 2010), and rather than being complementary or supplementary to the state, VSOs became providers of a wide range of services, not only taking a growing role in socially deprived areas but also taking on provision previously delivered by public agencies (Lewis, 2005). The innovative role for which VSOs were recognised in the past (Beveridge, 1948) and which New Labour also sought to utilise, initially informed the rhetoric of the coalition government (Maude, 2010). However, this recognition has been progressively relegated to VSOs being among 'a number of possible providers in the market-place' (Harris, M., 2010, p 32); and the efforts invested in VS service growth and adopting the necessary regulatory frameworks associated with specific service silos and contract demands may prove futile in the rapidly changing private public services market.

Rationalising markets in public and voluntary services

Encouraging markets in public service delivery has been justified over three decades on the basis that markets produce greater choice and efficiency, and give users greater influence over provision (Le Grand, 2003). Recent government statements (Cabinet Office, 2010c) re-emphasise belief in the superiority of the market in driving down costs and encouraging diversity. Improvements in quality, efficiency and responsiveness of services have also been promised as consequences of competition by governments from the 1980s onwards (Le Grand,

2003; Hills et al, 2007). However, research points to the damaging and undesirable outcomes of markets in welfare (Gewirtz et al, 1995), since marketisation is a poor guarantee of democracy, generating losers as well as winners, and unstable provision. As sites for markets, welfare services are flawed (Bode, 2006); users cannot be equated with product consumers and purchasers; and are rarely the actors with choice or most power, which is largely embedded in funding or commissioning agencies.

Much empirical work discussing the effects of public sector outsourcing in the VS, in the United Kingdom (UK) and internationally, is relatively recent (Proulx and Denis-Savard, 2007; Eikenberry, 2009; Baines et al, 2011) and documents an increasingly complex picture from the late 1990s when the UK VS gained a much higher profile under New Labour. Growth in contract size, diverse, multi-agency projects and cross-sector bids all increased competition for funds and service allocation. A consequence of competitive pressures on costs is to restrict the scope of services, encouraging providers to exclude more challenging service users or those least likely to meet performance targets (Muncie, 2009). Competition in public services is rationalised through public choice theory (Finlayson, 2003) but instead of service users being able to choose between different providers that best meet their needs, the efforts of organisations to meet contract conditions may well reorient service activities, leaving potential beneficiaries with less influence over provision. The differential power and skills already present between organisational workers and their users are aggravated in the context of neoliberal markets and tendencies towards more competitive and formalised service requirements (Piachaud, 2002); and users with the greatest needs are the least likely to access adequate services.

The increased external pressures on competing for contracts and funding to maintain provision has generated tensions between different VSOs and within individual organisations in determining key purposes and activities. Harris M. (2010) identifies that competing for contracts and funding and meeting associated demands have produced cumulative pressures on small VSOs, leading to a loss of autonomy. This has been a gradual and not always discernible evolution, resulting from institutional isomorphism (DiMaggio and Powell, 1983), as the norms and arrangements of larger and more powerful sectors and organisations have impinged on VS activities. Competition demands a privileging of motives around winning – bidding and gaining contracts for services – which necessarily entails shaping provision to meet funders' requirements and maximising competitive advantages.

This may well result in a steady process of mission drift (Billis, 2010) and potentially fragmentation among VSOs, as service winners and losers, and those complicit, accommodating or resisting competitive tendencies, become divided.

The studies

The chapter goes on to consider data from two qualitative studies in different urban areas, focusing on shifts in state–VS relationships. The first study, located in Rushley at a time when outsourcing was widely introduced, was completed in 2005; and the second in Wharton, when area commissioning was established in 2007. Some follow-up research has subsequently been undertaken in both areas. The background and approaches to the studies were described in more detail in Chapter Three. Together, the two studies provide insights into cumulative and differently experienced effects on local VS cultures and arrangements of instituting competitive funding regimes.

From joint endeavour to contract culture

Reframing cross-sector relationships

Significant policy changes affecting cross-sector relationships framed the study in Rushley. Extensive outsourcing of public services, coupled with the Third Way agenda, signalled a growing role for community-based organisations but entailed increased formality. Additionally, the national policy focus on social exclusion highlighted the need to tackle an apparently increasing problem of young people's disaffection from schooling. These policy directions generated cautious optimism among the three Rushley VSOs – Crossroads, Horizons and The Place – whose long-established work with disaffected young people had suffered erratic support following a series of local government budget crises. However, it became evident that the hopes of staff and trustees for greater recognition and secure funding based on clearly framed contracts were unfounded. Instead, a series of externally driven changes presented new difficulties and seriously damaged previously positive relationships with local government officers.

Key informants – longstanding staff and management committee (MC) members from the three VSOs – discussed the transition in relationships with the local education authority (LEA), as they moved from receiving grant funding for their provision for young people, to contracted services. Crossroads, Horizons and The Place expected that the contracts would improve stability of funding and services since they were promised three- to five-year terms, and that they would gain increased autonomy. They also anticipated better acknowledgement of their service reputation, since catering for young people excluded or truanting from school matched local policy priorities committed to tackling social exclusion. Studies in other areas (Martikke, 2008) similarly identified that some VSOs anticipated positive benefits from gaining contracts, including increased financial security and more widely recognised service reputations.

Before the proposals for service contracts, the three Rushley VSOs enjoyed a close working relationship with an LEA liaison officer, Claire. Shared discussions generated common understandings around both achievements and difficulties. The phase of negotiating new contract arrangements saw few of the anticipated improvements to stability and a serious deterioration in relationships, with attempts by Rushley Council simply to impose new conditions.

An early change was that Claire, the only local government professional with significant knowledge of the VSOs, was made redundant and replaced by a contracts liaison officer. VSO MC members contrasted the limited interest shown by the contracts liaison officer in their work with Claire, described as someone who "understands and values what we do. She wants us to succeed with the young people ... and shares our concerns ... she has that professional background and knowledge" (Anna, The Place).

This sharing of concerns and expertise had enabled difficulties to be addressed and improvements made through jointly constructed and unthreatening communications. Claire had visited the organisations regularly and her observation of everyday activities contrasted with the emphasis on specification and numerical performance targets in the contracts subsequently being proposed. Good personal relationships had been established over some five years; and there was positive motivation for improving services through shared learning from problems and achievements.

Reshaping VS activities and meanings?

With the introduction of more formal contractual relationships, the lines of communication changed. Visits to the organisations became rare and VSO workers believed that formal arrangements inscribed in the new contracts were threatening values inscribed in locally agreed approaches. VSO members complained that their achievements and efforts with extremely difficult young people were being discounted in favour of measuring performance against prescribed targets and outcomes. Earlier forms of exchange ended; communications became more limited and formalised; and because there was a failure to resolve the terms of the contracts, the VSOs' anxieties about future funding grew. Instead of greater security, difficult contract negotiations multiplied uncertainties; and rather than co-created purposes, discourse and meanings were defined and imposed by funders. There were effectively parallel but disconnected streams of communication and understanding operating, those associated with previous and new ways of working.

The VSOs identified several concerns about the encroaching contract arrangements: new requirements seemed to invade previously autonomous spaces, threatening to distort purposes and activities through the detail and rigidity of the proposed specifications. While flexible and creative attributes were widely identified as key advantages for devolving services to VSOs (Blackmore, 2006), this differed from the Rushley VSOs' experience. Birgit, the Crossroads' MC chair, gave the example of student attendance requirements to illustrate how flexibility was being undermined through inappropriate specifications. She highlighted the LEA's lack of realism in requiring similar attendance rates of young people who had been outside any education provision for months, to those demanded for school pupils nationally: "So it [the target] is now 87% – for each child ... they [LEA officers] don't see how different children's histories are. Some will never manage to come more than 60% but it's what they do achieve from nothing".

VSO staff and trustees regarded these new demands as undermining their work and restricting their ability to define appropriate approaches and goals through negotiation with individual young people. To avoid severe financial penalties for failing to meet such performance targets, they discussed needing to limit the kinds of young people they could work with to those more likely to attend or achieve the targets. Rather than sharing risks for challenging work, the proposals transferred risks for contract failures to the providers, with impossible odds of success for young people with seriously disrupted family lives and long histories of disaffection.

Over a 10-month period of contract negotiations, disagreements arising from conflicting assumptions about meanings, purposes and appropriate specifications and targets grew, reinforcing differences. During discussions among the VS trustees, there were increasing references to Rushley officers' deficiencies and lack of competence as professional managers. There was little sense of shared or jointly understood services and considerable damage to relationships.

The LEA contracts liaison officer interpreted the VSOs' reluctance to accept contract terms quite negatively, asserting the view that they should comply with managerial arrangements: "I mean ... they're living in the past.... I know these projects have been running a long time. I'm sure ... they try hard but we need clear accountability ... it has to be more specific now."These comments, reflecting a wider shift in operating culture, were reinforced by an elected LEA member, who observed: "It's a new regime now ... we need clear ways of showing we're delivering.... We want to disassociate ourselves from a laissez-faire past."

Among the various participants, different interests, motives and expectations were apparent, illustrating ways in which sector and organisational identities and ethos produce barriers to learning from, or listening to, others. Where power and pressures to conform to dominant modes of operation prevail, such barriers may be exacerbated, generating unanticipated outcomes.

Compliance, breakdown or resistance?

After several months of discussion, mistrust and frustrated communications grew, and the level of coercion in the contract 'discussions' increased, with the LEA insisting on its rights to impose terms. With a number of issues unresolved and legal information on the transfer of staff still outstanding, each VSO received a letter from the contracts liaison officer containing the 'final Service Level Agreement and Terms and Conditions of Contract', requiring immediate confirmation 'that you will sign agreements [within seven days] or indicate you do not intend to sign, so that we can develop alternative providers'.

The VSO trustees were shocked by this ultimatum and appealed in a letter to elected council members, explaining that the new documents imposed 'impossible attendance targets' and other previously unseen amendments, including '14 extra pages in legal jargon'. The trustees highlighted significant inconsistencies in the extended contract terms, which referred to 'production line standards, inapplicable to education services'. They went on to criticise the refusal to negotiate further as 'outside the normal codes of conduct in negotiation' and demonstrating 'a derisory attitude towards us as delivery partners'.

Although the VSOs thought they were involved in a process of negotiation, the experience evolved differently. Specifications for contracts associated with professional managerial systems are couched in a language and codes that often detach them from meaningful knowledge about the actual services, and officers determining criteria are similarly distanced. The example quoted here also included standards and benchmarks designed to monitor production line quality – hardly rational inclusions – as a result of inexperienced officers being pressured to conclude this 'agreement' hastily. However, attempts to coerce did not generate compliance but induced VS resistance. There was also disillusionment: rather than the greater autonomy and financial security anticipated, the formal contract requirements breached essential organisational goals and autonomies. In Cora's words, the whole process was "surreal. Just as the government recognised the importance of work we've been doing for years [Social Exclusion Unit priorities], Rushley wants to cripple us with penalties for not meeting totally unrealistic targets" (Cora, MC chair, Horizons).

The Rushley contracting process shows that even where VSOs are not in open competition, the coercive pressures embedded in contractualism can damage meaningful communications and marginalise local knowledge and experience about services and service users. In sending the ultimatum, LEA officers asserted their right to control arrangements, as understood in managerial regimes (Clarke and Newman, 1997), demonstrating mistrust of the more flexible VSO approaches. The VSOs' unwillingness to comply was seen as signalling their non-compatibility as providers, potentially relegating them to a fringe of difficult outsiders.

The Rushley VSOs expected to be valued as delivery partners because of their longstanding local service reputations and their publicly recognised history of success with challenging young people. The LEA assumed, however, that compliance and conformity with the discourse and arrangements were implicit prerequisites for providers in the new contract culture. This situation was complicated by the lack of open competition, the scarcity of providers able to offer similar services and the LEA's need for places. Thus, there were competing positions, with power located on the side of supply as well as demand, whereas often, powerful funding agencies dominate. Expectations about growing managerial arrangements competed for legitimacy with existing local knowledge, expertise and alternative approaches.

Better exploration or discussion of differences might have helped to develop mutual understanding but neither party identified relationship building as a priority in the new environment. As a result, diverse prior assumptions and subsequent actions cemented mistrust in relationships and rather than negotiations over contracts, resistance, competitive positioning and winning became paramount. The consequences, however, were damaging for future services and potentially for the

VSOs' survival, which will be considered in Chapter Seven, since ultimately funders' power is likely to prevail.

This case reflects the importance of exploring power within inter-organisational relationships and shows the transition from co-created meanings to different forms of power-based brokering – first persuasive, then coercive – as the LEA attempted to dictate the rules of play (Clegg, 1989) in instituting contractual arrangements. There were few examples of the predictable rituals of behaviour, which are often identified as sustaining cross-agency and client–contractor relations where shared discourse and arrangements provide surrogates for more meaningful communications. In this case, resistance on the part of the VSOs, a refusal to accede to the dominant rituals of behaviour, can be read as a struggle to maintain independence in a situation where compliance would have led to excessive compromise in activities, and ultimately in missions.

Cairns et al (2006) argue that accepting external definitions of services in a quest for financial viability may lead to VSOs becoming less responsive to local circumstances and stakeholders. Some VSOs may be able to accommodate new service contracts *and* remain focused on their core goals by continually revisiting their directions; and those dependent on varied income sources have often found this easier (Nevile, 2010). However, many studies (Macmillan, 2010) suggest that avoiding mission drift has proved difficult for small VS service providers. The risks of widespread compliance with poorly specified service contracts are that small VSOs may relinquish considerable influence over the shape of activities and reduce their effectiveness in responding to local need and beneficiaries, and as agents of community change.

Commissioning: responsive contracts?

The Rushley case highlights damaging changes in cultures and arrangements, which led to a breakdown in cross-sector relationships. Wharton examples discussed below, also focused on children and young people's services, point to different concerns arising as the scale of outsourcing rapidly increased. Widespread acceptance of the inevitability of service contracts was again coupled with aspirations that VSOs brought to area commissioning in 2006-07 – that new contracts would address criticisms around continued instability and projectitis (Harries et al, 1998). Local government commissioning and procurement were intended to generate coherent contracting processes, remedying the confusion of multiple, short-term contracts and project funds (HM Treasury, 2005). This mainstreaming of the VS (Kendall,

2000) was underpinned by the twin strategies of VS capacity building and workforce development to match increased public sector demand for services. In exchange, the VS was promised growth and sustained funding. However, as in earlier phases of contractualism, hopes were undermined as the simplified funding streams and longer-term funding – intended to support stability of provision in poorer areas – gave way to larger contracts and greater complexity in arrangements, presenting new barriers to small organisations.

In contrast to perceptions in Rushley, most interviewees in Wharton considered that there was a genuine intention to support community organisations among local government representatives and a commitment to improving services in disadvantaged neighbourhoods. There was a gap, however, between perceived intentions and practice, and many criticisms emerged concerning top-down aspects of planning and change processes, inadequate communications and dense, complicated and inaccessible contract guidance. Funding uncertainties and destabilising changes continued to be criticised for their effects on staffing and organisational stability. The increased distance in relationships between provider and procurer made the onerous nature of contracting arrangements for small VSOs of limited relevance to public sector funders.

Working or competing with others?

The rationale for markets (Le Grand, 2003) is that they will lead to service improvements resulting from competition among providers. This subsection, however, illustrates negative outcomes of competing for resources, highlighting potentially reduced quality and reach of services.

Wharton youth and play workers repeatedly pointed to ways in which competing for contracts had changed how they worked, inhibiting some of the cooperative discussion between different organisations that enabled them to learn from each other. In Dina's words:

> 'It changes how you think at neighbourhood meetings, I mean sharing ideas between groups … you still do but then you might hold back sometimes because next month you're going for the same money and the pot's only so big, even though you know there's more than enough young people and problems to go round.' (Dina, Redlands youth centre)

Another worker, Dan, ran a specialist service for young teenage fathers, supported by funders across several local government areas. As a specialist provider, he was fairly confident about winning sufficient contracts but was unsure whether this would mean developing new links in different neighbourhoods. However, he talked about 'massaging' the focus of information on activities and outcomes to match each funder's requirements and recognised that publicly, he could only talk about successes; and 'publicly' included funders and VS competitors. Competition for funding generated misgivings about sharing difficulties in everyday work among small VSOs working in similar fields, highlighting further dilemmas. Like Dan, Paul, a youth centre worker, talked about a reluctance to admit to failures, isolating workers from learning from other agencies – a barrier to collaborative working that is explored further in Chapter Six.

In order to overcome disadvantages of size in competing for large contracts, some organisations considered collaborating with others to pool resources or bid jointly; and in some cases, even discussed mergers. However, the spectre of competition often undermined trust in working together because of the complex weave of purposes and interests. As John, a youth centre trustee, emphasised, "partnering like that can be really short term and that's massive time and energy commitment for small groups, without being clear who gains what beforehand". Resolving issues of approaches, priorities and accountabilities requires considerable time investment, especially if rewards are uncertain. John's comment also offers a pertinent reflection on more recent criticisms of VSOs being drawn into partnerships as bid candy in tenders for the Work Programme.

Larger contracts reduce transaction costs for public agencies and other funding bodies but they demand a significant time investment from small VSOs to identify and manage the arrangements necessary for complex bids and contracts, whether singly or in collaboration. Most respondents from small VSOs, like Mel, working with a young women's health project, highlighted the extra challenges involved in joint bidding as too onerous and perceived potential threats around 'takeover' and loss of autonomy in ways of working. However, Mel acknowledged that in the future "if funding streams dry up and it's all super-competitive, we may need to think harder about joining forces. But it's no easy option".

There were also tensions between local branches of two national children's charities based in Wharton and their regional offices. The local groups resisted pressures to enter contracts in new fields, which they perceived as outside their understood mission, and were keen to maintain a resistance to being overly defined by either funders' or regional office demands. They believed that there was some integrity among local VSOs and wanted to avoid using the competitive advantages of their regional and national resources to poach provision that was outside their normal remit. Clearly, this conflicted with regional and national goals of growth and diversification and created dilemmas for local workers. However, it also demonstrates resistance to isomorphic tendencies, defying resource dependency theory (Pfeffer, 2003): that organisations inevitably seek to maximise resource advantages.

Local knowledge and expertise

Despite competitive bidding for contracts, local government officers in Wharton identified young people and families as collaborators in determining priorities and targets for future children and young people's services. However, most VSOs were sceptical about the extent to which they had reached or discussed service needs with less accessible groups of people. Few VSOs appeared to trust the mechanisms for deciding on future services and providers or that plans translated into contract criteria genuinely represented local views. A recurrent criticism was that the outcomes-led planning and procurement model, coupled with competition for funds, risked ignoring existing local expertise in favour of decisions based on bid presentation. As Jan, a community worker, observed:

> 'I don't hold with people getting funded year on year, just like that. But funders need to take account of the experience out there.... To build those connections locally, takes time, especially with young people. You start with a blank slate, lists of targets, outcomes ... and get people competing, smart bidders. Who knows, we might none of us get funded.... And they'll lose that local knowledge, experience altogether.'

Respondents argued that the planning model was mechanistic and inadequate: there was a need to map existing provision and commission new services where gaps, needs or poor services were identified. There was anxiety about the lack of value ascribed to local experience and good practice and fears that new arrangements would draw in new providers from private and entrepreneurial organisations with better resources to bid for increasingly large contracts but little local knowledge.

One of New Labour's key arguments for 'democratising public policy making' (Barnes et al, 2010, p 257) was to involve service users in planning decisions so that people whose lives are affected by services can have a say in how they are run. Participatory approaches to governance were intended to draw on local knowledge (Yanow, 2003), and remedy the perceived lack of responsiveness in services designed by local government professionals, distanced from the problems. Drawing on local knowledge and experience in shaping and delivering service activities are also central ideas in Big Society aspirations (Cabinet Office, 2010b), although in this case, local democratic structures are not identified as conduits. However, under both administrations, competitive procurement is the key mechanism used to allocate funding for services and implement provision, and these arrangements are increasingly distanced from the specific and the local. Instead, they rely heavily on commodified specifications and prescribed targets, and the fears expressed by Wharton's VSO workers in 2007 are proving disturbingly accurate predictions.

Polarising outcomes: locality versus scale and capacity

Competitive funding regimes in Wharton had begun to create a visible polarisation between large and small organisations – those able to manage large contracts and not – and between those identifying with a neighbourhood base and those with wider geographic roots or from outside the area. Respondents worried that new providers, especially bigger organisations, might have limited commitment to the local area and might start to absorb community-based provision across different geographic areas. The picture is not simple but perceptions of assimilation and concerns about polarisation and discounting local experience reflect experiences in other areas (OCVA, 2008; Simmons, 2008). Ali, working with young people out of school, expressed her anxieties: "You can be smart, show you meet the criteria, I mean, if you're big enough to have someone dedicated to fundraising but we should be judged on knowledge and reputation locally, how we do the real work, day in, day out, reaching kids and families."

Many respondents felt that this trend for larger contracts and organisations would generate poorer services, unlikely to engage some harder-to-reach young people, and ultimately result in the marginalisation of small local providers *and* disengaged young people. Larger organisations were reasonably confident of gaining future contracts but smaller and less experienced organisations felt that they lacked the time, skills and resources to compete adequately for funds. Expressing fears about the future, another worker reflected:

'If bids are open to all kinds of new service providers, you see groups who've spent years building links and local trust lose out to organisations coming in with smart application skills.... [A]nd long term, you [organisations] lose connections with the very young people we're trying to keep hold of.' (Jo, young people's drop-in centre)

Instead of larger and smaller organisations sharing discrete experience and skills, competition for funding or its perceived threats was generating insiders and outsiders in different settings. Members of larger organisations with greater resources could attend meetings with funders and local government officers regularly; were familiar with changing discourse and arrangements; and some identified themselves as effective sector boundary spanners. Small and longstanding grassroots organisations were effectively neighbourhood gatekeepers, with power in relation to local knowledge and service users but little influence over planning or procurement.

Larger contracts, capacity-building schemes and overall growth in VSO service delivery have been strong drivers towards VS change, exacerbating this polarisation, and creating winners and losers from the recent public service commissioning environment. Among larger organisations in Wharton, there was often a conscious strategy to construct good networks of relationships, and awareness of the competitive advantages to be gained. This runs counter to the rhetoric of fair and transparent competition – the level playing field scrutinised by the Audit Commission (2007). As, Marguerite, a manager in the regional centre of a large national children's charity based in Wharton, indicated:

'If you want to be successful in winning contracts, it's not just about bid quality – though of course that matters – you need to stay informed, read between the lines, keep in touch with service planners, commissioners – networking I guess. They'll know you can deliver, you're on side; and it helps if you're ahead of what's coming.'

Small VSOs, by contrast, had little time or resources to network, and as Wynne's (2008) research in Manchester shows, often failed to access the necessary information on opportunities for funding, or if they did, the timing, scale and complexity of the bids proved prohibitive, without specialist support. Other studies also point to the informal networks and relationships established by individual public and VS boundary spanners as providing 'insider' information and underpinning successes in gaining contracts (Bennett, 2008; Lewis, 2010).

In Wharton, it was hard to disentangle fears from the reality of whether large organisations had become preferred providers because of the range of factors involved. Competitive advantage could be gained from:

- knowledge and insider information about tenders, bids and expectations;
- resources and capacity to bid adequately;
- nurturing good boundary spanners among workers;
- networking and operating within dominant cultures of arrangements.

In early years and play work, relatively new providers, including social enterprises and others with a string of organisations regionally, had gained contracts while some small VSOs had lost funding. Combining service activities across areas and reframing contracts made it hard to assess specific losses. Equally, some small VSOs were reluctant to compete for increasingly large contracts or bid jointly with others, choosing to avoid being shaped by procurement demands. While these small VSOs can be viewed as disadvantaged competitively, their resistance to remodelling to meet funders' requirements can also be understood as driven by concerns about autonomy and commitment to local stakeholders and missions.

Remodelling provision

Local government officers in Wharton clearly intended to shape provision and encourage growth and development through commissioning but anticipated including both small and large providers. However, small VSOs saw no overt strategy to reassure them that local expertise and continuity of effective projects would be strong considerations in allocating contracts, and much in their experiences suggested otherwise. Moreover, there was some evidence that large organisations were consistently contract winners, not because commissioners doubted the abilities of small VSOs to deliver good provision but because they failed to communicate in a convincing language and style for funders. Although some small VSOs subsequently became subcontractors, a number failed to gain contracts altogether.

As one VSO worker said: "We just weren't on message ... that's sum-total of their feedback!" While commissioners reported that unsuccessful bids failed to reassure them about quality, informal commentary highlighted communication and comfortability, a story reflected in other research (Macmillan, 2010). Clearly, organisations with good boundary spanners were more likely to create good relationships with funders, share the same discourse and achieve funding success; and cross-sector networking was more prevalent among larger organisations.

In the longer term, if smaller VSOs are increasingly eased out of the market, the acknowledged advantages that they bring are lost, including locally accountable trustees from among area residents, good local knowledge and a history of networks for referrals across different services. In parallel, the flexibility that is possible in small organisations and the opportunities for users to influence services are diminished as providers grow in size and provision is increasingly defined and administered from a distance. Many small providers in Wharton feared that, as area fortunes shifted, large organisations entering localities would not stay: they would pursue new funding opportunities or easier challenges, leaving gaps in services. Conversely, Karen, a Wharton family advice centre worker, observed: "Local groups like us will stick; we're invested in the local area and people. But big organisations coming in, they won't be here for the long game or put in that extra mile to support people and argue for what's needed locally."

Whereas small VSOs often lacked the resources to cost services properly or to support staff to write complicated bids, larger organisations admitted that they could hide costs in other overheads, if they chose to engage in a new venture, undermining contract assumptions about full cost recovery and 'fair' competition. If costs and presentational features are privileged above other factors in allocating contracts, this resource competition is patently unfair, favouring large over small providers, despite apparent policy interest in local experience and responsiveness.

The competitive arrangements of commissioning have not only discriminated types of organisation, but seem likely to progressively reshape the landscape of provision, as small providers opt out, lose out or enter a downward spiral with underfunded services. Significant shifts in the service environment began some 30 years ago but the last decade saw changes accelerate with the growth of publicly funded contracts delivered through the VS. The claims for competition include fairness and improved service outcomes but the disparities in size and power of organisations and the dominant discourse and arrangements associated with increasingly large-scale contracts have created new rules of play, disadvantaging small VSOs. Moreover, there is little evidence of service improvements resulting from competitive contracting, and reverse evidence from recent reports (Long, 2012; Sanders, 2012), indicating worsening experiences for service users. Equally worrying are the longer-term and often unplanned effects of remodelling welfare provision, which are also transforming the profile of VSOs. The further contraction of local government and wider dispersal of publicly funded services promises a step change in privatising services, which, up to now, have been located largely with public and voluntary sectors. The consequences of these recent changes will be discussed further in the final chapter.

Dilemmas: choosing to compete or not?

This research belies the premise that markets produce fair mechanisms for generating effective and more responsive services. Rushley officers rationalised the move to contracts in this way but it subsequently became clear that they expected to cut costs and achieve contract compliance by pressuring the VSOs into a nationally driven agenda, paradoxically, more closely resembling the school provision that young people had rejected. In both Rushley and Wharton, VSOs entered processes of outsourcing and commissioning optimistically, keen to see ambiguous, ad-hoc funding decisions replaced by a properly costed basis for their future services. However, such aspirations proved short-lived, and the contract culture that ensued transformed the culture of inter-organisational relationships and the emphasis of services. Cross-sector relationships deteriorated and local autonomy in designing services declined.

Capacity-building schemes and joint bids have been promoted as ways to address perceived barriers to a level playing field for small VSOs trying to access contracts but these tackle some obstacles, while constructing others. Rather than improvements, examples above highlight ways in which resources and activities are diverted towards managing funding and contracting arrangements, away from a direct response to service users. Small VSOs have had options to change and develop capacity, to join forces with others and to seek competitive advantage by adopting, at least in part, the discourse and arrangements of funders. However, some have chosen to resist such transitions to sustain their missions and locally responsive provision, seeking alternative means of survival.

The pressure to compete on costs and meet contract conditions drives organisations towards restricting the scope of services delivered, excluding high-risk or high-cost users and innovative activities. Reduced flexibility and narrowing of provision; services less open to influence by user groups; and a gradual re-engineering of VSOs' activities and purposes – these are all visible outcomes of contractualism. With many VSO efforts channelled into competing for resources, this re-engineering seems of little benefit to service users, and undermines the kind of shared inter-organisational learning that promotes service alternatives and positive developments.

Paradoxically, VSOs' expertise in bringing flexible and alternative approaches to resolving longstanding social problems was sought by New Labour and has also been recognised in the coalition government's rhetoric and structural reform plans. However, neither government has questioned its commitment to market mechanisms as appropriate means to fund and decide between service providers nor recognised their damaging effects in welfare provision. Moreover, welfare resources have become scarcer but commitment to market competition in political ideology has strengthened.

Competition is rationalised on the basis that good services will be the ones demanded and therefore thrive. However, in a welfare 'market', commissioners rather than service users determine provision and exercise purchasing power; and as examples above demonstrate, local knowledge, expertise and users' experiences are often absent from the discourse and criteria associated with contracting. This leaves potential beneficiaries as the players with least influence over the nature of services, especially those who are least advantaged and have most need for services.

As Glennerster (2003) argues, marketisation is a poor guarantee of democracy and can be highly damaging in welfare services since competition is a defective mechanism for ensuring services responsive to the poorest in society. Where users are among the most marginalised groups in society, using competitive and, increasingly, financial criteria to determine provision reduces complex political judgements about how to fulfil socially responsive aims for technicist decisions. Where welfare services for marginalised users are subject to market pressures, as in the cases above, VSOs have often become preferred providers because they are seen to tailor services more effectively to the needs of disadvantaged minority groups, offering cost advantages over state and private providers for whom generic services are more economically viable. However, this environment is changing as Chapter Seven illustrates; and prescriptive specifications integral to the contracting process are superseding tailored or responsive options, serving users poorly and potentially failing to address significant social problems.

Change or independence?

Chapter Two highlighted transformations in the policy and organisational environment over two decades and questioned the extent to which VSOs had intentionally embraced or resisted changes. My findings here convey mixed messages. The VSOs illustrated here have neither succumbed to coercive isomorphic pressures nor slipped unthinkingly into changes in response to prevalent policy and organisational cultures. The three Rushley VSOs resisted incorporation into New Public Management values and practices and, similarly, some Wharton VSOs made explicit decisions about which changes they would adopt and which they would resist. Yet, there are also examples where VSOs, faced with more powerful agency cultures and requirements, felt unable to influence the shape of externally defined arrangements, recognising risks to funding from asserting resistance. To counter such threats, many small VSOs coupled resistance with a level of accommodation, seeking to retain their core purposes and their 'organisational soul' (Cairns, 2009, p 43).

The examples also illustrate VSOs attracted to changes, entering new arrangements with optimism, but this was often short-lived. Initial outsourcing and subsequent commissioning promised both funding stability and ironically greater VS independence, alongside increased status as service delivery partners – which in each case failed to materialise. In parallel, new organisations have emerged, and with larger VSOs, have generally embraced changes more enthusiastically, benefiting from growth in income and opportunities in the New Labour years. While the jury is out on longer-term effects of recent government reforms, initial assurances of an important service role for locally based VSOs reflect earlier experiences of broken promises, with criteria excluding small VSOs.

Retaining a strong sense of autonomous identity and organisational roots has been identified as a way in which VSOs remain resilient in the face of difficulties (Milbourne, 2009a; Nevile, 2010). That growth and increased capacity therefore strengthen sustainability is for that reason contested, since increased income may also restrict independence. Factors that affect VS resilience and survival are discussed further in Chapter Seven, which addresses the effects of contract losses on VSOs.

Changing cross-sector relationships: legitimate knowledge and arrangements

A key issue emerging from the Rushley study was the damage to cross-sector relationships following the introduction of contracts: local government officers became distanced from local knowledge; and instead of joint endeavour and shared information about local needs, contracts were framed within generic, top-down specifications and targets. Government policies have emphasised the inclusion of local knowledge in service planning and wider public inclusion in decision-making bodies but commissioning and competitive procurement have formalised and bureaucratised relationships between those procuring and those providing services, resulting in commissioners progressively more remote from service users, and decisions hidden from public view.

The Wharton examples similarly illustrate the conceptual distance between funders and small local providers as contracts grow in size, resulting in judgements based on trust and local reputation displaced by externally determined criteria, and meaningful dialogue about services supplanted by adherence to shared rituals of organisational behaviour. Privileging certain discourse and approaches over alternatives, constructs powerful cultures around service funding and delivery that largely exclude small VSOs but it also shapes providers' activities and ultimately redirects their purposes.

Findings both in Rushley and Wharton echo those of studies elsewhere (Martikke, 2008; OCVA, 2008) that there was declining knowledge among local government officers of community-based activities and users' experiences, as earlier practices of visiting projects dwindled. Consequently, the culture of expectations about ways of doing things, which is constructed from a confluence of policy influences and the dominant practices of large funding organisations, generate insiders and outsiders, with most small VSOs remote from the inside track. Nevertheless, the isomorphic pressures affecting the style and operational modes of many VSOs struggling to win contracts have encouraged the positive acquisition of new skills but also produced negative impacts on their independent goals and practices.

Ultimately, contract specifications embedded in cultures and arrangements that legitimate their design become divorced from the real quality of, or need for, provision. Consequently, competitive contract allocations have the potential for irrational outcomes since criteria underpinning decisions may be tangential to factors that match service needs with a contractor's ability to provide these well. The result may be to reshape local provision in unintended ways, which neither serve the interests of users nor improve services. Despite advocacy for more intelligent commissioning (IDeA, 2009), the cultures and discourse surrounding competitive bids and increasingly large contracts reinforce this separation between funder–procurers and local experiences, generating a decline in real intelligence informing contract design about the challenges of local services and needs.

The unwritten rules of the game, significantly shaped by the assumed cultures of contractualism, dominate what counts as legitimate knowledge and understanding about service provision. VSOs also adopt these modes of operation to maintain competitive advantage but as contracts become larger and encompass greater levels of complexity, small VSOs experience correspondingly greater difficulty in accessing service funding without significantly changing their activities. By legitimising certain information about services and obscuring other knowledge from public view, contractualism reifies this proxy information to establish service winners and losers according to their adherence to the rules of play. The landscape of services and providers therefore starts to reshape, whether through winners shifting their emphasis to match that of funders or whether through others' loss of funded provision.

Small VSOs in both Rushley and Wharton held a strong belief in the value and public benefit of their provision but often found it hard to convey more than anecdotal information on its impacts. There is limited widespread evidence on whether devolving public services to non-state providers has achieved improvements; the conditions in which outsourcing might generate better services; or the kinds of providers or sectors best able to accommodate these. Instead, policy ideology commending the benefits of markets and competition is interwoven with diverse procurer, provider and user perceptions and experiences of relative costs and benefits. Consequently, the transfer out of major segments of public services represents an accelerating but largely unproven social experiment.

Fragmenting providers and changing the landscape of provision

With growing differences between the cultures and finances of larger and smaller VSOs and resources converging in fewer larger organisations, the fears and initial evidence (nef, 2010) of large corporations being attracted to compete alongside VSOs for services shed by local and national governments are materialising. As the 'Tesco-isation' of the VS (Macmillan, 2010, p 5) advances, it is clear not only that there is fragmentation between large and small VSOs but also that corporates are starting to colonise service delivery spaces previously held by VSOs, with consequent closures in longstanding VS provision.

Alcock (2010a) has argued the political strength and importance of conceptual unity in the VS despite its evident diversity in size, purposes and operational styles. While others have contested the rationale for this argument (see Chapter One), there are values, motives and characteristics inherent in ideas of a VS that are fundamentally different from those associated with public or private sectors (Kendall and Knapp, 1995). These have to do with the 'public good' and relate to improving social welfare for those in need and may also involve advocating for social justice. Small VSOs are most often associated with these values but the missions of large national VSOs are also underpinned by philanthropic founding stories (Schwabenland, 2006), despite more recent shifts in emphasis.

The transitions in organisational approaches among larger VSOs suggest a greater cross-over of values and purposes between sectors, although Billis (2010) argues that even where there are strong elements of boundary crossing, sector identities remain powerful. However, if the values and cost benefits of VSOs, that is, their facility to offer low-cost specialist and bespoke services, are discounted in the drive for new scaled-up contracting arrangements, this loses sight of the reasons for choosing VS providers but it also facilitates the take-over of provision by larger contractors. The result is a sharp decline of small local VSOs among funded service providers unless they shift their approaches to become subcontractors to large contractors. As some VSO workers described above indicated, if contracts move towards the corporate sector, the profit motive means that as incentives arise or cease, providers may be short-stay in an area, and their services limited to broad 'off the peg' provision, ultimately leaving significant gaps in provision.

Contrary to the rhetoric of establishing fairness through means of open competition, the intensification of market-driven arrangements endorses the inclusion and exclusion of different kinds of service providers and beneficiaries, exacerbating existing social inequalities. It also increases polarisation among VSOs. Research already offers some cautionary messages about the inequitable distribution and outcomes of provision resulting from markets introduced into welfare services (Glennerster, 2003). The increased emphasis on marketisation encourages corporates to colonise new territory mostly occupied until now by public or community providers. The advance of mega-contracts, coupled with Payment by Results, further disadvantages small VSOs. Few have the resources to maintain services for challenging or high-risk users, faced with reduced funding and payment only on successful outcomes.

Rather than addressing the broken society (Blond, 2010), the coalition government's policies appear to retreat from state responsibility for services and social problems, opening the way to increased competition for remaining public funds. Ad-hoc voluntary action is assumed to cater for service gaps and those left behind. At a time when resources are scarce, the unplanned outcomes from powerful market bidders competing for service funding are likely to be exacerbated, and the re-engineering of public and community-based services accelerated. Marketisation, as these studies of earlier phases of outsourcing show, can be happenstance and produce unintended casualties among providers and service users; unexpected resistances; and an unjust reshaping of provision across different areas. However, VSOs are no longer facing simply a shift establishing public sector contracts and controls over previously ungoverned terrain (Carmel and Harlock, 2008) but a substantial transformation of public and voluntary sector landscapes, which relocates power with private sector and unpredictable market forces.

Some concerns arising from this discussion of accelerating marketisation and the changing landscape of services are addressed in later chapters, including the extent to which questions of 'local', size and sector matter among factors that will improve services for users. Organisational size and turnover clearly offer competitive advantage in accessing service contracts but do they, as some VSO workers indicate, diminish the responsiveness and value of services to users? In a changing political climate, contractualism and competition have weakened the position of VSO providers; and the scaling up of contracts has intensified threats to small community-based VSOs – organisations acknowledged by both the coalition and the New Labour governments as offering creative solutions to social problems. Since knowledge and judgements about services depend so heavily on proxy indicators – largely prescribed, measurable data – yet innovation is often seen as necessary for improvements, how can we really know what factors generate better services for users in the longer term? There is little research justification for the competitive service environment that has been constructed or for the service landscape that is emerging. The next chapter follows on this discussion by considering how services are assessed, debating the contradictions of performance prescription, service risks and innovation.

FIVE

Performance and shifting accountabilities: from trust-based to regulated inter-organisational relationships

Introduction

Competition and outsourcing, as is evident from the last chapter, have been closely associated with an increase in regulation, detailed service specification, targeted outcomes and performance monitoring. As Chapter Two outlined, a gradual re-engineering of dominant organisational arrangements over some 25 years has produced a burgeoning of regulatory frameworks, and command and control forms of governance and management that have gradually had an impact on voluntary sector organisations (VSOs). From roughly 2007 onwards, government policies began to acknowledge an over-emphasis on regulation, professional standards and excessive performance targets and their potential to undermine the development of responsive local services. More latterly this is visible in the rhetoric of localism and criticism of big government. However, as outsourcing and contracts have expanded, the opportunities for locally designed service targets and community-level transparency in narratives around services appear more remote. There is a contradiction therefore between recent policy aspirations to reduce the burden of audit, while rapidly advancing the outsourcing of public services. The recent shifts are in how the sectors and players are being aligned in the chains of accountability.

This chapter discusses changing cultures of accountability and reporting and their effects on VSO activities. First it considers the more concrete effects of a growing performance culture on VSOs and insights that could be gained from a trust-based approach. It draws on a variety of examples from the studies outlined in Chapter Three to offer insights into ways that particular approaches to audit have become culturally embedded in expectations and organisational arrangements, posing problems for small VSOs. As the title of the chapter suggests, the chapter explores the changing nature of relationships between funders andVSOs; and using the lens of trust, highlights ways that differential power exercised through frameworks of performance management and regulation undermine open communication in inter-organisational relationships. Paradoxically, the means used to ensure accountability and manage risks for funders may increase risks of concealed service failures, while also impinging on voluntary sector (VS) autonomy.The final part of the chapter also discusses recent evidence to assess whether the rhetoric of localism and reducing the command and control culture of the state (Kendall, 2010) is bringing benefits toVSOs.

Command and control culture: costs and benefits to the voluntary sector?

With the spread of public service commissioning from 2006 onwards, much discussion in both policy and academic debates has focused on the increased burdens that service contracts and monitoring have placed on VSOs, often disproportionate to the size of contract and level of service, placing unrealistic demands on smallVSOs. One of the policy remedies has been to invest in sector skills and capacity building (Home Office, 2004) and subsequently to promote clustering, partnerships and mergers (Cabinet Office, 2009); and these continue to be key strategies, albeit with reduced resources.The emphasis has been on buildingVS capacity to meet external needs, with little real attempt to reassess dominant approaches to accountability, which have become more problematic forVSOs, with theTesco–isation of services discussed in the last chapter. Contract compliance is increasingly being assured through performance criteria that have grown in technical complexity and are demanding high levels of legal and financial knowledge (Bennett, 2011).

Performance management, integral to New Public Management cultures (Clarke et al, 2000b), has expanded in parallel with marketisation and outsourcing of public services. It has been utilised by large funding agencies to ensure contract and project compliance, and to control financial and reputational risks. Trusting professionals or small VS providers in their areas of expertise has gradually been displaced by external regulation and by beliefs about meritocracy and competition (Sennett, 2005).The choice agenda and governance through managerial controls (Brown and Calnan, 2010) were promoted as remedies to perceived problems of excessive professional autonomy and unresponsive services, with price and performance frameworks established in the place of trust. The rapid spread and sophistication of computer–based information systems have subsequently enabled and accelerated what were already growing demands for more widely visible accountability through provision of measurable data.

For some time, therefore, there has been increased pressure on even the smallest VSOs to provide measurable evidence of outcomes, and considerable work has gone into helping VSOs to exhibit what they do more effectively (Ellis, 2009; nef, 2009; NCVO, 2010). More recently, the ability to demonstrate social and economic impact has also been integral to accessing certain contracts but often without clear concepts of the potential difficulties of evaluating these outcomes. As Macmillan and McLaren (2012, p 11) point out, there has been a vigorous debate on the 'assumptions, costs and relative merits of different approaches to assessing and measuring different aspects of value'. Social outcomes, such as improved long-term health and wellbeing and better local environments, are recognised as adding economic value, and as areas where VSOs can have a significant impact: an impact that is unlikely to result from the actions of either the state or markets alone. These discussions re-open questions about what outcomes are desirable from services and the best approaches for finding out what has been achieved if we are to understand the social value of processes involved and not simply to measure targeted outcomes.

Specified targets and outcomes serve to reassure public funders and provide evidence for wider public and political accountability but they often transfer both financial and reputational risks to service providers. The onerous demands of performance frameworks and their wider effects on the emphasis of VS work have prompted considerable discussion in non-profit literature worldwide (Moxham and Boaden, 2007). There have been questions about the appropriateness of measures used to assess quality in VS services (Shaw and Allen, 2006) and the extent to which user-responsive activities, for which VS providers are sought, are constrained by target-driven services (Cairns et al, 2006; Proulx and Denis-Savard, 2007). Performance cultures have also promoted competitive ranking and formal, potentially punitive, control mechanisms, which have become inimical to organisational learning (Ellis, 2009). This encourages gaming and discourages open communication, realism and authenticity (Cooper, 2001). Paradoxically, the measures intended to assure and improve services and to make the work of non-state providers more publicly transparent may well be diverting efforts away from real improvements to quality (Rustin, 2004).

For a sector valued for its ability to attract marginal users and to tackle challenging social problems in innovative ways, these contradictions raise significant concerns about impacts on VS flexibility. Brown and Calnan's (2010) discussion of health services illustrates how the detailed control of standards and monitoring frameworks can prove more dysfunctional than the trust in professional autonomies that they replaced. They argue that the innate tendency of performance management to reshape activities towards required targets encourages health professionals to lose sight of service users' real needs. For this reason, VS concerns have also focused on the potential for mission drift (Macmillan, 2010), as the need to meet targets successfully, impinges first on organisational activities and subsequently reshapes goals. As Power (1994) argues, audit reshapes not only the focus of activities but also eventually what counts as valuable in an organisation. The expansion in the VS share of service provision from the 1990s to 2009, coupled with the power of audit, have therefore presented a significant challenge to VS independence, leading Cairns et al (2006, p 1) to question whether VSOs are becoming 'agents of government' rather than 'servants of the community'.

The recent reduction of funds to the VS and the growth in corporate providers entering the public service field seem unlikely to lessen the performative culture surrounding service delivery; indeed, recent accounts indicate the reverse (Marsden, 2011). These shifts provoke questions about the extent to which VSOs may now become agents for corporations, as the local state carries declining responsibility for local service delivery. The powerful cultures that underpin performance management may be adopted by corporate contractors but what is easily lost in this transition is the state's underlying purpose in accounting for public resources: to ensure their use for the public good. VSOs also share purposes around public benefit and social value, although often related to specific groups in the population or specific localities; but in these new arrangements the legitimacy of local expertise is being marginalised (Bennett, 2011). As profit-driven corporate contractors permeate the public service terrain, lines of public accountability are increasingly obscured in complicated supply chains. Consequently, indicators of service performance are progressively removed from local or publicly accountable design, undermining the policy aspirations of both the current coalition government and the previous Labour government for locally responsive services. Performance management by state agencies impinges on the autonomous activities and purposes of VSOs, extending the governable terrain of the state (Carmel and Harlock, 2008) but in recent contracting processes, this terrain is being relinquished to the steer of powerful corporate agencies.

Critical understanding of trust

As earlier chapters discussed, a growing literature has examined changing roles between the state and the VS in this mixed economy of welfare but there has been limited consideration of trust in these relationships. As pressures on public sector spending and competition for funding grow, there is a shifting dynamic between 'old' and 'new' values, as the distinctive character of VSOs gives way to activities that have acquired legitimacy through dominant managerial cultures. Consequently, trust that formerly underpinned varied relationships between public and VS agencies is being widely displaced by formalised arrangements that control and manage meanings, normalising an asymmetry of relationships between the state and the VS, and more recently drawing the private sector into that arena. The growth of widespread service contracts, with associated performance controls and risk management, has produced an imbalance in the ways that risks are borne, with negative consequences for organisational learning and innovation (Milbourne and Cushman, 2012). Organisational identities and local accountabilities have also come under pressure, with conflicting interests, values and 'ways of doing things' (Hoggett, 2004, p 119) between purchasers and providers, creating barriers to building cooperative cross-sector work.

There are different approaches to understanding trust and this chapter draws especially on Hardy et al's (1998) critical theory-based framework, which can be contrasted with a more limited, positivist concept of 'trust' contained in the commonly used ability, benevolence, integrity (ABI) framework (Mayer et al, 1995). Hardy et al (1998) explore the difference between trust relationships, and power relationships masquerading as trust. They suggest (1998, p 79) two forms of trust: spontaneous and generated; and two forms of power-based masquerade: manipulation (where dominant actors manage meanings) and capitulation (where subordinate actors surrender to dominant arrangements). Trust and masquerade are distinguished by the process of constructing meaning and by the allocation of risk. In trust relationships, meaning is co-created and 'trust results from a communicative process in which shared meanings either exist, or are created through a reciprocal relationship' (Hardy et al, 1998, p 71). This necessarily involves all participants and demands forms of communication that make space for examining differences, not only harmonies.

Building and sustaining trust in inter-organisational relationships is challenging and often more complex than readily acknowledged in models that emphasise the benevolence of the trustee to the truster

(Mayer et al, 1995) or argue that trust and predictable behaviour are mutually reinforcing (Grey and Garsten, 2001). However, these understandings overlook power inequalities and the importance of communicative action in underpinning organisational relationships and motivation in service delivery. As Bachmann (2001) elaborates, patterns of power and trust operate at both interpersonal and structural levels. When what appears to be trust is a facade for power, meaning is managed, distorted or imposed by the dominant participant. Commonly, hierarchical arrangements and specified transactions underpin cross-sector relationships, controlling risk but undermining trust and motivation for mutual learning, since learning requires the possibility of audience for suppressed voices (Clegg et al, 2005).

In this masquerade, speech is often strategic and agreement suborned by the dominant organisational partner. Predictable but imbalanced relationships may be maintained based on assumed cultures or sets of arrangements; however, managed meanings often exclude or marginalise those with limited power, who may increasingly mistrust, or become disillusioned with, the process. Power within communicative processes needs to be recognised and addressed, if shared meanings are to emerge, rather than meanings being managed in ways that maintain or increase power differentials. It is only when trust is present – either spontaneous or generated – that speech approaches emancipatory discourse (Habermas, 1990), meanings can be shared and ventures are joint. In trust-based relationships, risk is shared; in masquerades, risk is passed by the more powerful to the subordinate. Governance through targets and performance indicators could be trust based, if these are co-developed and agreed, but as Davies (2011) emphasises, in governance networks, hierarchical power invariably reasserts itself.

Trust, control and risks in a changing environment

The previous UK government identified the VS as central to improving 'public services including ... as advisers influencing the design of services and as innovators' (HM Treasury and Cabinet Office, 2007, p 49). While the emphasis extends to innovators from all sectors, the coalition government's position (Cabinet Office, 2010b) is remarkably similar. Yet earlier discussion suggests considerable inequity of influence over the definition of services and outcomes; and experience in the UK and elsewhere (Burnley et al, 2005; Moxham and Boaden, 2007) shows that performance targets have continued to be centrally defined with only marginal room for negotiation. They are therefore an exercise in power. However, as Shaw and Allen (2006) argue, where trust-based relationships are dominant, narratives around activities and achievements often offer a better guide to funders' assessment of the value of services than prescribed and measurable indicators.

Walgenbach's (2001) research on the spread of standards and performance certification demonstrates that highly specified regulatory and performance frameworks fail to fulfil the purposes intended. While Grey and Garsten (2001) claim that trust comes from exercising control through ensuring predictability, Ghoshal and Moran (1996, p 24) argue that trust and risk management are inversely related, with rigorous specification signalling that controllees are neither trusted nor trustworthy and that 'surveillance ... threatens the controllee's personal autonomy and decreases ... intrinsic motivation'. Similarly, at the organisational level, audit surveillance, far from deterring opportunistic behaviour, may actively encourage it, enhancing the potential for moral hazard.

In analysing inter-organisational alliances, de Man and Roijakkers (2009, p 77) highlight two elements of risk as important: 'relational risk (that partners will deceive each other) and performance risk (that the alliance will not deliver the expected results)'. Public agencies, increasingly concerned with value for money, tend to prioritise performance risks but often discount relational risks. However, this research identifies high performance risks and low relational risks as generally best managed through trust-based governance, a message that seems to have had little influence on recent state–VSO or contractual relationships.

Government agencies carry significant risks for quality of provision, whether through poor service delivery, inadequate information on service needs or lack of innovation. Rather than looking to trust-based relationships, however, they have increasingly sought to control risks through a focus on audit and performance measurement and by transferring risks to providers. These growing performance cultures have similarly transformed some VS management practices through coercive and mimetic isomorphism (DiMaggio and Powell, 1983). However, the escalation of data collection can readily erode autonomy without ensuring accountability, providing 'rituals of verification' (Power, 1997, p 145) and exacerbating the inevitable tension between accountability and autonomy. Many VSOs experience data reporting as intrusive and time-consuming surveillance, which signals a lack of trust (Milbourne and Cushman, 2012) and generates an atmosphere where concealing failure is a rational response. Conversely, strengthening trust allows an environment that moves from blaming to learning, supporting innovation (Willcocks and Craig, 2009).

Recent governments have recognised the value of organisational diversity in promoting enterprising solutions to social challenges (OCS, 2010). Both past and current administrations have also recommended that funding bodies should not be 'overly risk averse in funding decisions' (HM Treasury, 2006, p 10), arguing against uniform and heavily specified frameworks of control (OCS, 2010). However, there is an apparent denial of the acceleration of such frameworks as public sector outsourcing has spread and magnified; and as Muehlberger (2007) describes in the private sector, despite outsourcing services, arrangements have been subject to progressively greater control, delimiting activities and approaches.

As Chapter Two considered, relationships between VSOs and state agencies are not neat, boundaried or homogenous: they are multi-layered and dynamic, influenced by both horizontal and vertical policy environments (Alcock and Kendall, 2011). Historically, many VSOs were, either wholly or partly, grant funded through public bodies; and services were often co-constructed with local government. With the decline of grant funding, contracts for VSOs to provide diverse public services have been accompanied by the spread of regulatory controls and risk management, producing increasingly asymmetric power relationships.

The multiple pressures on VSOs to engage with other agencies, within and across sectors, have intensified, and complexity and formality in relationships and governance have grown correspondingly (Maier and Meyer, 2011). Joint enterprise and joint service provision are typically characterised by evolving trust relationships, although this may not be the case; and trust is assumed to emerge from equal, although distinct, contributions. While contracted service provision *may* be governed by trust, procurement contracts and associated performance frameworks more frequently involve hierarchical power relationships (O'Brien, 2006; Baines et al, 2011). These may appropriate the language of trust but often coerce consensus and restrict alternative approaches, in a facade of trust.

In contracted services, the trust basis has been superseded by client–contractor relationships, often derived from private sector models, which may translate poorly into public service settings. Lessons from other contexts and sectors are therefore valuable. Reviewing outsourcing, Weeks and Feeny (2008, pp 140-1) distinguish between three types of trust: personal, competence based and motivational. *Personal trust* is based on a belief in the personal integrity of partners; while *competence-based trust* rests on a belief in the other's professionalism, which may be eroded through operational problems. *Motivational trust* is based on joint opportunities for reward from success and joint exposure to penalties from failure – trust underpinned by appropriate risk- and reward-sharing mechanisms. Comparing these definitions with the commonly used ABI framework applied to understanding trust (Mayer et al, 1995), personal and competence-based trust parallel integrity and ability. However, motivational trust differs from the individual, voluntaristic concept of 'benevolence': while benevolence carries no obligation, motivation-based trust assumes joint endeavour and a two-way responsibility.

Hardy et al's (1998) discussion of generated trust suggests that trust develops with experience of the other. However, McKnight et al (1998) argue that people frequently start by trusting but that this can be cemented or eroded depending on subsequent actions, local context and cultural factors (Hofstede, 1980). For example, initial VS optimism in strategies concerned with localism and devolution of power has been short lived, as VSOs across many fields lose funding and face closure (Crawley and Watkin, 2011), illustrating the tenuous nature of trust. Grey and Garston (2001, p 246) similarly highlight the ongoing fragility of trust, arguing that significant (post-bureaucratic) organisational changes demand a recasting of shared social practices from which to construct new trust-based relationships. In rapidly changing situations, the security of shared rules, discourse and values underpinning predictable practices are interrupted, producing a precarious environment for trust, and little prospect of the hoped-for growth in community engagement. Insecure settings enable powerful agencies to impose arrangements that provide welcome anchors but are rarely mutually constructed.

Understanding the conditions that can strengthen trust therefore become important considerations. McKnight et al (1998, p 480) identify initial trust as being secured at an interpersonal and group level through tendencies 'to share common goals'; and describe this as *unit grouping*, which could apply where a VSO and a public agency cooperate in a common project. However, to maintain trust, both parties must exhibit trusting and trustworthy behaviour and the conditions for motivational trust must be present. The variable outcomes from cross-sector developments described below and in the next chapter demonstrate failures to understand the conditions needed for successful joint endeavour, and the consequent erosion of trust both in the unit grouping and the project.

Erosion of trust

In what follows, the chapter draws on examples from two studies also discussed in the previous chapter, exploring issues raised above. The background to the studies was discussed further in Chapter Three. The examples highlight ways in which a growing culture of targets, measurement and specified services has impinged on small VSOs in Rushley and Wharton, affecting their organisational activities and independence. The examples consider the effects on VSOs of the performance demands placed on them, examining the erosion of trust between local agencies and the ways that risk has been managed and transferred in contracts. The displacement of trust in favour of performance management through data reporting is a common thread running through the examples, and prompts the question of whether rebuilding trust and shifting towards soft performance indicators are ways to improve quality of services and professional creativity.

The cases below illustrate both the burdens of increased regulation and monitoring and ways in which goals and the emphasis of activities can shift, even when organisations are self-consciously resisting mission drift. The initial case highlights the costs of moving from a trust-based relationship to a formal contractual relationship underpinned by complex specification and targets, emphasising the potential damage to services and the need to reassess alternatives.

From joint work to contracted services: shifting what counts as legitimate achievement

In Rushley, the three small case study VSOs – Crossroads, Horizons and The Place – had received grant funding for providing services for young people excluded or truanting from school for a decade or more. The local education authority (LEA) officers approached the VSOs, to start negotiations on Service Level Agreements as the basis of longer-term contracts, marking a key change in the nature of relationships. However, the first experience of change was the redundancy of the LEA liaison officer, Claire, who was familiar with the three VSOs' work and her replacement by a contracts liaison officer.

The VSOs and Claire had established a relationship, which demonstrates all three elements of Weeks and Feeny's (2008) typology of trust: personal, competence based and motivational, and this underpinned shared commitments to improving the service. Anna, a VSO management committee (MC) member, described Claire as someone who "understands and values what we do. She wants us to succeed with the young people as much as we do. She shares our concerns ... she has that professional background and knowledge, she can support staff when the going's tough" (Anna, The Place).

Mutual trust was generated through a willingness to explore difficulties and share expertise so that learning and improvements could take place, and a joint language of what constituted success was generated. Claire visited the organisations and monitored achievements as much through narrative and observation, as through reports on measured outcomes that the LEA increasingly required. Shared knowledge about the services; and valuing, and knowledge of, the other's work helped to sustain mutual respect for the other's competence. Good personal relationships were built up over more than five years; and joint endeavour – sharing difficulties alongside achievements – underpinned motivation to improve and develop services.

Not surprisingly, the decision to remove Claire from her liaison role provoked antipathy towards the new contracts liaison officer but his actions subsequently did little to mitigate this, suggesting limited interest in the VSOs' provision. Visits to the organisations became rare and VSO workers perceived that the value of local knowledge and achievements had been displaced by terms legitimised in the new contract, which seemed remote from their everyday activities. Rather than jointly created purposes and meanings (Weick, 1995), the VSOs were increasingly asked to adopt superimposed goals and arrangements but communications often lacked common understandings and disconnected models were operating in parallel.

As specifications for service contracts were discussed, the VSO MC members identified little respect for their achievements in an extremely challenging service environment with disengaged young people, despite longstanding, successful local reputations. Instead, the contracts proposed a plethora of unrealistic targets accompanied by financial penalties for failures, which became major concerns, posing significant risks and also barriers in the negotiations.

Anna from The Place graphically illustrated the wide range of risks that they could face, asking: "If the student who was deaf and had a history of arson that the LEA placed with us, had set fire to The Place ... that's our real world; what'd be a successful outcome for him? And the penalty for failure?"

Birgit from Crossroads went on to explain the difficulties of prescribing attendance targets and the constraints on how the VSOs could work:

'So, we raise a problem ... but do the officers see it? They don't.... So it [the attendance target] is now 87% – but for each child ... they don't see how different children's histories are. Some will never manage to come more than 60% but it's what they do achieve from nothing.'

These targets mirrored those set for mainstream schools nationally and yet were being applied indiscriminately to young people who had not attended any education for up to two years in some cases. The contract allowed no averaging of attendance but proposed a financial levy for each day a young person fell short of the target.

However, the new contracts liaison officer took a different view and believed that the VSOs should comply with dominant managerial arrangements: "They're living in the past ... I know these projects have been running a long time. I'm sure as individuals, they mean well ... but ... things need planning, targets, outcomes, it has to be more specific now."

These comments represent the wider shift in culture associated with contractualism and managerial arrangements, which the VSOs were seen to be resisting. As, Jude, an elected local government member explained: "The culture's changed ... we all need to be accountable....We want to disassociate ourselves from a laissez-faire past." Accountability seemed to rely not on service reputation or professional integrity but largely on measurable performance using indicators constructed outside the context of the provision.

Contracts were debated over a 10-month period and disagreements arising from conflicting assumptions about meanings, purposes and appropriate specifications grew, with mistrust dominating discussions and entrenching differences. During VS debriefing discussions, the board members referred to the deficiencies of Rushley officers as professional managers. There was no sense of jointly agreed service goals to support motivational trust in the process, and considerable damage to belief in the individual integrity and competence of the other.

As mistrust and frustrations grew, the imposition of contract conditions also increased. There were a number of issues pending from earlier meetings, including legal information concerning staffing, when each VSO received an ultimatum to sign the 'final Service Level Agreement and Terms and Conditions of Contract' within seven days. The LEA indicated that it would otherwise seek other providers.

Although the level of coercion in the 'negotiating' relationship had grown appreciably, the shift to an ultimatum was received with shock and disbelief, since this 'final' contract contained some 14 or so pages, previously unseen, a series of inconsistencies and had imported terms from other quality assurance schemes, which made little sense in an education setting. Commenting jointly, the trustees displayed their loss of trust in the process: "Officers' refusal to entertain further discussion is … outside normal codes of conduct in negotiations and demonstrates a derisory attitude towards … [us]."

Performance measures, integral to managerial modes of operation of managerialism, are often formulated in ways that produce little meaningful evaluation of service quality (Cochrane, 2000) and are often proxy indicators aligned to government priorities. This example went further. Standards and benchmarks designed to monitor production line quality had been added to the contract conditions, possibly as a consequence of inexperience among officers under pressure to conclude this contract in a way satisfactory to their superiors. This is not a singular example and cases cited elsewhere (eg, NCIA, 2011) echo both the obscurity and inappropriateness of indicators. However, in this case, coercion did not induce capitulation to the more powerful agent, although the loss of trust at all three levels – personal, competence based and motivational – was acute. Instead, pressure and mistrust generated resistance from the three VSOs but also a breakdown in workable cross-sector relationships.

This example illustrates ways in which coercive pressures from powerful organisational cultures exerted through performance measures can damage meaningful communications, devaluing locally defined goals and destroying trust in public agencies. While the ultimatum demonstrates local government officers' assumptions about their right to determine protocol and arrangements, it is also indicative of mistrust in non-specified practices and the competence of the other. Non-compliance and lack of conformity on the part of the VSOs exacerbated officers' perceptions of them as untrustworthy partners.

The VSOs expected to be trusted because of their history of success with challenging young people, while local government officers expected any trustworthy provider to share or at least comply with their discourse and arrangements. Neither party identified the need to build better relationships in the destabilised environment; whereas better exploration of differences might have helped to build mutual learning, enabling more meaningful communication about service goals and more appropriate performance targets. Instead, diverse prior assumptions and subsequently poor communication and actions cemented defensiveness and mistrust, enlarging the divide between cultures of operation.

Reporting burdens: eroding trust?

Unlike Rushley, most Wharton VSOs identified a strong local government commitment to supporting community organisations, and discussed positive developments in relation to various young people's projects. However, VS workers pointed to a mismatch in practice, criticising top-down approaches to planning and change, poor information, short-term funding and constant changes to monitoring requirements. Initial goodwill towards public agencies had declined because of their failure to show respect to community partners. The unnecessary complexity of contract specifications and onerous, often inappropriate, data reporting requirements were recurrent criticisms, and smaller, less experienced organisations experienced these issues more keenly. There was a divide between organisations with few paid workers who felt they lacked capacity and sometimes the skills or adequate technology to respond to these demands and larger organisations that regarded the requirements as taking disproportionate time and resources away from other activities.

As Dekka from a Somalian youth group explained: "Sometimes it's not worth it. I work part time and otherwise we're volunteers. It's so much to do, the information we have to give on every youth and forms to fill, for such small funds." Many small VSOs felt that they had to reassess whether management and monitoring demands outweighed the benefits of accessing additional funding for projects. By contrast, Shona, who worked for the local area office of a large national children's charity, discussed the value of audit systems. She believed that work in the VS had often been invisible to outsiders before and saw ways in which transfer of information allowed service users to influence activities more. However, she criticised the lack of negotiation around relevant indicators that could demonstrate the impact of activities and contribute realistically to reviewing and improving services.

Almost all VSOs commented negatively on excessive reporting of numerical data and considered that the lack of value or legitimacy given to less tangible or 'soft' outcomes created a partial and fragmented picture of their real achievements. They also regarded the shift towards more anonymous forms of reporting as eroding mutual trust between public agencies, VSOs and local user groups. As Jan, a youth centre worker, commented: "It diverts our time but it can also distort the value outsiders put on our work; and mostly it feels like local government demands all these numbers so they don't trust us any more." Other VSO workers reflected similar comments, for example that commissioners lacked knowledge about the services and had become increasingly distanced from user groups, progressively weakening already fragile trust in public agencies.

During the study period in Wharton, youth centres were invited to bid for contracts to run estates-based detached youth work as a part of meeting nationally defined crime prevention targets in 'problem' neighbourhoods. VSOs already experienced in the localities were sought to work with identified groups of at-risk young people in places and at times regarded as problematic. The bidding process and final contract took six months, and as Rick, a youth centre worker, described, it was "unnecessarily complex when we and Northside were the only two groups in the ring". However, during that time, the requirements from the initial contract model changed, and there were elaborate and time-consuming procedures and checks before the VSOs could start the work. Nevertheless, they were still expected to achieve the targeted improvements in antisocial behaviour within six weeks – the original contract schedule. Such examples show how small VSOs that turn local projects into practical realities are made vulnerable by coercive and technicist performance frameworks within which they have limited power. While VSOs' vulnerability and risks of poor performance are increased, motivational trust in a jointly understood project – the starting point for the agreement – is eroded. Performance targets are imposed to manage risks for the funder but exacerbate VSO risks and deter genuine communication about the challenges or realistic achievements of such work.

Balancing performance demands and organisational goals

Hoggett et al (2009) explore the tensions that community-based workers face in balancing external demands against their own values and approaches, referring to these as dilemmatic spaces. It is in these spaces at individual and organisational levels that the balance between VSO goals and independent actions, and acceptable compromise, is worked out. The following examples demonstrate the insidious nature of external performance pressures, which impinge on flexibility and autonomous ways of working. Staff from the three VSOs in Rushley shared much common ground in their approaches to working with young people: shared communities of practice (Lave and Wenger, 1991) that staff, MCs and young people all contributed to shaping. These communities and the social values that underpinned them were frames through which they made sense of, supported and developed their goals, ethos and working practices. However, most staff and MC members highlighted tensions between their practices and the performance demands of external agencies.

Staff expressed their strong commitment to providing young people with "a second chance ... a way of getting back into learning" (Jon, The Place) and Steve explained Crossroads' aims as creating "a worthwhile contribution ... to change the lives of the young people that come into contact with us". For that to happen, Steve believed that values focused on young people had to come first "because often what they get is dregs and what we offer might be their life chance, so you have to do the best you can for them in an impossible world".

Most staff shared this commitment to improving young people's lives but some were not optimistic about what they could achieve if external agencies continually narrowed the focus of their activities through targeted outcomes. During some four years following the failure to agree service contracts, staff identified a progressive increase in numerical targets, such as for monthly and termly attendance and accredited achievements. These presented particular difficulties when a third of their students had hardly attended secondary schools before coming to these VSOs. Sonia, the coordinator at The Place, described tensions produced by these kinds of measures: "There's all this, you know, numbers, attendance, accreditation targets. But ... you've got to be flexible or the young people won't be there at all."

Sonia explained that one student, Keisha, had found a placement several afternoons a week in a hairdresser's, which she regarded as a positive step. However, Sonia explained that the detailed attendance returns meant that she "couldn't square that to be honest". She had options of either misrepresenting Keisha's attendance or not letting her take time out of education, with the risk of losing her and her trust in the project altogether. Sonia tried but failed to negotiate a resolution with the Rushley contracts liaison officer.

Steve, the Crossroads manager, also recounted dilemmas about using conventional models to measure students' achievements: "These kids have been all over, their education has been so fragmented ... I know we're doing a good job but it's a problem when you have to measure it. And the insistence on what are really useless measures says LEA officers don't trust us."

Neil, the manager of The Place, echoed some of the Wharton comments about the enormous burdens that complying with quality monitoring schemes placed on their workloads. He described the plethora of performance indicators that had invaded their practices as conditions of continued funding, illustrating the shift towards increasing formalisation, and potentially diverting staff from their work with young people:

> 'The time we're spending on ticking every box – all these indicators – is huge. The problem is, voluntary sector staff are dedicated and their time is full ... supporting students mainly, but now I have to fill my days differently ... and it's not a good use of my time. But the villainy doesn't stop with Rushley ... it's a prevailing national wind.'

Neil described how monitoring processes redirected his work but also highlighted ways in which he saw VSOs becoming 'incorporated' into a broader frame of locally administered national performance targets and accountability. The managers of the projects often became mediators, mitigating onerous external demands, since the financial consequences of ignoring monitoring requirements were considerable.

However, the pressures to compromise, to accommodate audit requirements without demur, meant that the VSOs' sense of mission and values had to be even stronger to set limits on what they conceded, and Neil gave examples of VSOs that he believed had lost sight of their purposes. "For example, Willowfield, another local youth education project, hasn't been able to stay grounded, keep that breadth. It's just into throughput, getting young people in and counted."

Reflecting other research on the importance of strong core values for withstanding inappropriate mission drift (Cairns, 2009; Nevile, 2010), Debbie, the coordinator at Horizons, like Neil, considered that defining limits was essential, and this came from knowing what the organisation did well. She stressed the importance of maintaining a balance between recording and returning data and 'real' work with young people, seeing her role as preventing unrealistic monitoring demands from unnecessarily diverting scarce staff resources:

> 'I'm probably the one who says, stop, we can't ... fit ourselves around any more because it's too much ... that's how I see it. And we're stretched between systems that all want different things, while our main aim is helping young people access change. We have to keep their trust or we lose them and the work collapses but somehow all this monitoring is a poor signal from government officers about trusting what we do.'

Steve also explained the need for considered resistance since he observed that sometimes the information required was quite arbitrary and depended on local interpretations of, albeit powerful, gatekeepers. Seeking to placate gatekeepers, however, had the potential for compromising professional integrity and risked both local reputational trust and the trust of young people. These three VSOs thus occupied a space where they were balancing resistance with necessary accommodation, seeking to sustain core values and purposes against isomorphic pressures to change.

What can be trusted as success? Measurement, gaming and innovation

Dan, managing specialist work with young fathers in Wharton, had contracts from several different funders, and explained the advantages of being less reliant on meeting the demands of only one contract, "since across all the work we can usually show we have met the outcomes". As a larger VSO, monitoring work was spread across different workers but Dan still complained that information gathering and reporting consumed "unreal levels of resources", especially his own. As illustrated in Chapter Four, he also acknowledged 'massaging' information on outcomes to match funders' requirements. Discussing failures or the limited progress made with some young men in the targeted timeframe were, he said, "things you just can't talk about now. Funders are at arm's length, they want success factors, they're not interested in the work as such, how we engage, help build self-esteem – even though that's crucial to more concrete outcomes" (Dan, Changing Lives).

Competitive funding regimes are heavily underwritten by performance targets, which as interviewees stressed, were rarely negotiable and failed to recognise many less tangible achievements. The limited value attributed to less concrete achievements and the technicist approach to monitoring activities also suppressed discussion about failures and sharing difficulties among organisations working in similar fields.

The need to compete financially and the growing risks of jeopardising funding encouraged concealment of problems, as Paul, a youth centre worker, highlighted. He commented on ways in which this damaged openness and information sharing between different youth centres and with local government agencies, discouraging cross-agency learning and more creative work:

'Time was, our YO [area youth officer] knew us, now it's like membership targets, attendance, accredited activities ... but same time, for young people we're reaching out to, it's got to be informal.... But what we're faced with is competing for funding, that's the bottom line, and it creates dishonesty ... people have to make the pretence of meeting targets ... to survive now, so we lose that chance of working together, learning from others.' (Paul, St Jude's Centre)

Measures intended by public funding agencies to demonstrate accountability and manage risk may well exacerbate risks to quality, undermining shared learning and trust. VSOs respond to pressures to maximise the appearance of meeting targets to minimise their own organisational risks. Paul pointed to a conspiracy to paper over cracks in achieving attendance and accreditation targets, when failures could offer ways to reflect on the challenges they all faced. Competing for funding and fears about future loss encourage them to hide such problems from wider public view. Thus, governments (local and national) and broader society can be assured of certain local achievements, while challenging social issues may well remain unaddressed.

As Paul explained, the pressure on meeting performance targets produces centres and projects that focus pragmatically on young people "who'll make the grade" rather than those who remain outside the reach of many services. It also narrows the focus of activities and client groups, discouraging the development of innovative work; and generates a 'can do' culture among workers and agencies focused on meeting prescribed outcomes. The consequence is both that structural problems for young people's marginalisation are obscured from policy and strategy concerns and that institutional failures are reinforced, relegating some groups in society as disposable or outside safety-nets of projects – an outcome recently visible from the Work Programme. There are further risks that follow in terms of quality and reputation: the quality of provision will decline if performance targets and not service needs or a shared community of learning drive activities; and by narrowing their scope, providers may put in train a declining reputation, deterring already hard-to-reach user groups. The alternative, as both Paul and Dan indicated, is gaming in relation to performance reporting but this still jeopardises organisational integrity and developmental learning.

Paradoxically, the public sector has depended on VSOs to set up innovative provision where mainstream provision has failed, especially in socially disadvantaged areas and for excluded groups of people (Ellison and Ellison, 2006). As services are narrowed and funders are at a greater distance, less is known about the provision, eroding both VSOs' and local stakeholders' trust in the commitment of funders to service needs. As constraints and unrealistic targets grow, motivation for resolving challenging service problems may correspondingly decline. Small community-based VSOs have been sought for their expertise in working with hard-to-reach groups, and the small VSOs in Wharton and Rushley have taken on difficult services where the state has a record of failing. Innovation implies both risk and unpredictable outcomes since it assumes the development of new approaches; and establishing exacting targets for providers sought to work innovatively with challenging user groups is irrational, especially when state services have failed previously. As Cora from Horizons observed: "We provide education for disturbed and vulnerable young people; outcomes are extremely hard to predict or measure." If funders discount contextual information about services in favour only of measurable indicators, it underlines their poor understanding of provision and accelerates the breakdown of trust. As trust is eroded, so also is the space for innovation.

Controlling risk and eroding trust

Compliance with specified activities and outcomes is inbuilt into many recent contracts and, rather than there being any meaningful discourse about how to account for and continuously improve services, has increasingly become the rationale for measuring performance. Compliance protects the risks of the procurer but, as discussed above, may well lead to gaming or damage to potentially innovative services.

Contrary to much of the literature on trust, in which tightly managed risks and predictability are regarded as underpinning trust between partners, risk and trust appear in inverse relationship. As the state–VS relationship in Rushley moved from trust to a contractual basis, a number of risks were transferred; and this pattern of transfer is evident from wider literature on public sector contracts and outsourcing to VSOs discussed earlier.

In Rushley, a part of the process of outsourcing required the three VSOs to take on the employment contracts of all the staff: teachers, youth workers and administrators. Some staff had previously been employed by the LEA and seconded long term to the VSOs. Under the Transfer or Undertakings (Protection of Employment) Regulations (TUPE), they were entitled to no loss of benefits, such as in sickness and pension rights, but these entailed risks of costs that were effectively beyond the means of small VSOs. The new contracts also contained financial penalties for failing to meet targets, such as in attendance and attainment – figures that theVSOs had argued were not realistic and presented untenable financial burdens. Far from cementing trust between procurer and provider, these terms exacerbated relationships. Such cases, which are being reflected in deteriorating relationships in supply chains for the Work Programme (Bailey, 2012) (discussed further in Chapter Seven), raise questions about the failure to maintain trust through sharing risks for services, especially when disproportionate risks are transferred to small VSOs with limited financial reserves. Audit requirements are intended by public agencies to manage risk for both the quality of outcomes and the local reputation of services, ensuring public accountability. However, by transferring risks to contractors, trust is eroded and replaced by inappropriate performance controls, increasing risks to quality and reputation as services are compromised and constrained by targets, and encouraging providers to resort to gaming.

There is, however, a difference between large and small VSOs in what may be reasonable expectations of carrying risks. Small VSOs, as the examples illustrate, face conditions involving uncontainable financial risk, together with unlimited reputational risk, whereas the financial risks required of large VSOs are often containable within the size of the organisation. However, they are also asked to carry unlimited reputational risks: meeting funders' requirements may necessitate deviation from their core purposes with longstanding stakeholders; but failing to meet performance targets risks their reputation with funders, jeopardising future resources. Business and financial reputation has become increasingly privileged (Bennett, 2011); and the pressure on maximising the appearance of meeting targets is equally significant for large VSOs. The need to appear successful therefore undermines the greater influence they can exert on achieving more appropriate definitions of performance outcomes, along with the trust of user groups.

Risk, trust and innovation: how controls erode trust and jeopardise quality

As the examples above demonstrate, traditional grant-based relationships have increasingly shifted to contractual arrangements in which differential power relations have undermined communications and trust. All too often, compliance assumes consensus but masks a lack of trust between participants. Some trust literature endorses rigorous structures and predictability as creating positive conditions for inter-organisational trust but ignores the element of power. The power to determine norms of behaviour, discourse and performance arrangements, associated with dominant managerial cultures and heavily specified contracts, has in many cases pervaded and damaged trust-based relationships, with potentially negative consequences. Smaller VSOs, furthest removed from dominant cultures, and excluded from influence and large-scale contracts, experience little commitment on the part of public agencies purchasing services to supporting work on developmental provision.

The examples demonstrate an organisational environment that is often hostile to developing or sustaining cross-sector trust, pervading recent public–VS relationships: an environment where roles are increasingly governed by competitive interests and excessive levels of control through contractual frameworks and audit, with little attention given to relational damage or lack of meaningful communication. Such frameworks serve to manage reputational and financial risks for large funding agencies but impose new meanings and arrangements that should instead require renegotiation between participating organisations and individuals. With large corporations increasingly competing for contracts, the growing distance between purchasers and providers generates services that are poorly understood, defined and evaluated, and a shrinking relational space in which alternative approaches and reporting, which could better inform service planning, can be valued. Small VSOs are being relegated to roles as subcontractors or, disillusioned, may withdraw, taking valuable local knowledge with them.

There is a danger in simply highlighting the contradiction between a culture of externally imposed audit and organisational learning, a dichotomy illustrated through diverse examples above. There is a pressing need to reflect on alternatives that will improve service learning *and* fulfil public accountability needs. As Kendall and Knapp (1996) observed, many small VSOs are obscure to external observers and may not account well for their activities beyond local stakeholders. However, simply complying with externally imposed data reporting measures affords poor information for providing a serious narrative on the extent of the VS's contribution. Overall information on the efficacy and longer-term impact of the VS, following its significant growth as a service provider, is limited, and greater clarity is needed on what the VS does better – or could do – if monitoring burdens and restrictions are mitigated. As cross-sector providers become enmeshed in supply chains for mega-contracts, earlier efforts towards assessing VS impact will be hard to disentangle. The need now may be to consider the ways in which the VS can best contribute.

Summarising discussion from this chapter highlights the inverse relationship between unilaterally defined monitoring frameworks and high levels of trust, with the latter more likely to generate collaborative advantage (Huxham, 1996) and developmental activities. Conversely, high levels of control and pervasive monitoring demands, used to manage assumed performance risks, seem more likely to present risks to assuring quality among small VSOs, whereas increased trust in the purchaser–provider relationship offers ways to overcome barriers to knowledge about services and effective delivery. Rigidly applied performance targets and outputs signal a lack of trust in providers and, as the examples illustrate, may result in gaming or suppression of information. This environment is exacerbated by a distancing of funders from providers, whether through supply chains or increasingly complex contract arrangements; the removal of trusted local government intermediaries; and the privileging and legitimisation of measurable data rather than the parallel use of narrative reporting. The result is that funders and providers can retreat from open communicative processes to spaces governed by signals of mistrust, with negative consequences for dialogue about service needs or improvements.

Despite policy rhetoric around risk sharing and innovation, the disproportionate transfer of risks from purchaser to provider is exposed as a significant factor in damaging trust relationships, exacerbating the breakdown of communicative processes around services and VSOs' beliefs in the value of performance requirements. The examples are salutary in highlighting the challenges and growing, but often unsustainable, risks for small VSOs in a rapidly changing and highly competitive environment, with constant turnover in arrangements. The future offers little respite, with escalating contracts and an increasingly risk-averse public sector environment, including Payment by Results, devolving enormous financial risks.

The discussion in this chapter also reflects the significance of power within inter-organisational relationships and of assessing assumed agreements critically. The examples illustrate transitions from co-created meanings to different forms of power-based masquerade in state–VS relations, as the Rushley and Wharton VSOs moved from joint service projects to contractually based funding and delivery. While the use of coercive means to ensure compliance was marked in the Rushley cases, other cases illustrate the exercise of power, guaranteeing VSO conformity to avoid jeopardising funding. More powerful partners are able to determine the knowledge that counts: what activities and outcomes are required and deemed successful. By asserting numerical data as legitimate reporting, rather than the VSOs' less codified knowledge and practices, government officers can be seen as agents of the pervasive discourse and arrangements that extend governmental terrain, in which appearances of autonomy are insidiously steered or suppressed by powerful cultures of information (Rose, 1999).

However, while providers experienced a devaluing of their expertise, the gaming employed in reporting responses aptly demonstrates how superimposed cultures of arrangements can be subverted when there is little belief in their validity or the professional competence of those representing them. This highlights the frailty of such proxy measures as indicators of service effectiveness, when the motivational trust of joint endeavour and shared goals are lost. Knowledge about services and local needs is also suppressed from public view because of reporting failures prompted by the exercise of power over future funding. Inevitably, lack of transparency results in fewer lessons shared among VSO providers and impoverished service learning overall. Technical skills for managing data and reporting systems displace depth in professional knowledge, leading to what Sennett (2005) describes as a hollowing out of the old values of professional craftsmanship, with managerial and audit arrangements gradually embedding new professional values. The real information about wider or longer-term impact also remains invisible since it largely relies on unseen narratives. Recognising the power exercised by audit and enacted through purchasers provides valuable insights into understanding VSOs' growing mistrust of performance requirements. It also highlights the risks to long-term service quality of supplanting local trust relationships with scaled-up competitive contracts and performance frameworks detached from local knowledge.

Increasingly, small VSOs have been engaged to design innovative service approaches in relation to hard-to-reach groups in society, where provision has systematically failed in the past. Fostering innovation conflicts with a regime reliant on managing outcomes and risks through measurable targets since performance in new developments is notoriously hard to predict. The prescription of specific outcomes is therefore neither logical nor fair and undermines creative efforts. Unless risks are partially shared, failures are silenced, motivation for innovation is lost and learning denied. Maintaining trust in fair and shared outcomes is needed if innovation 'fails'.

However, the public sector persists in managing risk through audit and data reporting, which often leads to gaming and concealment, inhibiting learning and innovation. If instead, wider use were made of narrative reporting and building shared knowledge of local needs and services between purchaser, contractor and service user, there would be more opportunities for shaping contract specifications and for post-hoc description of what has been achieved and learned. These are all important for assessing new projects in more rational and relational ways, rather than guesstimating targets for what cannot be known.

This chapter has raised questions about how competence and knowledge are judged and legitimised, highlighting differences in sector practices and understandings. In an audit system, meaning is anchored in unilaterally and hierarchically defined targets instead of being co-produced; thus, legitimate understandings and local narratives, important to providers and users, are lost. The examples illustrate non-negotiable targets encouraging over-optimistic reporting as a way to manage the reputational and financial risks associated with unrealistic performance expectations in extremely challenging services. Data reporting, based on predefined targets and in the language of the funder, has displaced narrative-based reporting where activities and outcomes might be described through meanings derived from reflecting on practical experience. The strong emphasis on numerical data rather than meaningful communication about quality creates unanticipated consequences, posing risks to longer-term service efficacy.

The legitimisation of some approaches over others demonstrates how powerful agencies define the rules of the game (Clegg, 1989) in cross-sector and contractual contexts, undermining trust and the kind of openness that could lead to improvements in relations and services. The nature of public–VS, client–contractor relationships invariably cements a hierarchical imbalance of power that denies all but a masquerade of trust. Performance targets do more than require a level of performance: they powerfully structure discourse and define the categories of what is meaningful and marginal. However, if funding agencies adopted a more flexible stance to communications, to understanding and defining service activities, there would be potential for mutual organisational learning and building better trust-based services with community providers.

In highlighting negative consequences of the erosion of trust in cross-sector relationships, this chapter has also demonstrated the benefits of trust-based relationships and consequent advantages for improved organisational learning. The question then is why so little emphasis has been placed on trust building between large funding agencies and smaller providers and quality assurance has invariably relied on quantitative targets. For some years, dominant policy ideology has promoted the effectiveness of market mechanisms, enforcing greater competition between VSOs. With diminishing welfare resources and greater privileging of market forces, this has recently intensified. Quantitative targets are believed to be effective signals for service markets but insufficient distinction is made between the comparative advantages of approaches in different sectors in selecting providers for different kinds of service. Equally, the signals denoting effective performance need better correlation to service goals and differences. Consequently, little value is placed on the intangibles of community wellbeing and solidarity, trust in community-level experience and alternative reporting models, which the discussion above suggests are both necessary and possible.

SIX

Collaboration in community-based projects: solutions or new organisational challenges?

Introduction

In the past decade, collaboration, both within and across sectors, has been a strong component of UK public policy, often integral to funding decisions. Public agencies have increasingly been required to collaborate with non-state providers to plan, monitor and deliver welfare services, with voluntary sector organisations (VSOs) providing an increasing range of services from early years to old age. The voluntary sector (VS) role in socially deprived neighbourhoods has also grown until recently, with policy makers recognising its expertise in working with marginalised groups of people. However, as earlier chapters identified, collaborative ventures may well be driven by competitive funding regimes, raising questions about how different strategies intersect.

Recent arrangements have frequently involved VSOs in collaboration within and across sectors, and partnership work has underpinned frameworks through which many local services are planned, managed and delivered. Both the current and previous governments have encouraged shifts away from a silo mentality of services towards ideas of integration, emphasising locally designed projects. However, as Hoggett (2004) illustrates, structural change in various forms – devolving public services; inter-agency and 'joined-up' work; cross-sector planning; and community-led projects – have, at different times, been offered as solutions to varied problems. Over more than a decade these have included the need to: reform and modernise welfare; tackle challenging social problems; improve service efficiency and responsiveness; and, more recently, reduce welfare spending and loosen the hold of 'big government' (Cabinet Office, 2010b).

Yet the difficulties that need to be overcome to achieve desired changes or improvements, including the protracted efforts often required for disparate organisations to cooperate around common goals, have repeatedly been glossed over; and many local experiences of collaboration have been discouraging (Milbourne, 2009a; Mills, 2009).

Research has identified numerous barriers to collaborative work (Huxham and Vangen, 2004; Snape and Taylor, 2004) at interpersonal, institutional, structural and policy levels, and also factors contributing to positive outcomes (Glaister and Glaister, 2005; Glasby and Dickinson, 2008). While discussion of inter-agency working is not new, a growing literature has highlighted the complexity of issues involved, including individual and organisational values and interests; and the local contexts that intersect with different policy drivers (Glendenning et al, 2002; Rummery, 2006; Taylor, 2006), producing unpredictable social interactions, interpretations and outcomes. As Higham and Yeomans (2010, p 398) illustrate, the interplay of such factors is dynamic, and collaboration frequently depends on 'happenstance, pragmatism ... and improvisation' so that its form is likely to be highly contingent on local settings.

This chapter therefore explores 'local stories', the everyday experiences of people involved in VSOs, as a way of understanding processes of collaboration. It draws on a study of community-based organisations providing children and young people's services in Wharton, a relatively poor English inner-city area, to examine recent collaborative projects from a VS perspective. Before turning to discuss different empirical examples, the chapter initially locates ideas of collaboration within political and policy changes outlined in Chapter Two and recent shifts in children and young people's services favouring cross-agency work. It then considers conceptual debates around partnership and collaboration, which help to shed light on the VS examples discussed subsequently.

Collaboration in a changing policy context

The unprecedented growth in VS welfare service delivery over some 20 years has led to increasing concerns about its negative effects on the sector. Collaborative alliances – formal and informal – have been identified as ways to meet the demands for capacity while maintaining some independence against isomorphic pressures towards adopting new public management cultures (Harris, M. 2010).

The compact between central government and the VS (Home Office, 1998) signalled a first phase of collaborative relationships with the New Labour administration, and an apparent shift in public policy emphasis away from welfare state hierarchies and marketisation, towards network governance and new localism (Davies, 2011). However, while inter-agency and cross-sector collaboration characterised New Labour's Third Way and subsequently community participation agendas, markets continued to underpin political ideology and funding strategy.

The community turn in the coalition government's policy is now reflected within ideals of building local ties and community-led solutions to addressing local problems, and service and funding deficiencies. The previous government's integrated area-based approach to services – 'total place' – was replaced in 2011 by neighbourhood-level and 'whole place' community budgets in selected areas, with similar aims of promoting local integration and jointly agreed outcomes across different services. Similar broad policy developments linked to localism and communities are reflected elsewhere in Europe, where varied examples underline interdependent relationships between states and the VS, highlighting the intermediary role of non-profit organisations in generating innovative solutions to challenging public concerns (Evers and Laville, 2004). Studies from North America also consider the diversity of local organisation forms emerging – from strong independent charities crucial to welfare, to contractually dependent and co-constructed relationships, which underline the importance of collaborations for sustaining small non-profit organisations (Proulx and Denis-Savard, 2007; Sobeck et al, 2007).

In the United Kingdom (UK), partnership working and short-term, inter-agency initiatives characterised state–VS relationships for more than a decade, increasing interdependency. As Cairns et al (2010b, p 2) illustrate, 'collaborative working, in all its guises, has become a central feature of organisational life'. As a partner, the VS has offered a means to more effective and responsive services; and to deliver wider social change, including addressing concerns about active citizenship. Many VSOs have welcomed these policy transitions, identifying opportunities for their expertise to be recognised and to influence future approaches. However, there are also challenges involved in representing community voices and maintaining alternative approaches, which may be perceived as counter-hegemonic. Rather than a force for progressive change, collaboration and partnership work may also suppress cultural alternatives in favour of dominant or more prevalent models of operation, a process of institutional incorporation masquerading as network governance.

A series of government documents acknowledges the value of working with VSOs (Home Office, 2004; DCLG, 2006b; see also Localism Act 2011), applauding community knowledge and creativity, and the experience brought to engaging local groups. Since 2002, government reports have highlighted the need to build VS capacity and appropriate local support infrastructures; and to establish collaborative projects to improve support for small VSOs. More recently, the coalition government has echoed the first goal, while putting faith in entrepreneurial aspirations to achieve the latter (OCS, 2010).

Acknowledging the hard times that many VSOs were beginning to experience from the effects of economic recession, the New Labour government encouraged VSOs to collaborate and merge with support from a modernisation fund (Cabinet Office, 2009). Addressing charities on Big Society plans (Maude, 2010), the coalition government's focus on partnerships has also confirmed a similar commitment to collaborative work within and across sectors. Thus, the emphasis on partnerships, localism and collaborative strategy is a common, apparently ongoing strand of many public policies with impact on VSOs. The difference, more recently, is the reduced role of the state as a collaborator.

In later years, New Labour gave some recognition to longstanding criticisms (Geddes et al, 2000) that a surfeit of initiatives and short-term project funding were potentially damaging to the continuity of developments that could make a difference in poor areas. Addressing such criticisms underlay the rationale for longer-term, area-based commissioning, which was intended to promote collaborative work across traditional service and sector boundaries. With competitive service commissioning growing, local governments are becoming tangential in the coordination of cross-sector activities, and there have been rapid shifts in power differentials between 'collaborators' in cross-sector bids, with organisational size and financial reserves becoming significant factors. Moreover, some of the issues identified in earlier studies as barriers to collaborative work – including competition for funds, dominance of quantifiable performance measures, conflicting agency interests, differential power relations and a lack of trust (Kimberlee, 2002; Milbourne et al, 2003) – have re-emerged in more recent studies (Cairns et al, 2006; Marsden, 2011).

Voluntary sector representatives have also criticised the enormous investment in time, effort and resources needed for small VSOs to engage in partnerships, pointing to a lack of capacity among existing charity trustees and heavy reliance on volunteers (Andalo, 2010). To this end, in later years, New Labour initiated a series of capacity-building and skills development programmes (Home Office, 2004), intended to support VS growth in service provision and to develop the abilities and skills needed for multiple new requirements. Questions about the interests served in capacity-building schemes and other factors inhibiting collaborative work are discussed subsequently but first I consider changes in children and young people's services towards cross-agency integration in order to provide a context for the empirical examples examined later in this chapter.

Changes in children and young people's services

Examples discussed later in the chapter are drawn from projects working with children and young people and paragraphs below offer a brief policy context for understanding these settings. Since 1997, the following have been among a number of UK programmes aimed at improving social inclusion, also mirrored in other European countries (Colley et al, 2007): redressing child poverty; supporting childcare and low-income working families to encourage increased employment; promoting parenting and youth education; targeting disengaged young people.

Youth voluntary action, young people's engagement and participation and youth-led projects have been particular priorities, while integrating local children and young people's services and cross-agency collaboration have become means to deliver changes (DfES, 2006). Many of these projects have reflected United Nations directives, with a strong emphasis on young people's rights and engagement (Tisdall et al, 2006) but with the change of UK government in 2010, these programmes have suffered rapid reductions, and funded youth work has declined significantly and narrowed in focus.

In the remodelling of UK children and young people's services between 2004 and 2009, integration of key agencies and cross-sector collaboration were priorities but the reforms were premised on potentially conflicting features (Hudson, 2006): a collaborative planning model, drawing on the views of young people and families in designing local services, and cross-sector partnerships, which were, however, charged with delivering outcomes and strategies defined through national guidelines. Burnley et al (2005) highlight similar contradictions in the Canadian devolution of children's services, illustrating ways in which users' collaboration in service design is reshaped to match professional agendas and centrally driven performance targets, despite the development of cross-agency projects intended to trigger changes.

Since 2010, encouragement to VSOs to deliver frontline work with young people has been coupled with a half-billion-pound reduction to youth funds and services (NYA, 2011; Williams, 2011). Rather than working flexibly with a wide range of young people, the youth National Citizen Service, the government's recently launched youth scheme, is targeted at 16-year-old school leavers (House of Commons Education Committee, 2011), and participation involves required phases of activity – arguably at odds with active collaboration with young people over project design. While every UK teenager will be invited to volunteer, the material (House of Commons Education Committee, 2011, pp 55-7) reveals prescriptive participation for some and the potential exclusion of others because insufficient funding means that many providers will have to charge fees.

UK funding for children and young people's services has been complex and provided through multiple, often short-term, initiatives (Milbourne, 2009b). From a public agency perspective, increased integration and local area plans designed with community partners produce helpful coordination of young people's programmes through one partnership body; and the joined-up services for families (see Localism Act 2011) now propose further amalgamation. However, change in young people's services has repeatedly been superimposed, with the logic for changes poorly understood at community level or among families and young people; and collaborative involvement in decision making has been questionable (Barnes and Morris, 2008).

Conceptualising partnerships and collaboration

Much recent collaborative work affecting VSOs has been policy driven, creating a contrived or instrumental environment for collaboration. Policy discourse emphasises the consensual and inclusive nature of partnerships and collaborative community ventures (Cabinet Office, 2009, 2010a) but disregards inherent differences and conflicts between participants, the inclusions and exclusions that Brent (2009) describes as constitutive of communities. For example, while local strategic partnerships established in deprived local authority areas were charged with coordinating innovative neighbourhood renewal strategies by engaging community representatives alongside private and public sector agencies, studies indicate that the rhetoric of collaboration and valuing different approaches often failed to permeate the practice of such projects, with powerful agencies determining the discourse and arrangements (O'Brien, 2006; Taylor, 2006).

The rationale and policy drivers for collaboration may appear evident but the scope and nature of inter-agency collaboration are far from clear, and concepts underpinning strategies linked to collaboration and partnership work lack substance. Differences around what is understood by collaborating and different motivations for instigating and joining collaborative ventures abound, exacerbating ambiguities (Cairns et al, 2010b). Diverse participants may understand the purposes of working together differently, and a lack of shared understanding frequently constructs barriers to effective collaboration. Meanings and purposes are also shaped by local settings and individual actors, emphasising the contingent and dynamic features of partnership work (Higham and Yeomans, 2010).

Mergers, collaborative bids for contracts, integrated approaches to public services, cross-sector partnerships and hybrid organisations are more recent collaborative forms (Billis, 2010), but VSOs have a long history of informal local collaboration in campaign and advocacy work and referrals across services (bassac, 2010). Cross-sector work, as opposed to collaboration within the VS, inevitably raises different issues, and sometimes relies on proficient boundary spanners (Lewis, 2008). Poor collaboration between public sector departments has been identified as problematic for some time (Alcock, 2005) and, for example, collaborating with VSOs – assumed to be more flexible – was introduced to stimulate innovative work and overcome the rigid boundaries dividing the practices of different public sector professionals (Milbourne et al, 2003).

Collaboration can be identified at several levels of engagement. It may be a fairly cursory exercise of consultation where, for example, local government has been charged with promoting wider public participation in service developments, contributing (in name) to agendas of active citizenship and political renewal (Barnes et al, 2007). Dominant institutional practices, which legitimate certain forms of discussion and participation, and restrict attempts to engage individuals in meaningful ways, may well discourage ongoing or future participation in collaborative ventures. At its best, collaboration can be identified as a committed exercise, involving concerted effort by different partners to shape a jointly designed enterprise, creating shared purposes and meanings (Weick, 1995). Organisations from state, VS and private agencies have been encouraged to participate in joint endeavours to bring about mutually desired change in specific localities or for particular social groups. As Howard and Taylor (2010) demonstrate, despite the challenges, in positive examples, partnership work can stimulate new approaches and gain considerably from drawing together knowledge, experience and the best working practices from different agencies and sectors. Such joint enterprise is typically characterised by trust relationships, although these may take considerable time to build so as to value participants' distinct contributions (Milbourne and Cushman, 2012).

Understood simply, collaboration entails non-competitive interactions between individuals or organisations but, paradoxically, competition and organisational self-interest may underlie reasons for collaborating.

Organisations can engage in collaboration opportunistically or pragmatically to access funding or maintain existing activities, sharing skills, resources and back-room functions, even entering mergers. These partnerships can be described as instrumental. Other alliances may be less instrumental – concerned with strengthening local service provision or strategic influence – and more consistent with existing organisational goals and purposes (Cairns et al, 2010b).

For VSOs, there has been pressure to enter collaborative ventures and mergers in order to access increasingly large service contracts, to develop appropriate professional skills or to meet the terms of specific project funding; and the New Labour government invested significant resources in VS capacity-building programmes to these ends. Arguably, the benefits of capacity-building programmes have been reaped more effectively by larger agencies in providing infrastructure, advice and skills training (Harris and Schlappa, 2008), and by public agencies in the reduced transaction costs from larger contracts (Milbourne and Murray, 2011).

Whether formal or informal, partnerships and collaboration depend on individual relationships, and as varied studies confirm, they are often most effective when there is already a history of local connections or working together (Glaister and Glaister, 2005). One of the key barriers to effective cross-sector working acknowledged by the previous government (HM Treasury, 2005) is that members of public bodies frequently lack understanding of the VS; and other studies suggest that reasons for this are located in sector identities, which they argue remain strong, despite some blurring of practices (Lewis, 2008; Billis, 2010).

Howard and Taylor (2010) highlight successful cross-sector working, where key individuals have developed experience of different sectors and, crucially, are open to learning from alternative approaches. Their example aptly illustrates conditions for collaborative advantage (Huxham and Vangen, 2004), where through shared communication, ideas and mutual learning, the partnership has jointly created something new, achieving greater value than the individuals or organisations could have achieved separately. However, Howard and Taylor (2010) also discuss examples where values and differences are not addressed or resolved, and where ambiguous purposes and leadership exacerbate difficulties and tensions. Even in apparently hybrid organisational forms, 'key players continu[e] to operate according to the rules and operating cultures' of their originating organisations (Billis, 2010, pp 248-9), potentially constructing barriers to cooperative work. In the case of larger agencies, these are often visible in reluctance to relinquish their power; in the case of smaller VSOs, a reluctance to compromise independent approaches.

The multiplicity of organisational forms emerging not only obscures understanding of what it means to collaborate but also creates challenges for VSOs in terms of organisational identities and purposes, for local accountabilities and ways of working. New forms and arrangements generate considerable challenges for the smallest or least powerful organisations and those least secure in mission, finance or membership. Examples that follow raise questions about the extent to which successful collaboration depends on the formation of a new organisational identity, or whether mutual respect, reasonable trust and commitment to a specific shared venture are sufficient, if participants' motivations for participating are clearly understood. Instrumental forms of collaboration may safeguard the goals, identities and meanings of smaller organisations against external threats initially, while opening the way to learning *from* as well as *about* the other (Hoggett, 2004) and more committed collaboration subsequently. Much depends on the approach of more powerful partners.

The local context

Drawing on the Wharton study of children and young people's services described in Chapter Three, examples that follow explore the perceptions of changes on VSOs' work in deprived inner-city localities. The focus here is on relationships between community-based and public sector organisations from a VS perspective, as a means of shedding light on how collaborative work is understood. The analysis drew on interviews with VSO workers, members of the local voluntary action council and key local government managers.

Only a handful of examples from among the many organisations involved in this study are included, chosen because they reflect common experiences in this and other areas studied. After initially considering broader perceptions of cross-agency collaboration in the area, subsequent material is organised by themes, examining motivations, successful examples and barriers to collaborative work.

Broad local perceptions

In contrast to experiences in other areas studied, most VS interviewees considered that there was a genuine public sector commitment to supporting community organisations in their area and to improving services in disadvantaged neighbourhoods. They pointed to progress, for example, in relation to children and young people's projects established through programmes, such as the Children's Fund, teenage pregnancy services and extended school services. The local authority had gained a national Beacon award for its collaborative youth engagement work, which was disseminated as a model for good practice for other areas.

However, beneath the surface, there was a noticeable gap between perceived policy intentions and practices; and many criticisms emerged about relationships with public agencies. Confidence in statutory agencies was fragile and, faced with arrangements that set VSOs to compete with each other and an influx of new providers, mistrust and demoralisation surfaced. Small and inexperienced VSOs felt particularly vulnerable but even experienced community representatives, including regular attendees at consultative meetings, found collaborative relationships redefined by funder–contractor power relations in the competitive environment of commissioning. Criticisms included the top-down aspects of planning and change processes, poor communications and non-inclusive conduct of meetings, and underlined instrumentality in relationships rather than effort put into collaborating with community 'partners'. Constant changes and insecure, project-based funding, with consequent effects on staffing and workloads, were also sources of tension and criticised for unfairly destabilising small VSOs without financial reserves. Descriptions of having to redesign data and reporting systems annually, to repeatedly design new funding bids and a lack of timely information on continuity of projects added to the list of commonly cited difficulties undermining goodwill.

Mindful of these experiences, small VSOs were disinclined to trust new arrangements, regarding them as constantly "reinventing wheels" (Sharon, play centre), and diverting frontline workers' efforts away from service users. The rationale for local strategic partnerships was poorly understood by many small VSOs, with some viewing them as settings where larger, better-resourced organisations could participate. However, members of VSOs attending meetings on commissioning plans criticised meeting notes for failing to reflect suggestions they had voiced, and were therefore worried about unwillingly being 'co-opted' into decisions. Others felt excluded from discussions, seeing themselves as outsiders in arrangements constructed by local government. This sense of insiders and outsiders – "those that do and don't network with the council" (Kali, youth centre) – was a commonly expressed view, and highlights ways in which partnerships can also be divisive, fragmenting alliances between different individuals and VSOs, and excluding smaller VSOs.

Most VSOs were also sceptical about the extent to which local government representatives had reached or discussed service needs with less accessible groups of young people for the Wharton Children and Young People's Plan, which, nevertheless, identified local young people and families as collaborators in determining future services. Few respondents appeared to trust that the process had been collaborative or that it offered opportunities to shape provision. This scepticism is mirrored in other studies pointing to the lack of credence often given to local experience in service consultations (Barnes et al, 2010), questioning how, despite political aspirations, local knowledge can be legitimised and service users given scope to redesign services. Moreover, if individuals and groups, whose views have been sought, repeatedly fail to see their contribution valued and respected, they become disillusioned in the collaborative projects in which they have invested effort.

In considering these broad perceptions, it is evident that smaller VSOs experienced more disincentives to engaging in collaborative ventures, such as area-based planning partnerships and local strategic boards, while some larger organisations, such as a regional representative of a national children's charity, identified participation as an opportunity to influence strategy. In this sense, participation in local cross-sector partnership work is more likely to be instrumental on the part of VSOs, while for public agencies, it fulfils goals of improved local engagement. However, where organisations or individuals make decisions to collaborate for instrumental reasons, they may be less likely to give time to relationship building and learning from different approaches. Thus, they may fail to create the collaborative advantage or added value of working together.

Capacity building through collaborative work: who benefits?

Detailed examples below illustrate significant barriers to effective collaboration, as also some positive relationships, and these are examined, considering the conditions that work for and against meaningful collaboration.

A significant element in recent policies (HM Treasury and Cabinet Office, 2007; OCS, 2010) focused on building capacity among smaller VSOs, conceived as professionalising and developing the workforce and enabling growth in services. A key means to achieving this involved encouraging organisations to work collaboratively within and across sectors (Home Office, 2004). This development programme under

New Labour was also intended to extend the capacity of community-based agencies to reach hitherto excluded groups (DCLG, 2006b). For developments to be effective, it was recognised that growing burdens, including in data reporting, needed support (Cabinet Office, 2009). Collaboration between different VSOs by clustering resources through mergers, and between community and statutory providers exchanging expertise, were identified as a significant (and relatively cost-effective) means to achieve these several policy aims.

Considerable resources were put into establishing intermediary bodies at regional and local levels to coordinate local capacity-building initiatives. Again my studies indicate varied criticisms of these developments, including for drawing funding away from frontline work and for emphasising funders' needs in improving the managerial skills of small organisations rather than addressing locally identified needs. As outlined earlier, the policy focus on building community capacity via inter- and cross-sector collaboration has remained strong. However, where New Labour's Modernisation Fund (Cabinet Office, 2009) offered support for VSO collaboration and merger as safeguards in economic recession, the coalition government's emphasis on partnerships (OCS, 2010) highlights entrepreneurial activity as a key component of collaborative community capacity building.

Examples below illustrate mutual benefits from co-constructing community-based projects but also visible costs, including the investment of time and energy needed to establish joint working and to resolve and learn from differences. Others examples in this and subsequent sections suggest that larger organisations may gain most from collaborations, raising questions about the benefits and costs of collaborative work for small VSOs and the extent to which they can retain independent approaches.

Capacity building: gains and losses

The following example is of a capacity-building project involving a local government Children and Young People's Service (CYPS) officer, Kidscare (a large regional VSO) and several small community groups providing out-of-school hours activities. Commissioned by the CYPS, Kidscare provided advice and onsite training sessions for the small VSOs, aiming to establish a mutually supportive partnership, linked to community bridging and cohesion targets. The CYPS officer mainly took a monitoring role once the project was established. The support that Kidscare offered was generally well received because its staff knew the area well and were willing to tailor their advice or training to needs that VSOs specified. Although welcoming the support, a part-time worker for a young Somalians project stressed its limitations and voiced the concerns of other groups about the lack of time they had to engage collaboratively with other groups:

> 'Support, training, yes it's helped but we're small, we need more.... I don't see recognised the pressure, the demands, how hard, what we do for nothing at all. And taking time to meet others [groups] is not real.... But communication [from local authority officers] is more politics than respect, it says how they, not we, getting young people involve, not what we do each day, only with volunteers.' (Samia)

Many of the small VSOs worked with refugee communities, some longstanding, some more recent, and had quite disparate interests, with projects in different localities. Building commitment to collaboration demanded time invested in identifying shared interests and locations when the motivation for collaboration was unclear and resources were non-existent. As Samia indicates, the community groups understood the support offered but mistrusted the credit taken by local public agencies for outcomes achieved at the community level, referring to the Beacon award as an example. Thus, these VSOs collaborated instrumentally, identifying specific benefits, but failed to see the value of engaging further: the possible mutual advantages of organisational exchange (Huxham, 1996). This suggests that organisations limit their level of collaborative engagement if benefits are unclear or demands too costly. This is explained partly in this case by the nature of the project: promoted top down and driven by the policy targets of mainstream agencies rather than the concerns of the intended participants. Building better bridges between small VSOs would have demanded creating motivation towards more committed collaboration, including from representatives of public agencies, and considerable time and effort invested in jointly constructing purposes.

As critics of different government programmes have argued, often poor people (or poorly resourced VSOs representing them) are asked to work jointly to resolve wider social problems (Ellison and Ellison, 2006) – in Samia's case, growing concerns about youth crime among Somalian boys. Community groups, with few workers, are faced with acting as a first line of defence in tackling such problems where they are most acute: at the neighbourhood level. Their tasks are currently growing – increasing community engagement and tackling unmet service problems – and are increasingly reliant on volunteers. The paucity of resources accessible to such groups illustrates the fragility on which such policy aspirations are based, while efforts to achieve wider collaboration that fail to start from, or legitimise, local knowledge (Yanow, 2003) – the local conditions drawn from lived experience – are unlikely to generate motivation for more than instrumental participation.

Ambiguity of purpose, short-termism and an underestimation of resources needed to develop committed work towards mutual goals therefore curtail the longer-term benefits and learning from this cross-agency work. Motivation for small VSOs to explore the advantages of less conditional collaboration is undermined by their lack of capacity, which generates resistance to extending their activities in ways that could jeopardise ongoing activities with user groups. Harris and Young's (2010, p 55) study of bridge-building activities draws similar conclusions, highlighting the 'limited potential' of diverse grassroots organisations to extend their roles without compromising their autonomy. If infrastructure and public bodies assigned greater value to community-based knowledge, it could be significant in achieving improved collaboration across diverse VSOs, potentially constructing projects jointly regarded as meaningful. However, the more open communications entailed might also expose flaws in proposed collaborations: for example, in this case, expecting a diverse range of small, minority ethnic organisations to develop coherent bridging work may exceed realistic capacity and expectations of voluntary collaboration.

Capacity building: co-construction of projects

A project involving Family Links offers a more optimistic picture. Family Links is a small VSO working collaboratively with members of the Child and Adolescent Mental Health Service (CAMHS) to provide home-school liaison support for vulnerable young people and parents. Family Links staff regarded the project positively, identifying the CAMHS infrastructure as removing some time-consuming burdens, such as funding bids and monitoring systems, and providing essential access to school-based information. Staff felt that they had learned considerably from the joint work but that the effort to create the project and resolve complementary roles had been significant and relied on positive individual attitudes to working through and respecting differences in approach. For CAMHS staff, project work meant that they could operate more flexibly than if they were bound by the usual department regulations and they acknowledged learning from different perspectives. Paul (CAMHS) reflected: "We could develop more creative approaches and combine our different strengths."

However, these developments were not achieved through the comfortable consensus implied in policy documents but demanded a process of negotiation and opening up of relational space among participants. There were also elements of improvisation needed to deal with the uncertainties exposed when previously understood roles and organisational accountabilities became blurred. As Jan, from Family Links, recognised: "We had to sort it together, how we could work best ... thinking back now, that was good – no blueprint – but at the time, it seemed a bit, well, unstructured and daunting." Drawing in community partners, effectively as change agents, introduces new approaches to addressing past failures in mainstream services but, as Howard and Taylor (2010) identify, working through the ambiguity of new organisational forms can be challenging and lead to resistance in partnerships, as well as offering space for flexibility and risk taking. In this case, through willingness to engage with alternatives, the project work freed professionals from bounded procedures, facilitating a more responsive service.

In successful examples, such as this, collaborative relationships involve learning *from* the other but this can be problematic since it may involve reassessing individual assumptions and ways of doing things, opening up fields of difference and potentially conflict. If these issues pose challenges and dilemmas for cross-agency delivery work, the prospect of merger exposes VSOs to considerably greater threats in terms of mission and identity; and constructing the shared vision needed to merge successfully demands significant time (Moran et al, 2009).

Inter-organisational collaboration, nevertheless, depends on individuals; and key individuals committed to building a successful project emerged as critical to the success of the Family Links project. Donna, a VS worker for a home-school liaison project based in a primary school, similarly stressed how much "it has to do with the individuals that make things work or not". Because many VSOs in this area were small, individual commitment was crucial in moving collaborative projects forward. However, equally, commitment could be constrained by underlying institutional cultures: how much an individual's originating organisation (or sector) dominated their modes of operating and thinking, creating resistance to learning and change. This suggests that there has to be a level of trust: that collaboration does not mean takeover and relinquishing fundamental values and approaches.

In another example, community workers delivering extended learning projects within schools cited initial mistrust from school staff and agencies, including education welfare services, as a barrier to collaborating. Overcoming this often relied heavily on the efforts and credibility of individual workers. Otherwise, mistrust hindered access to key information about children and families, increasing and duplicating work, and undermining collaboration. Where collaboration worked well, key individuals with good local networks and a willingness to set aside organisational hierarchies were important, allowing a co-construction of goals and meanings that extended beyond individual and sector interests. However, individuals leave, organisations restructure, funding for sustaining projects or partnerships ends; and individuals' base organisations may prioritise other tasks for their time. Reliance on individual dispositions therefore underlines the fragile foundations on which community-level collaborations are constructed, and reinforces Higham and Yeoman's (2010, p 398) account of partnership working as locally contingent and 'happenstance'.

Barriers to collaboration: competing interests

The VS has been subject to contradictory policy strands: 'partnership culture' – encouragement to collaborate flexibly within and across sectors – has been promoted in parallel with competitive funding regimes and associated 'command and control' cultures, discussed in earlier chapters. As identified earlier, competition is a policy driver for instrumental or pragmatic collaboration, to meet the terms of funding or gain large contracts, but it often undermines motivation to collaborate in more committed ways.

In policy terms, small VSOs have been encouraged to collaborate on bids for increasingly large contracts. However, many small organisations in this study identified the detailed arrangements required to negotiate and manage combined bids and contracts as more onerous and time consuming than separate undertakings. For small VSOs with limited capacity, bidding jointly with bigger organisations was potentially more beneficial but also posed threats to autonomy over values and ways of working. As Seth, a play centre worker said, "one of the things about us is we're small – that's a plus for us – and unthreatening for the kids. We could lose all that ... get swamped in YL" (a large provider that had approached his VSO as a bid partner). Aggregating smaller contracts into larger ones benefited local government interests in reducing transaction costs but not those of small VSOs. However, solutions in VSO collaborations or mergers are complex, demanding affinity in goals and values, and time and commitment to work through detail. Some small VSOs otherwise perceive the pressures for collaboration as another form of incorporation or assimilation, reshaping how they understand and approach their work.

With only a few smaller VSOs involved in collaborative bids, larger organisations in Wharton were reasonably confident of gaining future contracts while the smallest, least experienced organisations felt disadvantaged in a growing and increasingly fluid market. Local reputation and co-construction of projects with user groups seemed undervalued in funding decisions, implying few benefits to users from cross-sector collaboration over services. Expressing anxieties about the future, Jo, a youth centre worker, reflected:

> 'If bids are open to all kinds of new service providers, you see groups who've spent years building links with disengaged young people locally and trying to work together, lose out to organisations coming in with smart application skills.... [A]nd long term, you lose those connections with young people we're trying to keep hold of.'

The spectre of competition lay beneath concerns about different forms of cross-sector work, underlining the complex weave of purposes, interests and motivations for involvement. As Gary, a youth centre trustee, explained:

> 'Partnerships can be very short term, there's a big time investment for small centres.... You have to trust it'll be useful somehow, not just a pretext for other agencies to access funds because community partners are fashionable.... They tick the box for community involvement, whether or not they took our views on board.'

Gary's mistrust of the benefits from closer association, especially with larger agencies, raises questions about whose interests partnerships serve; and points to intrinsic difficulties arising from the unaddressed power differentials of partnership actors. While competitive funding cultures lie under the surface of such work – whatever the overt purpose of the collaboration – creating better foundations for openness, shared purposes and trust is hard, as too is disentangling motivations for participation.

Mistrust of the benefits from closer association with bigger agencies, whether in the VS or not, were frequent comments, highlighting the different interests served, threats to independence and the compromises to local accountabilities implied. Proposed mergers of national and regionally based charities have been the subject of recurrent articles in the journal *Third Sector*,[6] and reports of staff and volunteers in local branches reacting with mistrust and sometimes resistance to recent mergers, such as of Age Concern and Help the Aged (Plummer, 2010), highlight the challenges in forging successful mergers. If competitive funding cultures underlie the reasons for merger or collaboration, it is hard for organisations to operate with openness and trust, to overcome differences in approach or to separate the drawbacks from benefits. As Campbell (2008) identified from studies of non-profit mergers in the United States, power dynamics strongly influenced the shape of decisions and had an impact on subsequent success.

Examples reveal how conflicting interests can destabilise the overall project of collaboration without the time, will and motivation to address these tensions. Repeatedly, small VSOs felt overwhelmed by a powerful consensus of arrangements, which were strong on form and structures but were experienced as sites of 'lifeless consultations' (Hoggett, 2004, p 123). As Kim, from another youth project, described: "It's hugely time consuming ... everyone's got their view but with officers it's one sided ... we don't feel like respected, valued partners ... there's a lot of meeting jargon and red tape ... and it's not about, even close to things ... young people want."

Larger organisations with greater time and resources to attend these fora were able to increase both practical and cultural advantages by engaging in networks, influencing service criteria and accessing key information, whereas small VSOs felt increasingly excluded from participating. Valuable opportunities to learn from diverse alternatives were therefore lost, while dominant cultural norms were reinforced, suppressing appearances of difference or conflict. Boundary spanners – familiar with the rules of engagement – marked out those able to participate in (and potentially influence) joint planning groups from the less experienced, creating hierarchies of inclusion, insiders and outsiders among VSOs.

Many VSOs participated instrumentally in collaborative ventures to gain or maintain funding, often identifying these as sets of relationships and procedures that they reluctantly engaged with. Some explained that the competitive funding environment obstructed meaningful exchange, and as Gary (cited above) underlined, multiple interests were in play. Competition for funding, coupled with unrealistic performance targets, generated misgivings about failing to do the best possible work for user groups. Paul from St Jude's community centre described the pressures on their work with young people, highlighting the lost opportunities to cooperate on exchanging information about challenging situations with other similar VSOs: "We have enormous problems.... So there's issues about working together with other local groups, sharing problems, professionally, like we used to. But what we're faced with is competing for funding, that's the bottom line, and it creates dishonesty."

Competitive funding regimes are heavily underwritten by quantitative performance targets and, as Chapter Five underlined, also discussing comments from Paul, these are rarely negotiable and may lead to gaming. They therefore undermine opportunities to collaborate openly and honestly because, as Paul argued, VSOs have to appear to meet targets to survive. Disclosing and sharing failures could offer means to reflect on ways of reaching young people outside many services but competing interests limit the potential of youth centres to tackle such challenges jointly.

The darker side of change: risks and casualties in collaborative work

The cases described above have illustrated factors inhibiting more open, innovative and engaged collaborative work, pointing to ways in which powerful organisational cultures often undermine VS partnerships with larger agencies. In many of the examples above, differential power in determining approaches has restricted the terms of collaboration, privileging dominant partners and arrangements and discounting the independent approaches of small VSOs. As a consequence, oppositional voices have often been sidelined and those with limited resources to participate excluded, highlighting inequalities in 'partnership' work. A further illustration below highlights the difficulties of building trust in such work, alongside the darker side of changes: the risks and damage resulting when collaborative ventures raise and subsequently destroy hopes, as fashions in policies and funding change. While large agencies may be able to manage and control their risks, as Chapters Five illustrated, small VSOs are asked to carry the risks and support the casualties of innovative, and financially and emotionally challenging, work.

Rather than acknowledging difficulties and risks involved, the positive and consensually driven message of the politics of change has apparently intensified in the recent coalition government's advancement of local partnership proposals. The coalition's goals have placed social enterprises and VSOs at the forefront of changing communities, 'as if change was simply a matter of seizing opportunities' (Hoggett, 2004, p 119), and presented no dilemmas or conflicts. Collaborative work introduces tensions and risks, especially when greater commitment is involved; but as other chapters argue, these are carried disproportionately by smaller VSOs.

The example below involves a Sure Start project developing collaborative work between an adult education provider (ACE) and three recently established parent–child education groups for whom ACE was providing accredited play-worker training. The ACE project coordinator described the participants: "Some parents are from ... two generations without jobs. The project helped a few feel brave enough to train. Now they're working in the community centre. They'd never have gone to college or got involved in something outside their immediate area. Building up that trust was from street level." The apparent success of this collaborative project was short-lived because of the end of Sure Start funding, highlighting the potential damage to collaborative community relationships produced by disruptive policy changes. As another professional commented:

> 'This funding stream ends in two months; local parents whose hopes have been raised will lose jobs and the children's projects. We're letting them down all over again. This is their project, their neighbourhood, what they've put effort into. They can't see their role in a big, new children's centre, starting again somewhere else. Why would they?'

The struggle of community-based collaboration, involving hard-to-reach, low-income families in designing self-help projects that increase local employment and provide better facilities for children and parenting support, relies on building trust and engagement over time. This is easily lost with no visible means of continuity in a neighbourhood, a loss of support structures and other local VSOs struggling. To expect the successful experiences of this collaborative work to be transferred into new, larger projects outside the immediate locality, with new professionals and within short timeframes, is unrealistic, especially in a hostile job market; and disregards individual casualties. From an outsider's perspective, mainstreaming Sure Start and related projects into large integrated children's centres may appear rational and cost effective but makes poor sense in communities where people see their efforts devalued and endeavours frustrated. Community-based development work is fragile and the risks for vulnerable individuals are high in a discontinuous policy environment over which they have little control. Mistrust and reluctance to engage in collaborative work are perhaps unsurprising then. This case also underlines the time, efforts and levels of professional support needed for successful self-help – the kind of community action envisaged under the Big Society banner – if community-based collaboration is to enlist those without the resources of existing professional classes.

Collaboration in theory and practice

In examining VSO involvement in cross-agency collaboration, this chapter has highlighted complex and conflicting features of policies intended to promote collaborative work. It illustrates a considerable mismatch between policy aspirations and local experiences and outcomes, generating disquiet about unanticipated consequences. Policy changes and mechanisms for their implementation may be constructed by central government bodies and local government managers but the community turn in policy has increasingly shifted responsibility for delivery towards community-based organisations collaborating with other local agencies. If this fails, blame is frequently located with frontline arrangements. The rhetoric of collaboration and partnership suggests something open, equal and democratic; however, examples here show that power to determine the rules of engagement resides with larger, mainly public, agencies, marginalising the interests of small VSOs. As a means to promote VS capacity and access large service contracts, collaboration is therefore problematic since it poses threats to the identities and autonomous purposes of smaller organisations, arousing VS mistrust.

In terms of mainstream agencies leading the way in collaborative relationships, the findings illustrated few examples of valuing or respecting VSOs in ways that allowed them genuine influence over services and arrangements. Removed from delivery, larger agencies often continued to collude in, rather than confront, cultures and structural limitations, which undermined co-constructive ways of working with community groups, despite the acknowledged value in policy of learning from different approaches. As Clegg (1989, p 200) argues, power, is 'inscribed within contextual rules', undermining the potential for cooperative working. The persistent exercise of hierarchical power in cross-sector work, as Davies (2011) highlights, is a reassertion of governmentality and undermines the less bounded aspirations of network governance. However, at the community level, it generates disillusionment in the goals of purportedly collaborative arrangements, hindering creative developments and devaluing the approaches and achievements of small VSOs.

However, there were also positive examples of cross-sector collaboration, albeit few, showing that agencies can break this pattern by sharing power and valuing local experiential knowledge. These examples demonstrated mainstream agency staff working alongside small VSOs in frontline delivery, with partners learning from mutual strengths and contributions. Being engaged in a joint project and sharing rewards and potential failures strengthened motivational trust (Weeks and Feeny, 2008). It is readily assumed that 'what works' can transfer across contexts but experiences from this research show that effective collaborative work is fragile, often depending heavily on the commitment, dispositions and networks of individuals, and situated experiences. If key individuals leave or contexts change, successful collaborations may not be sustained.

Similarly, if VSO capacity building, rather than mutual learning or co-constructed activities, had been the key driver in the positive example illustrated, the value added or 'collaborative advantage' might have been lost. Capacity building, as a motivation for collaboration, was frequently criticised by VSOs since growth and professionalisation often accelerated mission drift, threatening independent ways of working. Although some VSOs recognised the instrumental value in collaborating as a means to continue funding for services, capacity building appeared to privilege the interests of larger agencies and those purchasing services.

Competitive funding mechanisms posed significant barriers to collaborative work. There was considerable anxiety surrounding competitive bidding in procurement processes, which was identified as damaging cooperative relationships among VSOs and across sectors. There was also fear that costs rather than value of services would determine future decisions and that better-resourced, 'smart' organisations would gain contracts without the local knowledge to generate effective provision. This fear is currently being borne out in the allocation of recent welfare contracts (discussed in Chapter Seven). Service planning models based on broad abstract criteria and judged through proxy, numerically based indicators of outcomes highlight the contradictions between aspirations for locally designed collaborative solutions to social problems and competitively allocated contracts, drawn up without the local knowledge accessible to small community organisations.

Privileging the power of market-driven policy governance has the effect of relegating smaller VSOs to roles as state agents or as subcontractors for larger VSOs or private corporations, reinforcing the hierarchy of size, and undermining the collaborative aspirations of localism and cross-agency working. The parallel contexts of both collaborating and competing for funding underline ways in which policies are contradictory and can inhibit and adversely affect others. Despite the collaborative and mutual emphasis of the Big Society, the belief in market-based solutions has intensified in recent government ideology and policy, exacerbating the contradictory challenges.

In the current climate, collaboration may be a means for VSOs to compete and survive, allowing access to funds that small VSOs could not secure alone. Consequently, the apparent policy dichotomy of collaboration and competition may be better understood as interdependency, albeit employing instrumental collaboration. However, while competition drives some forms of collaboration, it simultaneously undermines the development of cooperative relationships, curtailing opportunities for collaborative advantage.

Competition necessarily privileges motives around winning – in this context, achieving individual or organisational vested interests in funding, influence or survival – over developing shared meanings, trust building and co-constructing goals. The extent to which trust and open communication can develop in inter-organisational relationships largely depends therefore on the motives and understanding brought to the venture and the willingness of individuals to invest in, and learn from, the process. It follows, then, that motivation to collaborate and the different ways in which collaborative work is conceived and operated must be better understood for collaboration, as a strategy, to be more effective. In some contexts, the best and only form of collaboration will be instrumentally driven. Provided aims and limitations are understood, this may be appropriate. However, the overriding aims of achieving improved community cohesion through collaboration in the project involving Kidscare, were neither well understood by participants nor shared; and were, in any case, perceived as unrealistic by most VSOs involved.

While research has theorised the development of non-profit organisations as responding to market failures (Salamon, 2003), paradoxically, the coalition government has identified markets and entrepreneurialism as driving the future shape of community services. However, asked to be co-constructors of local solutions, the most vulnerable community groups suffer most where discontinuities in policy or market vagaries curtail funding streams. Sustaining community-level commitment to collaborating on social problems must also entail an obligation from government and larger agencies to act responsibly, that is, not to raise hopes in an area and then change the rules, nor to open the door to unregulated markets in contexts where user groups have minimal market power.

For a decade or more, the wider public benefits of localism and partnership work have been declared in community policies but little attention has focused on drawbacks. The analysis in this chapter, however, questions the assumed benefits of greater collaboration and highlights challenges for small, already overstretched VSOs pressured to engage in time-consuming partnership ventures with significantly poorer resources and infrastructure than those of larger agencies. As Ellison and Ellison (2006, p 341) stress, participation and engagement can be 'ambiguous goods' with 'equal scope for disempowerment and alienation' because of the complexities of power and interest involved, the paucity of resources and lack of value accorded to legitimise efforts.

Policies envisage collaboration as involving locally based VSOs in change processes to generate innovative models and remedy poor local responsiveness in services. However, competition for funding and the pressures to accommodate mainstream organisational interests and arrangements undermine these possibilities, working against inter-organisational learning and alternatives critical of dominant approaches. If collaboration is to be effective rather than a further isomorphic force, the exercise of power and the coercive financial pressures involved need to be addressed. Otherwise the results may well be VSOs, at best, engaging instrumentally and defensively in collaborative work and few of the developmental outcomes intended.

Combining different individual and organisational cultures in partnership working is often conceived as if there were no material conflicts – a comfortable ideal that takes little account of diversity in local conditions. Paramount in policy rhetoric and expectations is the joint collaborative enterprise, portrayed as consensual, without conflicts or gaming. Thus, the outcomes from collaborating are invariably depicted as positive – gains from sharing different expertise – while the costs and tensions of the process are hidden; and the questions of who benefits and in what ways are rarely publicly articulated. Yet, social change – in which inter-agency collaboration is a deliberate strategy for shifting patterns of social relations in communities and service delivery – is essentially a conflictual process. Not only does this conflict need recognition but also, as the next chapter considers, the inadvertent outcomes in winners and losers, and the costs of casualties emerging from the darker side of changes, need disclosure.

Benefits and resistances in collaborative spaces

Achieving more effective collaboration, which benefits a wider range of participants, demands both better understanding and tackling issues identified above, especially the role of dominant cultures and hierarchies. Competition is advanced as a means of generating fair funding decisions and efficient services, while collaboration alongside capacity building and mergers are argued as means to a more level playing field for small VSOs. Such strategies serve government interests in devolving services and reducing transaction costs through increasing contract size but make unrealistic demands on the smallest organisations, closest to those in the most deprived neighbourhoods. Such changes create tensions internally and at organisational boundaries, potentially destabilising relationships with user groups. In these contexts, VSOs are likely to enter collaboration instrumentally, accommodating necessary changes but resisting threats to independence. Moreover, the powerful hierarchies that are often replicated in partnerships are hostile to co-constructing approaches, cooperative communication and building mutual trust, deterring VSOs from more committed collaboration, which might be built if there was a willingness to share power.

The benefits of collaboration are assumed to be in sharing knowledge and expertise across agencies and sectors but my studies identified limited evidence of shared practice and organisational learning. The examples also show that, at a number of levels, the legitimacy invested in dominant organisational cultures and arrangements exclude openness to alternative approaches, at the same time, obscuring conflicts of interest arising from underlying differences. As Davies (2011) finds, networks involving powerful actors who give emphasis to congruent interests appear more prevalent than those that are widely inclusive; and professionals, as the Family Links–CAMHS project illustrates, need to recognise and avert ways in which they habitually assert their legitimacy and dominance. Moreover, the presence of some VS representatives at planning and consultation bodies has been read as denoting wider VS concurrence, legitimising ideas of commonly adopted discourse and approaches, despite the diversity of organisations and views in an area.

Levels of power and influence between those involved in projects may differ widely, and experiences discussed above indicate ways in which partnership insiders and outsiders are generated. Larger, better-resourced VSOs may accommodate organisational pressure to collaborate more readily, identifying beneficial opportunities to influence outcomes. However, the effects of institutional isomorphism, as Chapter Two discussed, may result in insiders relinquishing autonomy or alternative models in exchange for gains in legitimacy, and competitive and financial advantage. In accepting this transition of identity, these VSOs may be renouncing the attributes for which they were initially sought in partnership. While insider status may be used to support VSO users' interests, in other cases, it may distance VSOs from their user groups, creating internal fragmentation.

The assumed benefits of building capacity as motivation for collaboration are often unwelcome to small VSOs whose identities rely on localism, smallness and links with specific user groups. Moreover, the professionalisation implied in growth often restricts the space for diverse approaches. Similarly, failure to recognise the lack of time and resources available in small VSOs for collaborative work is inimical to committed engagement. Thus, small VSOs' resistance to participating in the project of collaboration can be construed as contesting or subverting policy spaces, preferring to safeguard autonomy, grassroots identity and overstretched resources.

As Hoggett et al (2009, p 97) illustrate, organisational actors increasingly have to navigate a series of tensions – 'dilemmatic spaces' – in contexts where roles and boundaries are both blurred and contested. These occur across sectors and in ambiguously defined collaborative roles, reflecting more fluid, less conventionally defined structures but also demonstrate uncertainties around how the state may now value and resource the VS. Ambiguities coupled with the pressures exerted through different changes argue the importance of individual and organisational sense making (Weick, 1995) and inner authority (Obholzer, 1994) to sustain autonomous purposes and practices, rather than seeing the adoption of only those generated from new governance spaces dominated by policy ideology and powerful partnership players.

A new (cross-sector) hybrid identity might appear a logical, shared outcome from forming new collaborative entities but seems neither an ideal nor a probable outcome reflecting on the cases above. Despite some blurring of individual and organisational practices that has occurred as collaborative work has grown, ideas of sectors and their associated identities remain strong, as Billis (2010) also claims. Consequently, differences in approach, values and allegiances for accountability associated with different sectors need to be recognised and respected if barriers to genuine collaboration are to be tackled and trust in the process established.

Collaboration entails an ongoing and dynamic process of working, dependent on participating individuals who are crucial in fostering relationships. It is neither an entity nor a static event, and those who engage in instrumental ways may, in the future, engage differently, if the collaborative project allows sufficient time and mutual respect to involve participants inclusively. Distinguishing between superficial, instrumental and committed collaboration, therefore, is more effectively represented as a continuum. 'Good enough' collaboration at the outset, provided benefits and limitations are understood, may lead to better joint ventures and shared learning in the future. However, without recognition of the powerful dynamics and dominant cultures that currently threaten collaborative spaces, and the fragility of this work in an under-resourced and rapidly changing policy environment, small VSOs will inevitably resist engagement, and changes in public and community services will hardly emerge as intended. A mixture of accommodation, organisational defensiveness and subversion will continue to surface and deflect the course of collaborative policy aspirations.

Note

[6] A leading professional publication for UK non-profit organisations.

SEVEN

Community heroes, survivors or casualties? Exploring risk and resilience in the voluntary sector

This chapter considers the recent climate of recession affecting the English voluntary sector (VS), together with the political ideologies and policies underpinning related changes in state–VS relationships. Recent policies have simultaneously applauded the work of small voluntary and community organisations as components of civil society or Big Society and privileged corporate service providers through increasingly large contracts. The chapter draws on case studies of three voluntary sector organisations (VSOs) to explore questions of risk and resilience among survivors and casualties, considering the extent to which compliance and conformity are requisites for survival in this new organisational order.

For more than two decades, the UK government has increasingly relied on VS providers to deliver varied welfare services, generating unprecedented VS growth (Kendall, 2010). Service providers, infrastructure organisations charged with building capacity and small organisations engaged in regeneration and community engagement projects have all participated in, and gained from, this growth. However, as earlier chapters have discussed, this has raised concerns about the extent to which VSOs have become servants of government, overly dependent on public funding and with fortunes reliant on unpredictable government strategies. Yet, as historical accounts in Chapter Two illustrated, VSOs have shown considerable adaptive capacities.

Voluntary sector growth has now reversed, as has the sector's privileged position as a preferred service provider in New Labour's Third Way ideology. Voluntary sector resources have diminished rapidly, with some local government areas admitting reduced funding to VSOs of some 60 to 80%; and local VS infrastructure agencies struggling to survive (NCIA, 2012). Loss of income, a predicted £3 billion of nearly £13 billion VS income in 2008-09, now presents a high risk, especially for small VSOs (Slocock, 2012). In parallel, service contracts have grown massively in size, with financial and business acumen supplanting service knowledge or reputation in criteria for outsourcing decisions. The new political discourse emphasises the need for VS entrepreneurialism

(OCS, 2010), which is implied as a remedy for survival, displacing earlier rhetoric valuing community expertise.

This chapter first explores ideas of risk and resilience, providing a lens through which to consider how organisations can navigate recent changes. Resilience is often understood as a process of positive adaptation within a context of significant adversity (Luthar et al, 2000; Ungar, 2004) and has gained renewed interest in exploring the differential outcomes of socially excluded individuals and groups (Mohaupt, 2009). However, it has seen limited application to factors influencing organisational survival, especially in the VS. In examining risk, in particular the location and transfer of organisational risks, the exercise of power within inter-organisational relationships again emerges, reflecting ideas discussed in Chapters Four and Five on the isomorphic pressures that legitimise and spread dominant arrangements.

The chapter then explores empirical data drawn from studies in English urban areas described in Chapter Three, selecting three cases for closer discussion. The focus on seeking to understand organisational survival in adverse circumstances now resonates across international research (Jäger and Beyes, 2010). Drawing on this analysis of case studies, the chapter identifies a typology of *entrepreneurs*, *resisters* and *accommodators* among VSOs, considering how each of these positions can construct survivors and casualties. Any typology necessarily highlights differences at the expense of similarities and types often embrace overlapping elements. However, a typology offers a conceptual map for understanding the different ways in which VSOs have approached changing conditions and potential threats to survival. The chapter questions whether VSO survivors are replicating historical examples of successful VS adaption or whether recent conditions represent unprecedented changes requiring new thinking and approaches.

Risk, risk management and innovation

Risk and risk management have become significant concerns in organisational literature (Coutu, 2002), with disaster recovery and resilience strategies coming under scrutiny. In the VS there are significant threats as resources diminish after a period of growth, with few opportunities for diversifying funding sources. Previous chapters have outlined challenges facing VSOs with growing contract size, associated regulatory cultures and new forms of collaborative governance. While risk management, as discussed in Chapter Five, has increasingly become a feature of large funding bodies, their dominant organisational arrangements have also been promoted as appropriate ways of doing things. However, these arrangements contain inherent risks to VS independence, constraining the kinds of flexible and innovative approaches valued by user groups and rhetorically by policy makers, and therefore jeopardise the VS's reputational value for both groups.

Voluntary sector organisations' relationships with public funders have, for some time, maintained a tension between autonomy and accountability, partly consequent on the balance between public, voluntary and private sectors in the mixed economy of welfare. That mix is shifting with growth in corporate providers, further restricting autonomies. In the VS, autonomy is necessary to sustain the goals and actions mandated by community members and service users, and to respond flexibly to local conditions. However, with pressure to build capacity in service delivery since the first 'Changeup' policy (Home Office, 2004), resisting growth to maintain autonomy has been read potentially as risky behaviour, hindering organisational development. Such behaviour is risky in posing challenges to dominant organisational trends and risky because it fails to adopt the assumed protective factors to be gained from growth. Yet as other studies illustrate (Harris and Young, 2010), such developments may be wholly inappropriate for small VSOs whose key purposes and activities rely on maintaining trust and connections at the grassroots level. Risks to survival in such cases may be greater through loss of autonomy, since local relationships and reputation are crucial in engaging hard-to-reach users.

Over 13 years, New Labour substantially increased resources allocated to VSOs with the intention of promoting innovative and more responsive services but extended limited trust to VSOs to use the resources wisely, and instead, closely managed financial and (their own) reputational risks through highly specified contracts (Milbourne and Cushman, 2012). The coalition government's Big Society promised greater autonomy but the drastic reduction in financial support, alongside the rapid spread of outsourcing to corporate contractors, have significantly exacerbated VS risks.

There is an inescapable trade-off between autonomy and accountability that faces both public funders and VSOs but for VSOs it runs in parallel with managing survival. Taking risks in order to promote innovation and managing risks to demonstrate probity and measurable achievements are visible tensions. However, as Chapter Five identified, while there is pressure on VSOs to create new and flexible approaches that are inherently risky, these are undermined by funders' models for managing risks.

The previous and current governments have both highlighted the value of diversity in addressing social challenges, the need to avoid being overly risk averse and the multiple opportunities available for those willing to be enterprising (OCS, 2010). Yet such recommendations have mainly been disregarded in the relentless acceleration of heavily specified frameworks associated with public sector outsourcing. Therefore, while government rhetoric aspires to enabling innovation, funders' willingness (whether or not government agencies) to adopt this advice, share risks and welcome alternatives is little evident in the construction of contracts for projects and services.

The audit mechanisms inherent in the dominant managerial environment, as earlier chapters identified, have also transformed VS management practices through processes of coercive and mimetic isomorphism, and many VSOs have assumed organisational behaviours believed to manage risks. Paradoxically, such behaviours undermine openness and learning, often detracting from organisational missions and sense making (Weick, 1995), which may be crucial in protecting against external risks. The escalation of data collection can readily erode autonomy and creativity without ensuring accountability, offering 'rituals of verification' (Power, 1997, p 145) but few safeguards against longer-term risks.

The failure to share risks and the disproportionate transfer of risks to small VS providers from large funding bodies have been evident as welfare outsourcing has spread. This has recently been exacerbated in contracts that include Payment by Results, with risks transferred from government to prime contractors and then to VS subcontractors (Marsden, 2011). For example, VSOs may provide effective activities over several months but receive no payment until a client retains a job for six months. In a labour market where jobs are at risk and VSOs are working with high-risk clients, these conditions transfer untenable risks to many small VSOs with limited reserves to draw on. The risks for VSOs are thus intensifying.

Resilience

If the risks that VSOs face are growing, the obvious question is: what can help to protect them in an adverse environment? 'Resilience' is a somewhat imprecise term signifying the ability to remain strong and survive difficulties. It is a metaphor for sustainability, often applied in academic work to denote the capacities of individuals or businesses to overcome hostile conditions (Coutu, 2002; Seccombe, 2002). Resilience theories have been used across disciplines, including to consider adaptive capacity in ecology, but much work on resilience derives from psychological studies concentrating on behaviours and strategies (intrinsic and exogenous) that build or support individual, group or socioeconomic wellbeing (Edwards, 2007). Von Krogh et al's (1994) analysis of organisational adaption and survival is helpful for this discussion but little of this work has been applied to study VSOs adapting in hard times.

Features judged as promoting resilience are clearly not static but relate to dynamic processes of adaption and meaning making; and equally are interwoven with policy, socioeconomic, institutional and environmental changes. Personal characteristics and protective behaviours, which enable individuals facing difficulties to cope, adapt or succeed (Edwards, 2007), have featured prominently in resilience literature. However, the social resources and capital that support individual and group resilience can also be destabilised by exogenous changes; and elements of social stability are important in anchoring both organisations and individuals facing adversity (Luthar et al, 2000). By contrast, multiple reorganisations and changing staff roles can exacerbate already low organisational morale when funding and service cuts are taking place.

Although creative solutions may be particularly needed, Weick (1993) argues that people under pressure and facing hardship are unlikely to maximise creativity. They more often concentrate on a short-term fix to the problems, relying on familiar methods. Instability and creativity appear inversely related; and there is useful converse evidence in the VS: when resources have been stable or growing, innovation, developments and increased voluntary action have tended to flourish (Aiken, 2010). Recent challenges facing VSOs include major changes on all fronts: substantial funding reductions; growing privatisation of public services; and rapid shifts in the roles expected of VSOs in service delivery and community work (Taylor, 2011b).

Secure havens from which to generate creative solutions are in short supply.

There are, of course, different types of resilience:

- the emotional resilience of organisational actors;
- their purposeful adoption of protective behaviours and strategies;
- the strengths that an organisation derives from its history and values, often grounded in organisational narratives (Schwabenland, 2006).

The ways in which organisational actors utilise and communicate these strengths within and outside the organisation may be significant in addressing external threats or in achieving a meaningful accommodation of changes. Different fields of research emerge with remarkably similar abstract factors identified as supporting organisational strengths and resilience, including: clarity in core goals and purposes (Nevile, 2010); the ability to make meaning out of hardship (Von Krogh et al, 1994); the ability to be flexible (Coutu, 2002); the ability to recognise successes and failures (Williams et al, 2001); the ability to learn from differences (Jäger and Beyes, 2010).

Linking with some of these ideas, other work (Small and Memmo, 2004; Cairns et al, 2006) – again from disparate fields – emphasises the importance of strongly held values and beliefs in grounding necessary adaptive processes. Available social support networks are also identified as important in sustaining positive endeavour when faced with difficulties (Edwards, 2007). The recent significant damage to VS infrastructure organisations and resources then augurs poorly for small VSOs, previously reliant on local or regional bodies for advice and support.

The earlier focus in psychological research on innate qualities of resilience has ceded to ideas that key resilient behaviours can be learned (Coutu, 2002). As Chapter Two illustrated, VSOs have a long history of adapting to externally generated changes (Billis, 2010), with some adjusting more successfully than others, sometimes because of the diverse combinations of conditions present in different contexts. Such variations therefore highlight the difficulty of identifying characteristics common to resilient organisations, and as Ciborra (2002) stresses, it would be a mistake to assume that successful strategies in one context can necessarily translate into another.

Despite research that explores in depth how organisations adapt to and make sense of changes (Weick, 1995), the focus on adaptive behaviours and strategies reflects a tendency for resilience theories to present normative features assumed to be protective in overcoming organisational adversity. Abstractly described, these often echo approaches identified in policy priorities. For example, under the New Labour administration, capacity building and growth, and subsequently collaborative bids and mergers, were recommended as strategies that would shield VSOs from the effects of economic recession (Cabinet Office, 2009). Mergers can erode organisational identities and purposes, increasing distance from key stakeholders (Mullins, 1999; Baker et al, 2010), but such strategies suited both national and local governments generating large contracts as ways to reduce transaction costs and, more recently, to attract large corporations. Similarly, entrepreneurialism is applauded since it can draw in resources for services that have lost funding from the public purse. Arguably, therefore, resilience may be a proxy definition for success in conformity with recommended trends rather than describing autonomous development capacity.

There are further problems with resilience theories. Conceptually, resilience suggests a positive outcome from challenging circumstances, highlighting individual or group resourcefulness and achievements in overcoming misfortune. This chimes well with recent political ideology, with its emphasis on responsibilising citizens (and organisations) and reducing dependency on the state; but it ensures that those that fail, when funding is cut, projects close, infrastructure support is withdrawn or service contracts are reassigned, are blameworthy. The policy emphasis remains on success through competition – VSOs can survive if they adopt the right strategies; and responsibility for survival is individualised, locating failure as a deficit in individual organisational behaviours, rather than deficient policies, institutions or deeper-rooted social or economic problems. Defining normative behaviours that will generate resilience also implies that VSOs that operate with alternative approaches and fail are at fault for their non-survival. The message is clear: shape up or ship out. The myth is that all VSOs can succeed despite the current challenges and scarcity of resources. Underlying this myth is a controlling dynamic, which shapes and defines how organisations should address survival, illustrating the powerful hegemonic forces of governmentality (Rose, 1999).

Locating the onus of responsibility for success or failure with individual actors and organisations allows structural problems underlying hardships to be concealed; and theories of resilience have effectively been appropriated by neoconservatives as useful cover for divesting responsibility for failures and the social problems that ensue. Since only some individuals and organisations will prove resilient, it follows that others are effectively disposable in impoverished economic times but may be blamed for failing to adopt hegemonically constructed normative organisational behaviours. However, there are flaws: if the alternatives that VSOs have created to tackle social problems over the past decade are recognised as valuable, logically this space for diverse approaches has to be retained.

Building social and community resources and related social capital has been identified for some time as establishing a form of locality-based resilience. However, Gamarnikow and Green (2000) argue that such constructs are premised on consensual articulations of individual and organisational actions, which lay responsibility for strong or resilient civil societies on normative and non-contentious assumptions about local actions. This premise starts from a deficit model of communities, which favours bridging and linking social capital; and also masks differences inherent within ideas of community and community actions. Moreover, community building is greatly affected by individual and organisational resources, and they in turn by stability, wider economic resources and equity (Adger, 2000). This reveals as unsound the case for constructing community resilience as an effective protective factor when times are hard and inequalities growing.

What, then, are VSOs to do in this difficult environment? Maintaining alternative approaches – logical actions in terms of sustaining autonomous organisational purposes and meanings – may be regarded as a strength but conversely also as resisting mainstream arrangements. Since the ideas that underpin VSOs' meanings are drawn from different settings, sectors and frames of reference, resilience also needs to be understood as relative, and resistance potentially as strength and a form of resilient behaviour. However, resistance is often mistrusted and can prompt the exercise of power by dominant agencies in ways that marginalise or exclude small VSOs, highlighting coercive and punitive pressures towards compliance and the suppression of other (minority) interests.

Survivors and casualties

An analysis of cases drawn from the studies described in Chapter Three has been used to explore how VSOs have dealt with the challenges identified above. In what follows, three cases have been selected for this chapter to illustrate three broad organisational types identified: entrepreneurs, resisters and accommodators. Typologies construct ideal types since their value is in illuminating differences; whereas in the complexity of detailed organisational cases, boundaries are inevitably less clear than types suggest. Within types, some entrepreneurs, for example, adhered to social values while others sought greater market legitimacy; and some resisters exhibited different degrees of willingness to accommodate change. Equally, features associated with organisational types did not necessarily correlate with survival; and from the wider range of cases, stories of survivors and casualties emerged in each category, including among VSOs adopting similar strategies in different areas, suggesting that external, as well as internal, factors are in play. While some observations from these cases inevitably concern effects on service users, the focus here is on consequences for organisational survival.

Entrepreneurs

The first example involves a large national VSO – NetworkPlus (NP) – whose main work is with unemployed people. NP has been significantly affected by the recent Work Programme, the prime-contracting model used to outsource services for unemployed people. This began with the Future Jobs Fund under New Labour and is now integral to the coalition government's programmes.

NP has over a dozen local bases across England and Wales, many in large urban centres. It also works in partnership with local authorities and with a network of small community organisations running neighbourhood projects. In most areas it has developed specific schemes for young people not in employment, education or training (NEET) and for long-term unemployed people. NP began some 35 years ago, working in a few neighbourhood centres of one large English urban area; but grew steadily over the last decade.

NP has benefited from diverse funding sources, including: successful bids for contracts outsourced by public agencies; special local and national project funding; donor funding.

Volunteers contribute to service delivery and as trustees; and in the last five years, NP's strategies have become more overtly 'enterprising', with growth and fundraising targets, and separate trading ventures. Thus, the evolution of NP has reflected the kind of capacity building and entrepreneurial development encouraged as positive survival strategies by both the previous and current governments. However, NP staff acknowledge that they have experienced conflicts in internal culture between caring and business models. As Evers and Laville (2004, p 8) highlights of social enterprises, they effectively combine the 'different components and rationales' of civil society, state and market in one organisation, integrating competing purposes.

Managing the inevitable tensions of this hybrid form across multiple sites and localities is challenging, although as Nevile (2010) argues, an organisation that can maintain clarity in core purposes is less likely to simply become a pawn of the prevailing funding environment. NP still adheres strongly to values associated with maintaining its social legitimacy despite explicitly entrepreneurial approaches to growth and raising income, through dedicated regional fundraisers. It identifies its locally based staff and flexible, responsive approaches to community projects as important aspects of its overall success. For example, in one area, work placements and job clubs have developed, while individual advice sessions and group training have been prioritised in others. A small trading division has created employment for some service users;

and in one area a drop-in cafe established by ex-claimants as a social enterprise, also combines an informal advice service. Financially self-sustaining activities both provide jobs and augment service delivery.

Those involved in managing NP's funds and contracts are distanced from the main service activities, generating criticisms from some about funding spent on infrastructure rather than frontline service activity. However, NP managers argue that central and regional services are crucial for securing funding for projects prioritised locally. As Iona, one of the central office staff explained, "[t]he trick is matching funding criteria, local needs and sustaining the good schemes. That's part of the job".

At the initial stage of the Work Programme, NP collaborated with contractors in different regions, aiming to be a key delivery partner. As only one of these was successful, NP subsequently negotiated with other successful contractors but failed in all but one case. Key managers criticised the lack of consistency and transparency in the bidding and contracting processes and in how delivery subcontractors were selected, echoing other VS experiences (Marsden, 2011). NP managers also voiced anxiety about the meagre funding allocated. The organisation has an impressive success rate of maintaining service users in employment and estimates that the costs of supporting 'hard-to-help' claimants into work, with follow-up advice, considerably exceeds the government's estimate of about £1,000. Managers also highlighted the value to society of investing in worthwhile programmes, indicating that the social return on investment in young people's programmes can be tripled. As Laura, a regional manager commented: "with growing youth unemployment, think about the future costs multiplied – if we're saying we can't afford to help them properly now".

Prior to the prime-contracting stage of the Work Programme, the government (DWP, 2011) announced a commitment to including VSOs, acknowledging their expertise, especially in poorer areas. However, at this first stage, only two of 40 VSOs were successful in accessing contracts through partnerships (Slocock, 2012). As Bennett (2011) describes, some large VSOs focused considerable effort on enhancing their entrepreneurial attributes and meeting the financial thresholds, which excluded those with less than £20 million turnover. However, many like NP had insufficient scale to access contracts without partners.

NP's unsuccessful experience of collaborating as delivery subcontractors is confirmed in other reports (Slocock, 2012): many successful corporations have chosen not to take on previous providers, with only 18% of the provision likely to be delivered through VS subcontractors. NP's perception, as that of other VSOs (Crawley and Watkin, 2011), is that these decisions appear to be driven by cost reduction rather than concerns about effective services. Toynbee (2011, p 5), commenting more cynically, indicates that some 90% of contractors comprise 'a handful of big firms with success records worse than job centres'. Recent reports on A4e (BBC, 2012) and G4S (Hopkins, 2012) confirm Toynbee's claim.

NP views its limited success in only two regions as presenting a huge threat to the future of its many projects. However, staff also voiced concern about the whole Work Programme, which, by abandoning many VSOs, will, as Laura stated, "lose an army of experienced workers and a vast pool of local knowledge". Over a decade, NP had delivered diverse skills and unemployment support programmes, including Pathways to Work, the New Deal and the Future Jobs Fund, drawing in matched funds and volunteers for projects in different areas. It had created job clubs, mentoring and extended activities intended to tackle the underlying causes of unemployment, training some staff advisers who had been unemployed previously. With the unwillingness of new contractors to use existing projects and staff, these staff too will add to the numbers of local unemployed people, echoing Toynbee's (2012) report on a London VSO.

Surviving the present and prospects for the future

NP staff have other anxieties: service demand is growing and funds are declining. Even without the loss of multiple contracts, local projects are under considerable pressure to do more with less. Shelley, a centre manager, commented: "Talking to frontline staff, youth unemployment is so much worse than figures show, so they're swamped. Young people use our drop-in but won't bother with job centres."

However, for national managers, the key challenges are keeping provision afloat and surviving. Successful negotiation with a prime contractor in one region has achieved a partial sharing of risks but the second delivery contract contains worrying conditions. The Department for Work and Pensions contracts are heavily biased towards payment for results, with severely delayed payments. Even where NP has managed to negotiate part-payment once someone starts a job, this does little to mitigate the costs of advice or training needed to achieve this. The lack of jobs available, especially in poorer areas, exacerbates difficulties for those finding it hardest to access work, with employers likely to take on experienced or more desirable applicants. Consequently, timescales for supporting worklessness and therefore receipt of payments are inevitably extended, and activities undertaken with people not placed in work remain unremunerated, raising significant questions about whether the financial risks and investments are bearable.

NP managers believed that they had little choice but to 'chase the money' for the Work Programme, which represented a major source of income for their core business. However, like other VSOs entering this arena, they failed to anticipate the extent to which the costs and risks would be passed on both by the state and large contractors, leaving relatively small providers shouldering the burden of support for long-term unemployed people. NP managers now fear that other income streams and reserves will prove insufficient to sustain basic services in areas where they have lost funding and also carry the new delivery contracts, for which they estimate receiving only about 65% of their costs after some 12 months.

To avoid an inevitable downward spiral, NP has already planned to close several regional offices, reducing its direct workforce by nearly a quarter. While this is provoking unease among staff, a regional coordinator also highlighted the parallel loss of volunteers through removing infrastructure support. Additionally, instead of activities directed towards unemployed people, efforts were being diverted towards exit strategies as centres closed. Several centre coordinators identified that NP's withdrawal from some localities would leave an absence of provision in needy areas, certainly in the short term.

These are hard times for NP, as for other VSOs in this field. Although NP remains hopeful about its overall survival, it acknowledges that its growth since 2005 has generated greater problems, than if it had not chosen to expand and maximise use of external capacity-building funds. Since 2010, the marked shift in state–VS relationships, now mediated via large corporations, means that NP faces retrenchment of operations developed over a decade. By withdrawing from some regions altogether, managers hope to limit damage to activities elsewhere but regret no longer supporting some of the 'extended activities' that fall outside both the worklessness funds and the National Citizen Scheme for youth.

NP managers have considered how voluntary action could sustain some activities but doubt that this is viable in the longer term, especially in the poorest areas; and regarded 2012 as crucial in determining survival. As one manager explained: "Surviving at the moment, we really have to focus on our core business: supporting the unemployed … young and older. But activities may have to be narrower than we've been used to." Surviving, then, may depend on limiting vision and creativity, and restricting activities to service users most likely to succeed, reflecting conclusions discussed in Chapter Five about the negative effects for the most disadvantaged of funding focused on performance outcomes, when resources are scarce.

NP reflects other examples of VSOs threatened by insolvency and closure following unparalleled growth, where capacity building and enterprising income streams may no longer be sufficient to protect even large VSOs against the risks and harsh delivery conditions. Large VSOs, such as Citizens Advice, Mencap and the Prince's Trust have all entered this territory, including as subcontractors in welfare-to-work schemes. Time will tell how their reserves to underpin this work are sustained. Recent media report that 'some 85 charities working with large private firms ... have dropped out of the Work Programme since it was first launched' (Boffey et al, 2012), citing income and pressures to abandon 'hard cases' as growing concerns.

Much may depend on gaining funds for diverse activities; and NP's specialist focus in one service field – unemployed people – may increase its vulnerability. Conversely, NP's coherence of purpose provides organisational actors at all levels with a strong narrative for their activities, giving strength and meaning to their survival efforts. However, if successful organisations like NP falter, it raises disquiet about the effectiveness of the Work Programme and the future of similar welfare outsourcing planned; and similarly, questions the validity of encouraging VS growth and enterprise. As Adrian, a central office NP manager, rationalised:

> 'We've been through a sharp learning curve in business and financial skills. We've got partners, local bases, reputation, experienced staff, projects we've built up in places, it takes years to establish confidence. I'm not sure how a corporate can go in, even know where to go ... and succeed in this sort of service. It *needs* organisations like us to survive.'

Resisters

The Place, in Rushley, a relatively deprived urban area, is a VSO that resisted the kind of growth that would force it to expand beyond its local base. The Place was established some 30 years ago, providing adult education and advice services; and subsequently, established a project for young people (12- to 16-year-olds) out of school. By 2007, it offered full-time education to some 15 young people and part-time classes to some 150 adults. This case, described further in Chapter Three, has been a part of a longitudinal study that began in the late 1990s examining the effects of changing policies on small VSOs. In what follows, some external changes affecting The Place are explained to contextualise subsequent examples.

Significant cutbacks to Rushley Council's budgets and reduced funding to neighbourhood youth work and VS projects in the 1990s saw the closure of some community centres; and when Rushley withdrew grant funding, the local further education college took on community education work, sponsoring The Place to extend adult basic education. These changes to funding arrangements were accompanied by increasingly demanding management and monitoring, with activities shaped by accreditation schemes and extra documentation and reporting requirements for tutors. The balance of adult education work was shifting gradually from drop-in classes to accredited programmes because of funding dependency on the college.

In parallel with changes in adult and community education, the education for young people out of school was also in transition, with service-level agreements introduced to replace grant funding. The deterioration in relationships with Rushley local government officers reflected a shift from trust-based to coercive communications around funding and reporting arrangements (described in Chapter Four). This partly explains the kinds of choices that The Place made subsequently about compliance (or not). However, relationships with Rushley frontline workers, such as education welfare officers and neighbourhood workers, remained positive.

From 2000 onwards, pressures on the curriculum for young people out of school grew, with requirements to meet national curriculum targets in core subjects and to fulfil specified attendance and attainment targets, with negative impacts on flexible activities. The Place regarded these demands as perverse since they re-imposed in alternative settings, the kinds of requirements that young people had already rejected at school.

Resilience in resistance?

For many students at The Place, existing social, racial and economic disadvantages had been exacerbated by other disturbing events, such as family separation, illness, bullying or violence; and young people's experiences of difference and feeling undervalued at school often grew into opting out altogether. Both youth and adult education work, therefore, were premised on goals of ensuring a second chance because many students had been failed by the system, "pressured to fit in where they don't fit – or excluded elsewhere" (Terry, tutor). Staff stressed the importance of flexibility, as Sonia, the coordinator, explained:"I mean, it just had to feel different, otherwise why bother ... a second chance doesn't mean another bite of the same bloody cherry ... I'm not saying per se, school was crap, maybe they never went, but what could we do that was different?"

Many young people were at the end of a long line of referrals between different schools and agencies, and similarly, adults might be referred or simply arrive one day through word-of-mouth recommendation. Staff described their aims to respond flexibly and not to turn people away as considerable challenges, as pressure on activities and resources grew.

Students emphasised a culture of respect, including recognition of the difficulties they faced, as crucial to their experiences at The Place, especially being allowed greater influence than in previous professional settings. These features symbolise more expansive approaches to pedagogy and institutional rules, and different conceptual boundaries to professional relationships, which, however, staff regarded as jeopardised by changing arrangements.

Neil, The Place's manager after Sonia, stressed the importance of being a small centre, where students felt they belonged and had flexible access to advice, support and varied facilities: "Like the internet, a colour printer, they're learning skills but they also feel good because they make things for themselves ... and a centre has to be small to do that. So we don't want to lose that ... what we do well." Neil considered that sustaining this more flexible approach to education was crucial but was concerned about the "uphill struggle" against pressures to comply with external requirements. He explained:"It moves us away from what counts locally – our knowledge about students, their hardships, and legitimises ... pre-set systems and numbers, fitting students to moulds, not services responding to students."

With adult work increasingly focused on accredited programmes, the pressures to compromise aroused considerable debate about balancing survival needs and external demands, producing internal tensions. The manager and trustees – the boundary spanners negotiating external communications – worked hard to mitigate demands but also carried the awareness of jeopardising survival. Sustaining core purposes and meanings, while managing this tension between resistance and accommodation of external requirements, was integral to The Place's survival through a decade of barely workable changes.

Local difficulties were also compounded by national policies, echoing Ball's (1997) research on the contradictory experience of policy implementation. Neil described working with volunteers, illustrating how policy frameworks create perverse and frustrating outcomes:

'Even now [2003], when the government's promoting partnerships with the voluntary sector, they haven't a clue.... We rely on volunteers and support them with training – then we're told, that's remuneration ... pay a minimum wage. It says ... VSOs are cost effective but imposes regulations that thwart us from doing the good job they say we do.'

Faced with diverse pressures, The Place's staff adopted different responses. Some challenged proposals to expand the number of classes delivered offsite, arguing that it undermined their ability to sustain a flexible and secure ethos at The Place. Conflicts emerged around the extent to which this was simply defensive behaviour – "blind adherence to an untenable past ideal" (Ray, trustee) – or necessary resistance to avoid serious damage to their purposes and activities. As manager, Neil, commented, he often became the mediator between other staff and unwelcome external demands, since the consequences of ignoring these could also be serious: "Like Owen [part-time teacher], he'd blithely ignore the monitoring forms and we'd lose income with a downward spiral for students." However, Neil believed that organisational values had to be even more strongly defined so as to limit what The Place conceded; and he identified his role as preventing unrealistic demands from impacting needlessly on other staff. He highlighted other local VSOs that had found it hard to withstand pressures, referring to Willowfield, another local VSO that had lost its ethos as a secure, supportive centre where people could just drop in.

Ali, a longstanding tutor with young people, like Neil, considered that defining limits was essential and believed that these came from knowing what an organisation did well, "where its heart is". Ali saw this knowledge as partly embedded in the organisation's history, giving it the grounding for a strong community of practice (Wenger, 1999), which enabled staff and trustees to resist external pressures for change: "I'm someone who'll say, we have to stop ... we're stretching ourselves between real people with needs and systems all wanting different things ... but we can't stretch any further or we'll snap.... And I can say that, because I have that history, knowledge of the projects."

Community hero or casualty?

Up to 2007, The Place sustained a balance between resistance and some accommodation of external demands but a series of events subsequently combined to undermine its stability. Uncertainties arising from funding and contracts, involving both the college and Rushley Council, continually threatened to destabilise its work. The Place had rejected the service-level agreement that Rushley had initially proposed for young people's education because of its punitive terms. Subsequently, ad-hoc arrangements were implemented annually, dependent on two staff seconded from Rushley and a small grant, but performance demands grew. The Place had a strong bargaining position as there were insufficient local places to meet needs for disaffected young people but direct discussion with Rushley officers was limited and resource and monitoring decisions were simply imposed. Some seven years after the failed outsourcing negotiations, a simpler service-level contract was introduced. However, The Place was also notified that its buildings would be transferred from a charitable to a commercial property rate, with apparently no compensatory funding increase. This designation was disputed for 12 months and a series of local government changes subsequently left this unresolved.

Ongoing uncertainty destabilised staff, and in 2007, Ali left to retrain in educational psychology. John, another key tutor, still technically a Rushley employee, was transferred to the recently extended pupil referral unit after 14 years at The Place. The Place then directly employed two teachers but could not offer them the permanence or employment conditions that Ali and John had enjoyed since income for salaries depended on uncertain arrangements with Rushley. Thus, the level of risks increased significantly, and new staff – outsiders to the community of practice and without the organisational history to ground their understanding of its purposes – joined The Place.

Later in 2007, Neil also left for a new job and was eventually replaced by Richard who met the trustees' need for someone who could apparently coordinate the organisation and share the managerial discourse of external agencies. However, he failed to gain the confidence of other staff and longstanding volunteers, who questioned his commitment to The Place's underlying mission. Richard ostensibly responded to trustees but staff and students' comments, like Terry's, describe an outsider, "who doesn't understand of what we are or do; he's not a voluntary sector person".

The contracts for adult work also became problematic. College and Rushley budgets for adult and community education were under pressure and payments were reduced. Aware that different providers were receiving differential rates, The Place challenged the reductions and argued for real costs, successfully raising the price. However, the following year, The Place lost most adult contracts to a private company and another VSO, willing to work for less. Despite campaigns involving several VSOs about the poor quality of the private company's provision and underpayment of staff, the contracts eventually proceeded. Tutors from The Place were forced to leave, as much of the adult work closed. Whether this decision reflected price only or Rushley's desire to sever relationships with The Place because of perceived difficulties in attitudes was hard to establish. After limited success in raising alternative funds, The Place decided to relinquish its young people's work, which was unsustainable without parallel adult work because of inadequate overall funds and the contribution that adult students made to the centre's ethos.

By the time The Place officially closed its services, several staff and trustees with a strong sense of The Place's original purposes had left. However, students and 'friends' of The Place celebrated its role as 'community hero' and established a campaign stretching over nine months. Despite small donations, without sustained funding for staff or for maintaining the centre, neither the youth nor adult projects could offer more than sporadic advice sessions. As Anna, a trustee, regretfully explained:

> 'Looking back, we should have depended less on public funding. We had a mission and fought off the worst compromises. That was right ... but did it make us a less comfortable provider? Would that adult contract have gone anyway? I don't know. But we began to lose our way – once you do that, it's hard to recover. To get funding elsewhere you need a success story.'

A reputation for resistance and overreliance on diminishing public funds may have accelerated The Place's demise in later years, but earlier, a strong internal coherence and stability had sustained The Place in delivering services within an autonomous framework of values for a longer period than many other VSOs studied.

Eventually, in 2010, The Place surrendered the education centre to Rushley for sale or rental and joined the ranks of community casualties. At the outset of the study, The Place was one of three full-time VS alternatives to schooling in the area. By 2011, only one VSO remained. The Place was also an experienced adult education provider with an excellent local reputation for drop-in advice. Although several community centres and one private provider continue to offer classes in basic education and English for Speakers of Other Languages (ESOL), most provision lacks the breadth previously offered by The Place.

The Place's earlier resilience in maintaining its values and practices alongside changes is characterised by resistance with elements of accommodation; and the organisation's attempts at sense making (Weick, 1995) signified important areas of organisational autonomy. However, from an organisation with a strong identity and a cohesive community of practice, in a few years, The Place was weakened by external and internal changes, opening up considerable ambiguity in identity and, consequently, its means to survive. However, compliance with dominant orthodoxy around growth and diversification seems unlikely to have ensured The Place's survival. If small VSOs shift their accountability away from key stakeholders, focusing on upward rather than downward accountability, organisational mission often becomes confused. Tensions and uncertainties of any kind, however, amplify tendencies to defensive organisational behaviours, making it easier for external practices to shape patterns of activity. For The Place, as internal strengths and values fragmented, and friction between old and new perspectives grew, coherent resistance based on clearly defined strategies declined, and with them, the energy for survival.

Among other VSOs studied, there were examples of resisters surviving, including Concord, providing mediation services for young people and families in Wharton. A different local government environment, generating fewer tensions, allowed Concord to gain strength from its local networks but with mounting service demands and declining funding, in 2011, Concord reported increasingly difficult conditions for survival.

Accommodators

Horizons is also a small VSO in Rushley, with some 30 years' history of working with young people in the youth justice system. It offers full-time education, practical workshops and recreational facilities to some 18 students. This case is part of a longitudinal study in Rushley that began in the late 1990s, described in Chapter Three. Horizons caters for some of the most disaffected young people in the area, as an education welfare officer commented, "taking young people rejected elsewhere, helping them avoid custodial sentences ... often turning them around".

Horizons also experienced a similar deterioration in relationships with Rushley local government officers in the late 1990s, leading to a breakdown of discussions around service contracts. Previously, it had experienced relative autonomy. Following this communication breakdown, a period of high turnover among Rushley officers resulted in a lessening of direct pressure on Horizons. However, funding and monitoring changes began to be superimposed without discussion and

Horizons had particular difficulty in meeting curriculum requirements since it focused as much on informal education and practical skills as classroom learning. With the establishment of youth offending teams (YOTs), Horizons decided to review the direction of its work, and to limit it primarily to young people referred through the Rushley YOT. Trustees believed that this would allow more flexibility and a stronger youth work emphasis, playing to their strengths.

From its establishment, Horizons had focused on young people who had committed, or were at risk of committing, offences but staff felt that their remit had gradually broadened under external pressure to provide for a wider range of young people. Re-focusing on its specialist mission appeared a logical step, and a strong organisational narrative from its past helped to anchor its values and activities in an uncertain present. The choice to retain this focus and not to diversify again runs counter to encouragement from recent governments to expand services and could be read as undermining normative resilience strategies.

Despite previous negative relationships with Rushley officers, Horizons identified working with the YOT as a new start in communications, reporting generally better experiences, perhaps because of its specialist expertise in work with young offenders. Improved relationships appeared to reflect a higher degree of convergence between funders' requirements and Horizons' aspirations, and staff were not faced with a 'one-size-fits-all' contract, as Debbie, the coordinator, described experiences in some other local VSOs. This mirrors other cases, such as SHA, a youth project in Marsham, providing advice on sexual health, where key workers felt that commissioners were familiar with their service. Reducing distance between purchaser and provider in these cases resulted in a beneficial bridging of knowledge and information between contract specifications and locally experienced service challenges, enabling local modification of performance targets.

Maintaining a coherent mission?

Horizons' emphasis on informal learning, coupled with a youth work tradition, involved more egalitarian relationships between staff and young people and more flexible and interdisciplinary approaches than were often present elsewhere. The growing emphasis on meeting national curriculum and attainment targets had previously threatened to undermine the balance of cooperation in relationships with young people – a significant factor in Horizons' approach. In contrast to more conventional schooling, staff placed greater emphasis on including students' prior experiences and knowledge than on transmitting predescribed knowledge, as Trevor, a youth worker, explained, highlighting group sessions where behaviour management, activity choices and project rules were discussed openly:

> 'They [students] shape what happens. Essentially they bring an experience of their only power is negative, rejecting things. So we're trying to rebalance that, offer space for something constructive. If we lose that time to standard classes, what does that say about respecting their views, how we value them? It's no all over again and we're destroying their trust in us.'

Like The Place, Horizons emphasised the importance of a small centre that could offer a safe and flexible ethos, an environment that would foster social as well as educational development. When the YOT in a neighbouring area proposed that Horizons took on a contract for services, it decided against expansion. Debbie, the coordinator, explained the compromise it had suggested instead:

> 'There's such strong pressure towards big is best, and Riverdon YOT wants us to sign up with them too. But that's a whole new negotiation and there's always hidden catches. So what we've said is we'll take a few young people if we have space as we are ... but we won't have a whole new contract with all the effort and different demands that might involve.'

Other staff joining this discussion acknowledged concerns about dependency on one public agency. However, they agreed that it gave them more opportunity to determine approaches, instead of "being caught between different sets of externally defined conditions", as Cora, the management committee chair, explained. Horizons' staff recognised that involving a wider range of gatekeepers had the potential for greater compromise and, as Trevor emphasised, pleasing them was sometimes "quite ad hoc ... because officers interpret what's set out". These discussions illustrated an overall coherence of views, and while individual staff and trustees had left and been replaced over time, bringing in different ideas, the adoption of new approaches was gradual, allowing the ongoing strength of the community of practice (Wenger, 1999) to be retained.

Cora also described Horizons' involvement in a crime prevention project in neighbourhoods identified as foci for antisocial behaviour.

She attended meetings with Rushley YOT in an advisory capacity to discuss potential activities, and Horizons participated in pilot work, subsequently being invited to bid for some of the work. However, the formal contract specification had been reframed significantly to address performance indicators required for the Home Office, introducing what Horizons' staff regarded as unrealistic timescales for succeeding in diverting antisocial behaviours. The work targeted two housing estates but there were seemingly arbitrary requirements, such as restricting outreach work to young people from specified postcodes. The funding depended on successful outcomes, defined as young people enrolling in local education, training or sports coaching schemes. However, as Debbie reasoned, "within a six-week project, places might not be available, and it's much better if they make their own decisions on how best to stay out of trouble, not being marshalled into schemes they may not want".

Unrealistic performance targets and payments weighted towards outcomes would have considerably increased Horizons' risks. Its experience suggested that a high level of success within the limited timeframe proposed would be problematic, especially with narrowly defined success criteria. Consequently, the trustees withdrew from all but the pilot project.

After an improved period of working with the YOT, this scheme evoked previous experiences of prescriptive specifications and unrealistic targets. Trustees and staff had already spent considerable time on planning outreach activities for the pilot. The additional efforts demanded for tendering, business planning and establishing new monitoring systems therefore caused considerable concern, even before confronting the challenges of delivery. As Cora explained:

> 'We got involved because it's prevention work with the kind of young people we recognise, it's what we do, only offsite. But what they [YOT] wanted, the criteria ... even for the formal bidding stage, it's not worth it, not good use of our time. They invited us to pilot some ideas, activities, because they recognised our expertise, which helped them access Home Office money. But now ... it's a big risk ... so no. They're puzzled why we're not going forward; but chasing money at any cost isn't right.'

Debbie added her interpretation: "There's a kind of 'we want you involved, we value your work, so can't you change a bit to meet the spec here?' But it's not just a bit, is it? That's the point."

While Horizons' staff and trustees emphasised the need to negotiate and to meet external arrangements part way, these compromises demanded a significant diversion from their core activities. There was a willingness to take reasonable risks to sustain income but this case also shows understanding of demands that might be destabilising. Nevertheless, Horizons' specialist focus and the lack of alternative providers maintained its value for contractors and also its bargaining power.

Just surviving or thriving?

Many small VSOs working with young people have been encouraged, until recently, to expand their activities, with both positive and negative consequences. Horizons' survival to date appears to have relied on clarity of mission and meaning making in the organisation, underpinning a strong community of practice, characterised by alternative approaches to working with young people and pragmatic management. Where trustees and staff identified threats to approaches that they regarded as integral to their success, they set limits on compromise and drew on their strengths to resist. Continuity among trustees and staff reinforced a coherent organisational narrative, also supporting necessary adaptive practices. Peripheral insiders (Wenger, 1999), those joining the organisation with new ideas, could gradually become integrated, generating changes in practices, without destabilising the organisational community because of its integral strength. Similarly, Horizons was more able to deflect coercive pressure at external organisational boundaries, while gradually accommodating agreed changes.

Horizons' approaches and history were, however, embedded in alternative models of practice, which, although successful, effectively challenged new orders of contractual arrangements. At times, this allowed Horizons to negotiate compromises from a position of strength; at others, it presented resistance, which was poorly understood by external agencies. Horizons' resilience is visible from ways that it balanced this alternative narrative with external transactions, weighing up the limits of compliance. It seems probable that organisational growth and diversification in services, rather than providing protection in recession, could have produced unhelpful changes for a small VSO, like Horizons. Horizons' size, specialism and its alternative approaches were fundamental to its successes in changing young people's future paths and therefore to its organisational reputation and survival.

Resource reductions and an increasingly hostile environment for small VSOs prompt questions about whether Horizons can survive into the future. Its approach of combining accommodation with resistance is potentially challenging to mainstream arrangements and therefore carries its own risks. Much may depend on the continued value of its specialist provision to purchasers. If Horizons had acceded to pressures to undertake the proposed additional contracts between 2009 and 2011, the consequent growth and additional staff would have had little guarantee of continuity. With political changes and widespread reductions in youth project funding through 2011 and 2012, much similar work has been discontinued, with ensuing destabilisation. Survival at the expense of collective goals and values produces short-term 'fixes' to organisational problems, whereas Horizons' survival owes much to its relative stability and specialist purpose, enabling adaption from a secure foundation. Its resilience is embedded, not in the kinds of growth and diversification strategies recommended for surviving hard times, but in its cohesive identity as a small community-based VSO. This strength has given it the ability to withstand not only coercive but also mimetic isomorphism (DiMaggio and Powell, 1983) and retain its distinctiveness and autonomy. How successfully it weathers recent threats may be in question but some form of survival seems likely.

Risk, resilience and community survivors

As dependency on state funding has grown, the flexibility of VSOs for providing alternative service models and creative approaches has been increasingly constrained by survival needs, potentially limiting organisational spaces for challenging dominant arrangements and producing instabilities as such funds decline. Engaging in enterprise and trading, merger, expansion and diversification of services – the mimetic isomorphism discussed in earlier chapters – have often been assumed as ways to address threats and construct protective strategies in hard times. However, as VSOs have grappled with capacity to meet changing requirements, insufficient attention has been paid to damage caused to the value of activities and the importance of VS roles in providing niche rather than generalist services. The VS has often been theorised as compensating for state and market failures, fillings gaps to provide responsive and specialised services that would otherwise be uneconomic. Adopting every opportunity for growth, then, is illogical as a survival strategy for small VSOs.

The cases above illustrate the contradictory outcomes of pressures to change in destabilising organisational missions and directions. Establishing the limits of compliance and resistance generates tensions but has also proved a strength where organisational actors had a cohesive sense of purposes. However, staff and trustees operating as VSO boundary spanners have also experienced growing pressure to mitigate the effects of external changes. Clarity of goals and organisational sense making (Weick, 1995), more than other features identified earlier as encompassing resilient behaviour, were significant for adapting and surviving.

The cases three have been identified as types that emerged from a wider range of VSOs studied, and highlight different approaches adopted for dealing with a rapidly changing environment. However, the typology emphasises pitfalls in different strategies, rather than correlating types with the probability of becoming a survivor or casualty. Clearly, distinctions between types are not clear cut, and the types identified could be subdivided, highlighting for example social enterprises that sustain their social values (or not) and resisters who adapt to some degree (or not). However, all three cases emphasised the importance of a coherent identity for sustaining efforts towards development and survival and offered insights into ways that organisational purposes and activities are destabilised or strengthened by different external and internal conditions. Organisations may draw strength from successfully recovering from challenging circumstances, a process of 'steeling' (Small and Memmo, 2004, p 6), as was visible at Horizons, after it broke away from unrealistic education targets. This may also apply to NP if it manages to weather recent hardships following the failed bids for the Work Programme.

Even before recent funding crises, contractual requirements often divested VSOs of their accustomed levels of autonomy in defining purposes and activities. However, the stage-set into which VSOs are now cast is heavily circumscribed, and carries higher levels of risk, not only limiting the extent to which VSOs can offer the advantages of an informal and flexible environment but also increasingly affecting their survival. As NP shows, growth and partnerships have proved risky in a world of severely rationed state resources, where government and corporate contractors are devolving operational costs and risks to VSO subcontractors, highlighting contradictions at the heart of policies purporting to support VSOs.

Enterprising VSOs, such as NP, have successfully embraced entrepreneurial activity to extend services at local levels, and their survival in a more favourable economic environment appears more secure than small VSOs wedded to grassroots activities. However, among recent instabilities, winners and losers are less certain, and VSOs are being displaced as preferred providers for work with disadvantaged groups. Analysis of these cases therefore challenges normative understandings about the adaptive behaviours that will protect VSOs in hard times. Compliance with recommended trends – capacity building, growth, entrepreneurialism and collaborative bids – have been integral strategies for NP but have failed to secure survival. Its clarity of purpose, autonomous goals and resistance to diversifying services may be more significant in surviving current threats. However, its growth strategy now means that it faces tougher decisions around retrenchment. Organisational actors may willingly or unwittingly be drawn into compromise through isomorphic processes but still become losers, not least because dominant players persistently change the rules of play to the detriment of less powerful actors.

As outsourcing has spread and contract size increased, the financial and reputational risks of failure have increasingly transferred to providers, even in innovative projects, where outcomes are unpredictable. Up until recently, government agencies carried risks for quality of provision, albeit tightly controlled. However, the failure of large corporations to carry these risks as prime contractors, and their transfer to much smaller VSO subcontractors, raises ethical concerns and also doubts about the survival of even large VSOs.

The small VSO cases – The Place and Horizons – tell a different story. To varying degrees both cases here aimed to sustain grassroots' identities rather than espousing external cultures. The work that these VSOs delivered for society involved containing the threat that some young people posed through non-conformity. That these VSOs sought to retain autonomy by resisting certain changes may be unsurprising, then, since both achieved effective work through approaches based on sharing some professional power. Such projects, then, always tread a fine line between public acknowledgement of their effectiveness and the threat presented through models potentially challenging to mainstream approaches. It is perhaps less paradoxical, therefore, that powerful agencies might seek to incorporate these VSOs, despite the jeopardy to their service value.

These cases illustrate how the survival and longevity of VSOs are often embedded in their alternative models and the narratives that underpin them. Maintaining a balance between placating gatekeepers and preserving alternatives, between excessive compromise and resistance, was crucial; and failing to do so, resulted in destabilisation, endangering service reputation and funding loss for The Place. Horizons' capacity for sense making and a clearly defined direction amidst diverse changes signified important areas of autonomy, which it successfully retained.

All organisations and staff necessarily undergo change; and whether this is externally driven or not, organisations need coherence to support decision making and actions. Lack of coherence and recurrent instabilities intensify self-protective organisational behaviours, blocking developmental practices and more constructive outcomes. Without the ability to articulate a strong and unified purpose internally and for others, small VSOs can readily become prey to strong external pressures and succumb to unintended changes, ultimately resulting in casualties, as at The Place. Adaptive capacity, as in the Horizons case, may depend on strength and reasonable stability at the organisation's core, which effectively delimit the destabilising power of changes and coercion towards unwanted compromise.

Policies located with ideas of capacity building and resilience rely heavily on individualistic and competitive agency. However, as the cases illustrate, there is little recognition of external social and structural factors that exacerbate risk and destabilise VSOs; and few attempts to identify how increased burdens and risks might realistically be supported or shared. VSOs that have adopted supposedly resilient behaviours are also under threat and show, paradoxically, that such directions can undermine autonomous values and purposes – features for which VSOs have been sought and applauded. It is precisely these features related to clarity and integrity of mission that seem most likely to help VSOs survive. By contrast, ambiguities and rapidly changing activities often damage organisational coherence and generate significant mission drift, leaving organisational actors struggling to make sense of external hardships alongside the internal goals of their organisation.

Despite the evident power of external influences (of state, market and the economy) on VS changes, the idea of resilience positions individuals and organisations – here VSOs – as key actors that bear responsibility for their successes and failures. However, leaving VSOs to thrive or fail, reliant on their own agency or that of individual staff or volunteers, masks the complex and challenging nature of the social problems that many were established to address; and inappropriately absolves collective social responsibility for their failure. The cases above suggest that amidst these uncertainties and changes, negotiable spaces are also decreasing, provoking questions about the future terms and conditions of survival. The need for greater recognition of the social and economic value of the VS's contribution to welfare is pressing. Otherwise its survival path as a service provider may be relegated to one of corporate servant and the distinct and independent approaches, which governments and communities have valued for over a century, may be lost.

EIGHT

Advocacy and democratic participation in a changing environment: room for challenge?

Introduction: changing approaches to advocacy

Successive United Kingdom (UK) governments have increasingly turned to the voluntary and community sector to not only deliver welfare provision, but also to address concerns about civic and civil participation. Consequently, understanding the role of voluntary sector (VS) advocacy in addressing such concerns has assumed greater importance. The coalition government's Big Society agenda has arguably accelerated this 'community turn' in policy, re-emphasising responsibilities associated with active citizenship and local schemes mobilising voluntary action. However, contradictions and challenges are apparent: resource dependency and increased professionalisation among many voluntary sector organisations (VSOs) have affected the kinds of advocacy tactics adopted (Mosley, 2011) and the maintenance of independent approaches. At a time of significant reductions in public funding, increased competition for resources and a context where policy governance is progressively dominated by neoliberal ideology, the challenges for advocacy are becoming more marked.

Advocacy distinguishes the goals of many VSOs from those of organisations in other sectors, and VSOs play an important role as intermediaries between citizens and the state, representing diverse communities of interest and enabling pluralism of expression (Boris, 2006; Bass, 2007; Smith and Pekkanen, 2012). Understanding VSOs in this way assumes that they are political organisations to some degree, even though their advocacy activities may be limited by capacity, law or concern about alienating relationships with funders. However, as VS survival becomes harder, questions arise about sustaining VS advocacy and social change roles, which have traditionally constituted an important contribution to civil society and democracy in liberal democratic countries worldwide (Phillips, 2006). Chapter One considered the longstanding roles of VSOs in the UK as both service providers and advocates. While many VSOs combine these roles, others have focused primarily on campaigning. This chapter considers changing roles and activities in VS advocacy, together with inherent contradictions and challenges as dominant government and governance cultures shift. Concepts including resource dependency theory (Pfeffer, 2003) and new institutionalism (DiMaggio and Powell, 1991) (discussed in previous chapters) underpin debates through which these changes are examined, prompting questions about the extent to which changes are infringing VS independence.

Research suggests that the predominantly neoliberal political and economic environments in Western democracies are marginalising the legitimate participation of VSOs (and others in civil society) in influencing policy (Onyx et al, 2010). More challenging campaigns and forms of advocacy are constrained, with negative consequences for an active and healthy democratic society. Conversely, governments have also been concerned with a decline in civic and civil participation and, for example, recent UK administrations have promoted initiatives intended to enhance community engagement and active citizenship, with a sizeable government investment, up to 2010, although with an emphasis on responsibilities. Mosley (2011, p 452), discussing service providers in the United States (US), argues that growing opportunities for participation have extended VS advocacy and influence on policy but she illustrates a parallel shift in emphasis to 'insider tactics', more institutionalised and elite forms of advocacy. As market-oriented neoliberalism is increasingly privileged in UK policy discourse, questions therefore arise about expectations of contemporary democracy and the part that VS advocacy can play within this; the reasons for VSOs adopting certain approaches; and the extent to which policy and funding environments are instrumental in shaping these (Donaldson, 2007). These questions have prompted discussion in US and Australian work but, with a few exceptions, little in recent UK research (Cairns et al, 2010a).

If the first challenge for VS advocacy is the shift in dominant political ideology, a second challenge is that funding streams have focused increasingly on service delivery linked to specified outcomes, highlighting the largely unfunded nature of advocacy work (Cairns et al, 2010a). For over a decade, growth in the UK VS has overwhelmingly been directed towards service provision, with little regard to funding lost from other parallel activities, despite concerns about declining civic participation. Conflicts of interest arise therefore for many VSO service providers in challenging the policies and priorities of funders (often the state) since such criticism risks damaging future funding relationships. However, not doing so undermines the potential to influence local services and decisions, limiting the diversity of publicly accessible information that may help to shape services. Such dilemmas are inevitably exacerbated as overall funding declines, suggesting that any changing emphasis in VS advocacy methods may be linked to resource concerns, coupled with increased involvement in cross-sector projects, which tend to encourage assimilation of different ways of doing things.

There have also been critical challenges to VS advocacy practice, questioning the extent to which VSOs represent different constituencies (Phillips, 2006) or discourage active participation through increased professionalisation (Skocpol, 2003). However, what may be regarded as partial in terms of representation, reflects a theoretical rationale for the formation of VSOs (Weisbrod, 1987) in providing an advocacy path for minority groups and unpopular causes where governments otherwise fail to hear or satisfy such demands. VS choices in undertaking different actions and dialogues may be crucial in enabling a hearing for some marginalised groups in society. Yet the processes of decontestation, which Alcock and Kendall (2011) argue have been promoted by recent UK governments, generating cultures of policy consensus around the VS, suggest more limited space for dissent and difference or to advance minority interests. Whose voices are represented may reflect differential power and the ability to share a common discourse with power-holders rather than VSOs' goals. This chapter thus highlights further challenges for advocacy work related to minority interests and their future within a healthy democratic society, which rhetorically at least, values active and diverse participation in democratic debates.

The chapter turns first to the changing emphases of advocacy activities within UK VSOs, within the frame of concerns identified above. It considers different purposes and approaches to advocacy, identifying advocacy conducted at various levels:

- on behalf of specific individuals and groups to access rights and services;
- activities involving influence to bring about wider changes;
- and activities designed to empower groups to promote their own programmes.

As in previous chapters, it draws on a series of examples from the studies described in Chapter Three, to illustrate approaches and recent challenges in VS advocacy. Examples focus mainly on small VSOs combining service and advocacy work but data from larger VSOs have been included since, as other research suggests (Berry and Arons, 2003; Smith and Pekkanen, 2012), size often affects the potential to undertake influential advocacy. The chapter subsequently examines barriers to effective advocacy and constraints on independent action, exploring the space available for pursuing and sustaining goals of social change.

Attempts to influence policy and strategy, as in many cases illustrated below, often occur at the local level but may also concern wider consultations. International literature identifies a similar breadth of VS influence at local, regional and national government levels (Onyx et al, 2010; Mosley, 2011). While policy advocacy appears to be a common activity among VSO service providers, empirical research on reasons for different advocacy approaches is limited, contrasted with widespread studies on political activism and social movements (Lofland, 1996; McAdam et al, 2005; Jenkins, 2006). However, distinctions between service and campaign organisations are also blurred, and Mosley (2011) argues that even campaign groups have become more institutionalised in approach.

Despite the priorities of recent UK governments to promote wider citizen engagement in shaping local services and decisions, it appears that advocacy strategies are increasingly becoming 'insider' activities, adapting to the dominant rules of play (Clegg, 1989). This trend inevitably marginalises smaller groups with limited resources and those campaigning for change in other ways. Does this signal a co-option of VS advocates and an associated loss of independent views? These questions are considered through examples and discussed in the final part of the chapter.

Advocacy, citizenship and democratic participation

Understanding the role of advocacy and VS influence in wider political and policy debates overlaps with discussion of citizen engagement and the need for an active and participant civil society to ensure a healthy democracy. In the UK and internationally, community participation strategies have been closely allied with discourses on citizenship, democratic participation and social inclusion (Newman and Clarke, 2009). Policies, including *Governance of Britain* (Cabinet Office, 2007), *Strengthening local democracy* (DCLG, 2009) and the Big Society agenda, all emphasise strategies to increase active citizenship, drawing on the expertise of community-based VSOs. Integral to these civil renewal strategies are schemes specifically focused on the engagement of young people. However, as Lister (2010) highlights, the emphasis is increasingly towards an understanding of citizenship associated with responsibilities and not rights or addressing injustices. The question raised by such initiatives is the extent to which the social change aspirations of many VSOs have been harnessed into more institutionalised and non-adversarial forms of advocacy and participation (Cummings, 2008), fulfilling government concerns to engage potentially disorderly citizens in times of high unemployment. However, few policies, whatever their intentions, are implemented unswervingly; and understanding the extent to which these contexts have also offered valuable openings for VSOs and their constituencies to influence and change local issues and governance is equally important. As Barnes and Prior (2009, p 1) identify, citizens may, purposefully or not, 'act in ways that modify, disrupt or negate the intended processes and outcomes of public policy' despite recent expectations that together with professional workers, they have responsibilities to implement governmentally defined policies.

Active citizenship is therefore visible as a more complex and ambiguous process than is often conceived in policy, and three levels of citizen activity are differentiated below in order to help explore concepts of 'advocacy' and 'participative democracy' in the empirical examples that follow. First, advocacy can be conceptualised simply as accessing rights to services and facilities, on behalf of either an individual or groups but this is a somewhat limited, individualistic model aimed to secure inclusion in existing institutions and may have little effect on ensuring adequate or appropriate services.

A second model for understanding advocacy relates to political participation and civic engagement, addressing concerns about the wider democratic deficit. This concentrates on participation in existing systems of decision making but stops short of systemic changes. Arguably, it also meets the demands of governments and mainstream institutions, securing apparent consensus in existing institutions rather than demonstrating needs for change. The later New Labour years saw a focus on citizens' involvement in shaping more responsive local services. This was intended to improve service outcomes and create more actively engaged service users, especially among disadvantaged groups. As Barnes et al (2010, p 254) recognised, 'by the end of the first decade of the 21st century, [citizen] participation' was embedded in official policy but did not necessarily generate the desired changes.

Community empowerment networks, youth empowerment projects and, more recently, the national network of community organisers illustrate strategies aimed at tackling citizen engagement and democratic renewal, which depend on the involvement of VSOs. Many of these projects can be identified as representative forms of advocacy, with key groups of local people shaping projects on behalf of others, such as in 'youth-led' projects, school and neighbourhood councils and community organisers promoting the voice and participation of others in their areas. Such action is hardly new (Butcher et al, 2007), and community development work has for several decades involved community-based organisations in promoting citizen engagement through advocacy and local projects, often adopting a critical stance to mainstream institutions. As noted earlier, VS advocacy may fulfil some aspects of policy *and* conflict with others.

Engaging a wider range of citizens in local decision-making processes reflects a third model of advocacy linked with community participation as a form of communitarian action (Etzioni, 1995), promoting a sense of community belonging and improved community cohesion through collective endeavour often directed towards social change. In this model, VSO advocacy both enables a collective voice through which local groups can campaign and organise local changes, and helps to build self-advocacy, sharing collective skills and expertise. Where this action is policy led, the extent to which it entails developmental learning and social participation with wider impact on changes to existing institutions, or facilitates hegemonic inclusion, is, however, debatable. If community-based advocacy projects can extend beyond the purposes initially prescribed, they may evolve as sites of constructive political activity, involving a more radical collective habitus (Bourdieu, 1992).

While there is broad acknowledgement of the value of citizen participation, there are also conflicting understandings of the interests and purposes served by different models. Active citizens are also constructed as assertive consumers, advocating choices, and consumerist strategies, integral to neoliberal policies, are embedded in outsourcing public services, in turn, intended to limit the power of public professionals and the state, increasing that of the market. Essentially, in this market-dominated setting, consumers assert individual rights by choice of service. However, since services are rationed by funding, this is not an open market, and arguments that highlight reliance on consumer choice to improve services are flawed. Moreover, some 'consumers' (such as unemployed people) have little power or influence and have to endure inadequate services through financial dependency, raising concerns about the diminishing spaces for the voices of vulnerable groups in society.

VSOs, especially service organisations, also have conflicting interests in relation to advocacy. Those that have benefited from growth may have strong vested interests in protecting their resources, which depend on maintaining good relationships with local government and funders. Service needs and the funding required to sustain provision determine priorities, so that advocating for maintenance or expansion of service activities may be privileged over other wider issues (Marwell, 2007). Closer interdependency with governments and the growth of cross-sector collaboration, coupled with resource dependency, have encouraged greater VSO conformity with institutional norms and growing use of insider approaches to advocacy, illustrating forms of isomorphic institutionalisation. Underlying the motivation to institutionalise, resource dependency theory (Pfeffer, 2003) suggests that organisations seek to maximise their advantages in competing for funding by investing in professionalism, shared networks and arrangements (insider tactics). Adversarial advocacy is necessarily discarded as are projects that devolve power; institutionalisation and insider identity become norms, and the range of concerns represented narrows.

VSOs that have engaged in these ways or yielded to isomorphic pressures may have more numerous advocacy opportunities but also an increased risk of co-option by either government or private funding agencies, and less likelihood of promoting power-sharing models. However, if we understand all forms of advocacy as essentially political activity, it is important to explore the underlying purposes for advocacy – the why as well as the how – to better understand the extent to which recent challenges have restricted the nature and autonomy of VSO advocacy work.

Understanding different approaches to advocacy

Blurred boundaries in perceptions of advocacy

Earlier chapters focused on the VS's changing role in service delivery. However, alongside this role, VSOs often have a long history of providing advocacy for both individuals and stakeholder groups, whether through campaigning and lobbying activities or through formal representation of a case or cause. An overt emphasis on political lobbying or campaigns is limited for VSOs benefiting from financial concessions under UK charity law, as elsewhere, although there is latitude for varied activities that might be deemed political but not party political. The values attributed to the VS around the public good, social justice and supporting the underrepresented, while ostensibly political, can also be encapsulated within UK charitable purposes. The combining of service and advocacy work and the massive growth in VSO service delivery have tended to obscure recent ways that VSOs have campaigned on behalf of their user groups, but as Cairns et al

(2010a) identify, VS advocacy is a longstanding tradition and intrinsic to the values and identities of many VSOs, from community groups to national and global charities.

In the examples that follow, the changing and often unclear boundaries for VS advocacy and service work are explored, as are distinctions between different types of advocacy. Advocacy may take the form of: direct advisory work at a one-to-one level; representation of a case or cause to outside bodies; or coordination of information and people in a purposeful campaign to gain more resources for services or to change the shape of policy or its implementation (Cairns et al, 2010a).

These models may overlap or one (supporting an individual case) may lead to another (a wider campaign).

Despite the importance of advocacy in VS traditions, VSO staff or volunteers often have no explicit role for advocacy yet regard it as embedded in their jobs. For example, Dan, coordinating a project for young fathers in Wharton, described his advocacy role as both implicit and crucial in exposing local needs for services, with his support for individuals interwoven with making this wider case:

> 'It's part of what we do, for the groups we work with. I mean it wouldn't be much use, would it, if we ran a session for the guys, get them to attend – then we didn't try and improve the situation more widely. It's to help our service users, yes, but it's about making sure Wharton Council knows ... the consequences of what's *not* being funded. So it's not what my job says as such, it's just part of it.'

Historically, the emphasis of VS advocacy was often on supporting the rights of individuals. However, more recently, it has been widely understood as giving a voice to underrepresented groups or campaigning with, or on behalf of, local groups to influence policy and changes, and is often regarded as taking place in professional settings, such as city council or local government meetings (Onyx et al, 2010). Some organisations, both longstanding and more recent, including various, largely web-based movements, can be identified primarily as campaigning groups but, conversely, there are many large VSOs that predominantly deliver services. However, many locally based VSOs combine advocacy and service functions, taking up the cases of both individuals and groups. The boundaries between these roles are ambiguous and often interlinked, as Sonia, the coordinator from The Place, a small VSO in Rushley, identified:

'Someone may drop in, ask for help with a problem, benefits, housing, they're not being listened to, and it may be just that – a phone call, help with a form. But often, they're there because they want something more as well, maybe classes, only they might not be confident to sign up....Then again, we might get more cases linked to that same benefits office and realise something's wrong there – so then there's a wider issue and we'd try and locate a manager; and it'll benefit people we don't even know yet locally.'

Other small VSOs described similar ways in which they had helped individuals and groups that they regarded as having limited voice to promote their own concerns or challenge injustices, and this often started with individual advice, helping individuals to access information or rights to services and resources. Alongside advice and support, insider tactics were also deployed to raise the profile of problems and to highlight poor practice but these could involve confronting the status quo. Cora, a trustee at Horizons, a small Rushley VSO, went on to discuss its advocacy for young people following the public disorder in English cities in the summer of 2011:

'We had students recognised on VCR [video cassette recording] – they don't live far – and because they're in the [justice] system and could be recognised, they were assumed guilty for being there. It shows how young people get branded. So we met with the YOT [youth offending team] manager and local police reps and put a different viewpoint – because the focus was criminal gangs – and most of our young people are not in gangs.'

At times, supporting vulnerable groups demanded challenging mainstream assumptions, entering potentially contentious terrain. Nevertheless, staff and trustees also relied on insider tactics, seeking to influence accessible official representatives; and their prior reputation in successful service work with young offenders was critical to being heard. At other times, advocacy reflected what VSO staff and volunteers regarded as 'facilitating communications, a route in for those without access', as Steve, from Crossroads, a small youth education provider, explained. VSOs could be conduits for information between agencies and in this sense, VSO advocates often acted as boundary spanners, affording less advantaged individuals or groups access to goods, services or influence previously out of their reach.

Size also seemed to be a factor in the advocacy approaches employed, not least because of the direct demands on workers' time, as Jan, coordinating a Wharton after-school project, observed, highlighting limitations for small VSOs in policy advocacy:"Whether it's networking to influence policy or campaigning to resource more projects, we don't have the same time a bigger organisation would to get our heads round all the information, so it's hard to be as effective in that way."

For the majority of small VSOs, attempts to influence policy and strategy were mainly at local levels but a few organisations in each of the study areas were branches of large national charities, often involved in wider networks. In Wharton, there was a contrast between large national charities represented on the local strategic partnership body and small community-based groups who felt they were outsiders to the discussion and decisions that took place. Large VSOs were more likely to be involved in cross-sector collaboration and to use insider advocacy methods, rather than more challenging tactics. Although advocacy and influence were used to advance the interests of their services and service users, their insider legitimacy gave these VSOs strategic advantages over smaller organisations.

Kidscare, based in Wharton, was a large national VSO, involved in a capacity-building scheme with the local government Children and Young People's Service, intended to support small VSOs in the area working with different minority ethnic groups. This collaborative work, discussed in Chapter Six, entailed training and development work to help groups access different funding resources and to respond to monitoring and regulatory requirements but the small VSOs had mixed views about the scheme's value set against the extra demands on their already overburdened time. However, Alison, from the national Kidscare office, regarded this work as an important form of advocacy since Kidscare workers had good local knowledge and could provide more focused advice to these small VSOs than local government workers, whose advice could be mistrusted. She also viewed the organisation's regional and national committee involvement as reinforcing local work, ensuring that "issues of concern to the minority groups are represented in ways that can influence consultations at different levels". She acknowledged that having a head office located in Wharton was helpful in legitimising its influence at local as well as wider levels. However, Zohra, working with Somalian families, remained unconvinced and expressed worries that minority "views get dilute because Kidscare and local government people, they all familiar, spend much time in meetings together, so they not going to make enemies are they?" Effective advocacy requires trust-building in its purposes and activities, since insider legitimacy may well create mistrust and concerns about what is really being advocated.

Insider or outsider tactics?

Many of the advocacy activities above can be identified as employing forms of insider tactics to influence more powerful institutions accessible to VSO workers. Most activities, however, could not be regarded as co-opted, in the sense of being disconnected with stakeholders' experiences or demands. Often being able to access and potentially influence these institutions relied on legitimacy achieved through a successful track record of service delivery, especially among challenging or hard-to-reach user groups. Such legitimacy was secured through demonstrating a good local knowledge of service needs and by fostering alliances with other local groups and across sectors. However, reputation and future funding were interwoven: larger organisations were more likely to be involved in a range of influential networks, where reluctance to threaten their insider status discouraged them from engaging in the direct campaigns or more adversarial activities that were more typical activities among smaller VSOs.

A Sure Start project in a Wharton neighbourhood with high unemployment identified its advocacy work as mainly at grassroots level, encouraging parents not only to participate in playgroups, but also to train and potentially run future groups. Parents' initial involvement was often about accessing individual advice and information but, as in examples above, this extended to education and wider social participation. When the project funding was threatened, workers initially used insider tactics to lobby support for continued resources but subsequently engaged parents and friends in a campaign, including letter writing, petitions, a protest group and placards at local government meetings.

The Place, in Rushley, had a long history of engaging in direct campaigns, and as the previous chapter suggested, trustees believed that their more adversarial stance may have ultimately affected their loss of funding for adult education courses. The Place had access to good legal advice through its trustees and challenged decisions taken by local government officers over education facilities for young people with disabilities, pursuing the cases via the ombudsman, gaining media support and ultimately a favourable court ruling. The Place had also campaigned jointly with other local VSOs, successfully challenging funding criteria for the introduction of service contracts and inviting local councillors and Members of Parliament to visit its activities.

However, subsequently The Place's trustees and student members were less successful in campaigns around funding decisions, which eventually led to closure. Arguably, much depended on the resources that The Place was able to marshal, and while the earlier disability cases drew interest in a wide campaign and sustained interest in its work, much had changed both internally and externally by the time the 2010 campaign for funds was launched. Internally, there was a degree of trustee and worker fatigue, changes in personnel and a resulting loss of coherence in the organisation's purpose. The cultures of expectation surrounding advocacy had also shifted with the mainstreaming of VSOs in service delivery, and most VS service providers being more likely to adopt insider tactics. As other studies indicate (Marwell, 2007; Mosley, 2011), even some social movements and campaign groups are relinquishing reliance on direct action or combining this with insider tactics to increase their likelihood of being taken seriously. There is a fine balance then between cultivating and maintaining an independent voice and adopting strategies that might produce effective outcomes in the contemporary climate.

Transformative activity?

As discussed above, there are distinctions between helping people to access rights and services; seeking influence on behalf of marginal or underrepresented groups; and developing environments where people can establish their own means of advocacy or participation. As examples of the last of these, youth projects resulting from policy and funding initiatives between 2004 and 2010 were intended to empower young people in designing facilities and services and to develop participation in democratic decision making. A key aim was to attract hard-to-reach groups of young people (DCSF, 2008). Local youth participation workers were appointed as advocates to support young people in developing youth-led projects, and young people involved also became advocates and advisers to others (Milbourne, 2012). This form of advocacy work, not only limited to youth projects, was intended to facilitate civic engagement and 'empowerment through community participation' (Taylor, 2011a, p 158); and before the change of government in 2010, had become a key element of government responses to underrepresentation and exclusion. In some cases, projects encompassed broader aims for civil renewal: promoting improved community action and cohesion through participation in collective endeavour. While localism and Big Society agendas have now incorporated this policy ground, via schemes including the youth National Citizen Scheme and community organisers, nudging behaviours and emphasis on the responsibilisation of citizens are more marked within these programmes.

Some evidence on the New Labour youth participation projects has been encouraging, suggesting progress in improving young people's engagement in voluntary, political and service activities. In the Marsham study of youth services (described in Chapter Three), which focused especially on youth-led projects, the youth council had adopted a particularly inclusive approach to its own organisation, rejecting a formally elected structure. Instead, it encouraged as many young people as wished, to become involved, the proviso being a willingness to commit regularly to task groups. Youth council members were supported by a youth participation worker and used community centre facilities for meeting. Among its developments, the youth council provided peer training, mentoring and advice for other young people's groups, undertook research on local needs and decided funding criteria for youth-led projects. A key strategy was to involve young people from 'hard-to-reach' groups.

One of the youth-led projects that has received funds through the youth council is MediaBus, supported by a consortium of four VSOs. Launched in 2009, the bus is equipped with a music studio, information technology suite, coffee bar and spaces for advice and training. In 2010, there were four workers, 20 young volunteers and trainee counsellors, illustrating a highly successful example of advocacy and support for a youth-led project, which is also perpetuating the engagement of further young people. Akeisha, a member of the youth-led steering group for MediaBus, outlined the process of project planning and developing funding bids and the importance of the support received from the workers in the 'parent' VSOs. She explained: "First out, we didn't know how hard it'd be, there's a lot of persuading, and we needed help how to present things ... when mostly people don't listen to young people." This support in building self-advocacy skills was crucial in overcoming barriers and maintaining young people's involvement, especially when many of them lacked self-esteem and had erratic social and educational histories.

Mutual trust and respect also emerged as significant in young people's willingness to participate in such projects: young people trusting adults; and adult power-holders trusting young people and promoting or advocating wider trust in young people's abilities. Lister (2007) reaches similar conclusions concerning the inclusion of marginalised adults in policy making, identifying mistrust of powerful adults among the reasons for doubting the advocacy processes that promise institutional inclusion. As Kwame, involved in the MediaBus project, explained: "It's been hard to trust it's not just a con, make sure we're busy so we can't cause trouble." As in other contexts where power and trust interlock (see Chapter Five), trust may be fragile or need to be earned through joint endeavour. Despite the policy focus on using local experience to develop services, young people often felt that their knowledge was given little legitimacy, undermining their trust in the process and responsibilities of participation.

Research carried out by young people on a large, predominantly Asian housing estate in Marsham gained 150 survey responses and found that existing youth facilities were limited and unattractive to many young people. The findings were submitted to local government officers but the young people reported that no action had resulted, nor had there been a response. However, they felt that neither they, nor existing community organisations, were "in a strong enough position" to pursue recommendations from the study. The young researchers appreciated their learning from undertaking the project but aspirations identified initially, such as "making a difference" and "creating change" in their area (Hajera and Sabia, aged 17), remained unmet, potentially discouraging future involvement. Like earlier examples, this project raises questions about the rewards and expectations implied when young people are encouraged to engage in this kind of community advocacy.

As in many education processes, collaborative learning develops confidence over and above the specific skills or knowledge accessed, and can therefore develop its own momentum. As Kristen (aged 15), a member of the youth council, identified: "What we do's good, it's helped me with speaking out and presentations, how to research.... But most, I think I've grown, I'm confident from working with others who've been here a while. It's kind of changed how I see things." Another youth council member, Ebo (aged 18) stressed other positive outcomes, including gaining legitimacy to influence changes on behalf of others: the power of 'office' and power over resources. He contrasted this with potentially risky behaviours: "At youth council we have status, we get views from area youth forums, different clubs and make decisions. Funding's important, gives you ways to make changes ... instead of getting into bad stuff because you got no status otherwise."

Many of the examples above suggest possibilities for transformative 'self-help' projects, led and designed by young people, demonstrating ways in which participation in collective endeavour has affected their lives and self-perceptions. However, they also illustrate mistrust in the process of realising change because of the persistence of powerful institutional norms and arrangements, which often discount alternative interests and approaches, retaining outsiders.

Barriers and challenges to advocacy

Exclusion, inclusion and representation

What forms advocacy and community participation take and the extent to which they are viewed as constructing inclusion into dominant cultures, arrangements and modes of governance, are important questions in establishing who benefits from advocacy. How professional power is handled, the skills and capacities that VS workers and volunteers develop and those that they promote among user groups or members of their organisations are closely related concerns. On the one hand, legitimacy and success in advocacy endeavours – an inclusive hearing at the policy table – seem to call for advocates able to employ appropriate means and discourse to participate: effective boundary spanners. On the other, this achievement of legitimacy can also distance them from those they seek to represent, and constrain the ways in which they organise and the kinds of cases presented.

In the youth empowerment context, as described above, key strategies included the election of local youth mayors and the establishment of youth councils. However, as Marsh et al's (2007) research on young people's participation shows, strategies that mimic existing systems and fail to challenge dominant structures and institutions often perpetuate exclusion of minority or marginal groups of people. Many areas, including Wharton, established youth councils conventionally through elected representatives from schools councils and area youth centres, but in several small youth projects, young people were either unaware of these structures or felt distanced from those elected, indicating that their views were not represented. Examples from Marsham illustrate a different approach where young people, despite pressure from the local government committee, persisted in a more fluid form of organising youth council membership. They argued that elections favoured the self-assured, discouraging others who lacked confidence or did not belong to a recognised youth forum. Josh (aged 19) outlined what he described as the 'vexed question' of representation, with the local government committee periodically exerting pressure for formal elections, as in other areas:

> 'It's been a big discussion all my time here ... and this latest proposal with representatives from each school, the

organised clubs, four from hard-to-reach groups ... excludes people ... and we've more chance to reach people our way, than if we limit numbers, have elections. We concentrate on letting people know what we're doing ... and most say they prefer our way, it's more about inclusion.'

In the same discussion, others questioned how hard-to-reach groups could form an electorate and which groups would be represented. Ebo, another youth council member, expressing this more graphically, asked: "One single mum, one disabled, one ... minority ethnic, should we have 90, one for each language in our area?" This youth council, like many VSOs, was concerned with drawing in underrepresented groups, and using conventional representative models is often inappropriate, whereas alternatives may avoid further marginalising those least likely to participate. However, purposes and actions may aim for inclusivity but the ability of the youth council to promote alternatives also faced the power embedded in local government structures, which underpinned institutional resistance to discordant issues and voices. As Barnes et al (2007, p 31) suggest, institutional resistance 'limits meaningful exchange', presenting a cultural barrier to efforts towards changes in approaches and outcomes.

Even before the growing transfer of public services to for-profit agencies, the effective management of participatory and consultative spaces to ensure inclusion of diverse constituencies was questioned (Barnes et al, 2010), also highlighting misconceptions around representation. For example, partnership bodies that include representatives from larger VSOs, often claim the inclusion of VS views, when multiple VS voices exist. At the same time, state agencies have accused VSOs of not being representative (Phillips, 2006), whereas, unlike public bodies, many small VSOs are concerned with specific groups or issues, which would otherwise remain unheard. Representing wider constituencies or interests is therefore often outside VSOs' immediate advocacy goals, although some may join groups involved in wider campaigns.

Many small VSOs challenge conventional ideas of representation, as illustrated by the youth council members, but how they define their advocacy roles, and the groups and issues represented, also pose conceptual and practical challenges. As Brent (2009) points out, community-based work can generate local inclusions and exclusions, with VSOs or neighbourhood centres perpetuating the values and beliefs of some groups and marginalising others. For example, in Wharton, a mediation group working with young people was initially established by a church-based community centre, with volunteers trying to defuse conflicts between different groups of young people. However, one dispute was around sexuality; and refusal to support alternative sexual identities, contrary to the centre's values, divided the workers. Eventually, a break-away mediation group was formed to support this group of young people and lobby locally for service changes. Tomlinson and Schwabenland (2011) recount similar challenges among small VSOs struggling to resolve values of respect for diverse cultures and competing religious beliefs expressed among service users.

The latter examples illustrate dilemmas experienced by small VSOs faced with questions about whose values and beliefs they can accommodate and represent. The dilemmas for large VSOs appear less acute, and it is often assumed that their size, the wider reach of services or links to national campaigns make them more representative. However, many also concentrate on particular kinds of service users, such as older or disabled people or children, and their advocacy concentrates on these interest groups or their carers. The knowledge and geographic scope of these larger VSOs is generally more extensive but they still represent certain segments of society divided by interest, and not others. The value to a healthy democratic society of VSO advocacy is to facilitate avenues for expression for diverse social groups or constituencies whose interests are often not represented through mainstream elected bodies, rather than to seek to duplicate area-based representation. Nevertheless, the more that insider tactics are adopted and some VSOs gain seats at the policy table, both public and some VS bodies may misconstrue these roles as more widely representative than they are. Arguably, the reduced role of the state as arbiter in local planning may simply facilitate the most powerful voices, silencing others, in the absence of arbitration. Advocacy and campaigns are important components in allowing expression to diverse minority groups in an active civil society but the tenets of localism have anarchic potential without the traditional role of elected local governments.

Biting the hand that feeds us? Resource dependency

One of the tensions highlighted earlier is the potential conflict of interest for VSO service providers between vigorous advocacy roles and jeopardising funding. As Steve, coordinating a youth education project, acknowledged, discussing relationships with local government officers:

> 'They're the gatekeepers I have to be pleasing but it has the potential for compromising integrity, if we want to argue

> what's best for young people. That doesn't mean we always
> take what's given – we have to strike a balance because
> often there's no one else to stick up for these young people.'

Steve explained that placating gatekeepers was not simply about future funding but sometimes meant agreeing to ill-advised placements and reporting what he termed 'senseless' performance indicators. As competition for resources intensifies, the pressures to withhold criticism and to advocate 'with gloves on' are all the greater (Onyx et al, 2010).

However, where members of the youth council in Marsham attempted to adopt insider tactics, they often felt marginalised, prompting discussion about whether they would have gained more notice through controversial behaviour rather than seeking legitimacy through the youth council role. Temi described presenting a case to the local government committee: "Some of them.... Like we bring an idea or decision, they'll listen but it's discounted. You can see they're thinking like ... why have them here? Has it put us off? No, but it's demotivating."

Like Steve, in Rushley, the youth council was conscious of needing to placate gatekeepers by meeting performance indicators, with Temi suggesting that the committee's interest in the large events organised to involve more young people "seems more about ticking their boxes". Michael (aged 18), also a youth council member, explained that to gain funding for any kind of event was "hard going" and essentially meant that "we gotta produce the goods or they [committee] going to put us down": withholding future funding and support for activities.

While the youth council's advocacy role on behalf of other young people is fairly new, Cairns et al (2010a) argue that the advocacy role in the wider UK VS is sufficiently embedded in values and practices that many workers do not view the dual role as service provider as conflictual, and this was borne out among VSOs in my studies. As Jan, a Wharton youth worker explained: "it's part of our ethos, what we do alongside running the projects, or we'd only be doing half the job", but she also acknowledged that "if a group never rocks the boat and is always ready to fit the brief" (by meeting new contract specifications), their funding was less likely to be threatened. This does not suggest that adversarial approaches are necessarily silenced but that the asymmetrical relationships between funders and funded may have a significant impact on suppressing unfavourable messages, with consequences for those less able to exert influence. It also strengthens the hand of collaborators and insiders, weakening the influence of alternative views and more direct forms of advocacy.

The Place considered above and in the previous chapter had a long history of direct action, campaigning locally for the service needs of vulnerable groups of adults and young people. As Sonia, the coordinator, argued: "If not us trying to even the score, then who? Some really vulnerable people will just go under the radar – disposable as far as mainstream systems go. If you know that, then how can you not shout about it?" However, a local government officer regarded these actions differently, articulating fears expressed by other VSOs:

> 'The Place is like a thorn in everyone's side; winning their disability case cost the council money. People remember, so it's not surprising they're losing contracts for adult work really. Price was an issue too; their staff costs were higher. But you know, they're stuck in the past ... VSOs operate differently now, it's a competitive environment and if they want to do business with us, we expect professionalism, not antagonism. They need to choose between campaigns and providing a service.'

Not all local government representatives took this same view of services *or* advocacy but most agreed that VSOs were more likely to gain ground from insider tactics and less likely to alienate funders. Effectively, this understanding of insider tactics could be read as sharing 'legitimate' information about service needs in the area, and made doing business more comfortable, albeit on the funders' terms. Other research suggests that anxieties about undermining funding have encouraged much greater use of insider tactics, with a shift away from more confrontational approaches to influencing policy (Smith and Pekkanen, 2012).

There was also a clear division in expectations around advocacy roles between longstanding and newer VSOs, and sometimes among workers, suggesting that assumptions about job roles may be barriers to advocacy, especially among recently established service providers. In Wharton, a small, recently established VSO offering extended school hours projects, did not expect its workers to engage in advocacy work on behalf of families or children. As the manager said:

> 'If it's about the hours or activities we provide, then I might lobby the school for equipment or make a case for extra resources but we work with families with multiple needs, so we'd refer them to specialist advisers, we just don't have the time or expertise, it's not our role. We're paid to deliver a service, not an advice agency.'

Most examples in previous sections reflect the contrasting expectations of more established VSOs but where new workers joined, there were sometimes different assumptions. As Kelly, joining Horizons in Rushley, commented: "It's impressed me how much the others did extra that wasn't written down in their roles anywhere, like lobbying the police authority meeting, helping parents write letters to the estate office." Debbie, Horizons coordinator, explained how her interpretation of VSO roles was more fluid:

> 'Kelly's experience is mainly public sector work, they're maybe jobs with clearer boundaries, specialist referrals.... It's not a criticism but it means she stops short whereas we go that extra mile. We're often young people's last stop before they're locked up and maybe there's a desperate parent ... and nobody to speak for them.'

These contrasts in advocacy practice suggest a shifting picture, with not only the approaches adopted subject to change, but also, as new workers and organisations enter the field, different cultures and expectations emerging around VS work and roles – intensifying the dilemmatic spaces of community work that Hoggett et al (2009) describe.

For VSO service providers especially, funding dependency and the associated cultures of arrangements have encouraged changes in approaches to advocacy, potentially limiting its acceptable forms. Young people acting as advocates have also faced challenging lessons about the difficulties of outsiders gaining legitimate status and notice. Unsurprisingly, small community organisations and youth groups are most likely to face barriers, experiencing marginalisation despite attempts to adopt insider approaches, and may resort to alternatives and direct forms of action. Wider research has also identified the increased professionalisation of language and arrangements surrounding advocacy work (Dalrymple, 2004; Cummings, 2008; Onyx et al, 2010), leading to disquiet about the effects of growing reliance on insider tactics and its potentially exclusive impacts on those unable or unwilling to assimilate these rules of play.

Resource dependency theory (Pfeffer, 2003) suggests that organisations professionalise structures and arrangements and invest in shared networks with power-holders to ensure legitimacy and therefore maximise resources and strategic advantage in competition for funding. Not only does this argue a reliance on insider advocacy activities but as institutionalisation and insider identity become embedded in a VSO's culture, other forms of more contentious advocacy are necessarily excluded, along with unpopular concerns. Thus, resource dependency and isomorphic institutionalisation (DiMaggio and Powell, 1991) work together, shaping calculated choices in approaches and issues presented.

Do changing forms of advocacy matter?

This chapter has identified diverse approaches to advocacy across a variety of VSOs, including models intended to promote self-advocacy, and community, civic and civil participation. It has also considered different trends, recognising that in a decade of growth among VSOs, as service providers and in delivering multiple government-sponsored initiatives, cultures and expectations underpinning advocacy practices have shifted, becoming more professionalised. Increased access to public funding and a higher profile in government strategy have raised expectations of advocacy activity, with VSOs seeking more influence on policy outcomes locally and nationally. Changing forms of governance and interdependent relationships with government agencies have extended opportunities for VSOs to be involved in consultations and meet with political representatives but have also altered methods of participation.

The picture is not simple and there are significant challenges for advocacy in this altered terrain: for small VSOs that may lack the resources and capacity to engage; similarly, for young people; and for participating VSOs concerned not to jeopardise relationships with funders. Gaining legitimacy to become influential as an insider may depend on a good local reputation as a service provider and fostering appropriate alliances but can also be fragile if based on ambiguous goals. It also disables outsider tactics. As discussed above, changing expectations around advocacy tactics, coupled with funding dependency, can neutralise activity, privileging insider voices and issues and marginalising outsiders. Effectively, this sets limits around advocacy practice and around the VS's independent role as an intermediary between state and citizen. Nevertheless, many small VSOs appeared to combine challenging messages with insider tactics where necessary, and advocacy purposes were clearly grounded in organisational goals.

Not all VSOs in my studies assumed the same path: some adversarial activities were adopted but these were mainly the province of smaller, longstanding or campaign-only VSOs. Concerns about policy, resources, services and conditions for different VSO constituencies increasingly involve non-adversarial means, and for larger organisations often rely on investing in networks and gaining places in policy committees. Being able to manage knowledge and information, and keep abreast of changing developments, confer authority and status, increasing levels of influence. Alliances also feature in the advocacy work of smaller VSOs, with local expertise an invaluable attribute in providing influential knowledge. However, without the inclusion of professional insiders, they may well be regarded as marginal pressure groups and largely discounted by local government and related bodies. As examples illustrate, local government representatives increasingly regarded advocacy involving direct action as outmoded in contemporary governance.

That the trend towards insider advocacy methods is also visible in other countries (Chaves et al, 2004; Cummings, 2008; Onyx et al, 2010) gives rise to wider questions about how far VSOs' commitment to advocacy has become incorporated within dominant cultures and structures of policy governance. The latter seem to offer little space for challenges or contentious issues, or for the role that VS advocacy has hitherto played in exerting pressure for social change in relation to minority voices. These openings for protecting marginalised individuals against the weight of majority interests are apparently shrinking.

Shifting forms of governance have therefore prompted contradictory changes, constraining some forms of advocacy and promoting opportunities for others, such as through participation in networks, partnerships and cross-sector decision-making fora. Such fora are often assumed to be consensual but power embedded in these processes often suppresses differences and contentious debate through dominant discourse and arrangements. Where policy agendas have promoted citizens' participation, they have emphasised hegemonic inclusion, discouraging independent, unpredictable or transformative outcomes.

If advocacy is curtailed in this way, its operation is limited to the level of enabling access for individuals and groups to services that they may currently be denied or engaging with government agendas intended to promote good citizenship through desired forms of community and democratic participation. While such interventions are valuable, the emphasis is on inclusion, rather than institutional change; and strategies concentrate on deficits of the excluded, not the barriers integral to services or institutions that exclude. Thus, advocacy activities that simply make the case for unproblematic inclusion, and those that are overly invested in insider activity, may avoid addressing underlying collective and institutional difficulties and the agendas needed for change. Advocacy thus becomes contained within incremental changes, in which private sector and public bodies may be allies, and contentious political changes are suppressed. Among my data, there were few recent examples of significant contentious issues being successfully challenged and won. Thus, the contemporary picture of civil engagement shows considerable adaption to normative models of social and political institutions, with VS advocacy potentially a collaborator in this process.

However, this chapter argued at the outset that VS advocacy was essentially a political activity, and integral to the values and purposes of many VSOs; and this longevity is borne out in many of the examples above. Not only forms of advocacy but also its goals and purposes are crucial to understanding the extent to which VS advocacy has been compromised. Although insider tactics are becoming dominant, many examples demonstrate that VS advocacy continues to work as a purposeful political activity. It is the clarity of purpose and not only the form of activities that are important for defining the autonomous or restricted nature of advocacy work; and when VSOs are alert to the pressures on them to become professionalised, constraints are more likely to be balanced by intrinsic organisational goals.

This chapter illustrates some tensions and contradictions surrounding independent forms of advocacy within political and associational life, offering mixed predictions about the future. There is a tendency in research to regard VS advocacy as an unproblematic good: as a route to pleading the case of underrepresented individuals or groups (Evers, 2010); whereas in any given context, there may be conflicting vested interests and constituencies driving the advocacy efforts of different VSOs, with the least powerful often remaining unheard. The ways in which legitimate participation for minority voices is retained, which groups and what types of knowledge are deemed appropriate, are important ongoing concerns for VS advocacy and more widely for a healthy democratic society.

VS advocacy has hitherto played a significant role in lobbying the state at different levels, and the longevity of advocacy work embedded within the UK VS ethos has tended to safeguard its ongoing role, despite the pressures to pull punches and the withdrawal of funding not related to specified service outcomes. Whereas opportunities for influencing the state grew over the last decade, there is now a rapid shift in the scope of VS–state relationships within a more entrepreneurial environment. The transfer of significant responsibility for services to agencies whose activities are profit driven rather than user or welfare focused means that they carry no embedded purposes around public good, benefits or fairness. This moves the goalposts for advocacy work and the shape of potential dialogue. Where VS services and advocacy roles have often been combined, and opportunities for influence have been gained from interdependency with government agencies, rethinking more direct campaigning models may now be needed.

In recent years, VS advocacy has narrowed in scope but gained impact within a more limited domain. As this sphere of influence changes again, it is important to think beyond current concerns about retaining the space for the political activity of advocacy following the growth of insider approaches. Infringements of rights may instead need challenging through harnessing wider movements, as accountability through local and national government bodies becomes more remote. Increased outsourcing in the UK, especially to large corporations, marginalises small-scale collective VS advocacy in relation to local state services, since prime contractors, not the state, control supply chains. As current trends in governance and mega-contracts develop, VS advocacy will also need to adapt its forms.

NINE

Values and visions for a future voluntary sector?

This book has been located within particular policy changes, positioned in place and time, but as Back (2004) argues of contemporary social research, we are also writing against time, often attempting to capture and critically reflect on what may be relatively short-lived social phenomena. A book focused on making sense of a rapidly changing voluntary sector (VS) environment therefore produces significant challenges, not least in considering what the future holds. Most of the empirical research included in this book was undertaken during the New Labour administrations but the subsequent analysis and writing have inevitably been coloured by insights drawn from changes after this period and by historical perspectives.

The book started by questioning how VS autonomy has been circumscribed as the sector gained increased importance in government projects. A retreat from interdependent funding relationships with the state might augur well then for future independence. However, it is clear from preceding chapters that recent political and policy changes foreshadow unprecedented hard times, especially because of the roads that many voluntary sector organisations (VSOs) have travelled during the New Labour years. How VSOs adapt to contemporary challenges will be crucial in sustaining the kinds of social values that have characterised many parts of the sector and for retaining its significant experience in tackling intractable welfare problems.

For VS actors undergoing rapid and destabilising changes, there is little time for thought. This chapter aims to give space to the kind of reflection often absent, drawing together discussion from earlier chapters and implications for the future. Preceding chapters have highlighted a number of themes concerning the exercise of governmental power; the isomorphic pressures of dominant organisational arrangements; and ideologies associated with the state, market and new models of collaborative governance that have framed discourse and processes of change surrounding the VS. Within these frames, concepts around performance, risk, trust and resilience have provided valuable lenses for insights into VS experiences of change and concerns about survival. In particular, the depoliticisation of potentially contested territory, such as in VS advocacy, prompts questions about the extent to which the independent choices and actions of VSOs have been curtailed through being progressively drawn into discharging state purposes. This chapter draws on these ideas but rather than revisiting these debates, frames discussion in terms of three questions: the concept of a distinctive role for the VS and its potential erosion; the future role of the state in shaping VSOs; and the space within contemporary changes for resistance and positive opportunities.

There is much to feel pessimistic about but as Taylor (2011b) concludes of community development work, there is a case for adopting a Gramscian stance of intellectual pessimism while retaining optimism around VSOs' willingness to resist and engage in practical developments. By concentrating on the cases of small VSOs, preceding chapters have illustrated that pragmatically, the values and contested spaces that effectively underpin the recognisable habitus and logic for actions (Bourdieu, 1999) of many small VSOs are being sustained within their ethos and communities of practice. That is the value of research into everyday conditions, which can explore the sometimes unintended power of agency to deflect the apparent course of structural changes. From a macro-level perspective, however, negative pressures are clearly increasing, which will require particular adaptive capacities from VSOs. Among these are: rapid reductions in funding; declining powers and responsibilities retained by the local state; and the ascendancy of markets and of civil society roles.

A further question therefore emerges in considering the potential shape of a future VS: the extent to which dominant influence on the VS has shifted from the state to the business sector with the growth of privatised public services. This is discussed alongside the issues outlined above.

Earlier chapters have highlighted the problematic outcomes from many recent government interventions, and with other authors (Ellison, 2011; Murray, 2012) have expressed anxieties about the direction of travel. The experience in the United States (US) of decentralising responsibility for welfare, with heavier reliance on ad-hoc voluntary action and philanthropy (Fairbanks, 2007), demonstrates regressive outcomes, including inadequacies in services and inequalities in access. A government withdrawing from social responsibilities, albeit opening opportunities for others, has nevertheless defined political and ideological choices that delimit the actions of other sectors. As corporations take a bigger share of public service contracts, with VSOs as subcontractors, the temptation is to shift the focus of study to VS relationships with business. These will be an important aspect of future research; however, state ideology and policies underpin understanding of a future VS; how its relationships with business are cast; and its role in social welfare. Moreover, the state continues to impact on themes highlighted in preceding chapters and drawn into the discussion below, including:

- compliance and resistance;
- risk and survival;
- collaboration and competition;
- trust and regulation;
- and the location of power.

A distinctive and independent role for the VS?

Exploring the limits of VS independence presupposes that there is, and continues to be, a defined VS, with distinctive features and rationale. Maintaining independence has been integral to VS identity, and identified as crucial to 'what makes it distinctive, effective and necessary' (Baring Foundation, 2012, p 3): voicing diverse views, challenging consensus and providing alternative service approaches. Separation from the state, a specialist focus on specific groups in the population, specific localities, campaigns and activities have been distinguishing factors, helping to convey VS value and legitimacy. Commitment to altruistic values, retaining local stakeholders' trust and developing alternative approaches and locally valued communities of practice have contributed to ways in which VSOs have been differentiated from other sectors, rationalising their importance.

Earlier chapters have examined ways in which ideas of VS distinctiveness have grown and subsequently suffered erosion, with some VSOs adopting characteristics, activities and arrangements that identify them more closely with public agencies or businesses. These transitions also prompt further questions about the extent to which distinctions continue to be recognised, understood or significant. Despite the acknowledged diversity among VSOs studied in this book, and their often complex cross-sector relationships, most confirmed a strong identification with the idea of sector. This was commonly expressed in terms of mission and purposes, and differences in practices.

The voluntary nature of trustees and management committees and widespread use of volunteers differentiate the VS from other sectors, while other features may be more ambiguous. However, VSOs in these studies frequently emphasised commitment to socially worthwhile values and purposes; undertaking activities of benefit to others; and non-profit motives. Some VSOs also identified forms of resistance to dominant organisational arrangements, ways that they subverted procedures and campaigning or advocacy activities, as key to understanding their role. There was also a strong sense of accountability to user groups and local stakeholders, especially among small VSOs, which contrasted with public agencies and new private contractors, often viewed as increasingly distant from knowledge about service users. However, where VSOs were engaged in trading or organised more as hybrids or social enterprises, the conventional non-profit features had more ambiguous boundaries. Volunteering has also spread, as both public agencies and private companies use internships to reduce expenditure, although motivations linked to personal benefits and limited volunteer roles contrast with the broader culture and motivations associated with voluntary action in the VS (Rochester et al, 2010).

The VS service role has changed rapidly and is now being displaced by private sector contractors; and the distinctive approaches and alternatives for which the VS was recognised no longer command the same governmental respect. VS expertise in community projects is also being positioned more ambiguously as a part of broader and more fragmented civil society action within a Big Society dependent on volunteers. While this may reflect associational identities characteristic of grassroots VSOs, it is a different role from the one enacted by many community-based VSOs in the latter years of the New Labour government. These changing contexts emphasise current splits in the VS sector and a blurring of former boundaries, highlighting the need to reassess thinking about distinctiveness and VS value and construct a more carefully crafted narrative for the future.

Within and outside the state? Benefits of a distinctive VS?

The discourse of VS distinctiveness is not new; but it grew under the New Labour government, denoting VS independence of the state, significant for both New Labour's Third Way discourse and VS identity. While distinctiveness has provided a rationale for the logic of VS action, like other aspects of VS change, it is contingent on external factors. The location of boundaries around sectors and alliances of organisations therefore reflects shifting perceptions and cultures of arrangements, with boundaries, therefore, both permeable and overlapping (Billis, 2010). As Chapter Two identified, VSOs undertook a significant historical role in welfare provision, often providing vital safety-nets and compensating for inadequate or non-existent state services. As public services grew, VSOs offered alternatives, providing services for specific groups in the population and more flexible, informal approaches, offering advantages over larger providers (state and private sector) for whom such specialist provision was uneconomic. In promoting alternatives, and in campaign and advocacy activities, VSOs challenged the bureaucracy and formality of public welfare, marking themselves out as different. However, since the widespread outsourcing of public services and projects, they have been reconstructed both as within mainstream welfare provision *and* as alternatives or outsiders.

This duality of role reflects current divisions among VSOs but also prompts questions about the extent to which they can continue to shape their own destinies and distinctive features as both insiders and outsiders, echoing 1980s' debates about the potential to operate both 'in and against the state' (Holloway, 2005). Chapter Eight, discussing the increasingly common use of insider tactics in advocacy, highlighted the continuing relevance of this debate, as did conclusions from Chapter Seven on approaches to survival: the coupling of accommodation with resistance. In the coalition government's discourse, there is encouragement to identify others – business, civil society organisations, communities – and not the state, as responsible for shaping welfare outcomes, making more ambiguous the ways in which VSOs and citizens can present criticism or navigate relationships with the state locally. However, the state remains integral to shaping the ideology, arrangements and communications that frame the operational settings for these actors.

Under New Labour the state's interest in granting the VS a higher profile, especially in welfare provision, coalesced with the strategic interests of the VS in having its worth recognised, and consequently, the sector grew more visible. The erstwhile 'loose and baggy monster', as Kendall and Knapp (1995) described the nebulous amalgam of VSOs previously, had become less opaque and more intelligible but partly at the expense of suppressing diversity – the different interest groups discussed in Chapter One. Rhetorically at least, New Labour applauded VS difference and independence, legitimising the sector's value. Ideologically, the sector could be positioned in uncontroversial political terrain: a third sector able to offer alternative solutions to social problems that neither state nor market had succeeded in addressing.

However, New Labour's recognition of the VS's distinctive value ultimately did little to protect VSOs from hegemonic governmental power defining the discourse and rules of play, even within new governance arrangements and apparently more fluid partnership work. New Labour needed to occupy this terrain to ensure that governmental projects were pursued even within non-governmental spaces; and many examples in earlier chapters illustrate VSOs experiencing pressure, or adopting tactics, to placate local government gatekeepers. Recognition of distinctive value drew VSOs closer to the state and many yielded to isomorphic pressure to change, paradoxically, undermining their distinctive characteristics. Large and medium-sized VSOs were encouraged to participate in domains where they could influence policy and strategy but were expected to operate with insider tactics to do so.

As Chapters Five and Six illustrated, national and local governments sought community-based providers to design and deliver innovative projects, for which outcomes were necessarily unpredictable. However, these were controlled through unrealistic performance targets to limit the financial and reputational risks to large public agencies, accentuating risks and challenges for community-based providers, and encouraging them to limit their activities to service users most likely to succeed. Thus, based on distinctive value, VSOs were drawn into initiatives and service contracts to offer difference and to provide innovative solutions to 'wicked issues' but were pressured to imitate approaches legitimised through dominant managerial cultures and funding arrangements. Distinctiveness was both applauded and undermined, generating dissatisfaction and ultimately mistrust, especially among smaller VSOs. The sector had begun to lose its political innocence (Kendall, 2010).

Narratives around VS distinctiveness and independence have underpinned the rationale for VS activity both in research and among practitioners (Alcock, 2010a; Baring Foundation, 2012) gaining momentum during the New Labour years. However, dissatisfaction with false promises from governments has exposed contested territory, raising questions about what really defines VSOs. It has also created splits between a minority of larger charities heavily engaged in service contracts, and the majority of small, community-based organisations, many unfunded or largely reliant on volunteers. In this contested VS territory, independence from state and business interests is potentially reasserted as a new badge of honour: a fundamental facet of VS identity; and overly compromised independence regarded as a sign of retreat (NCIA, 2012).

It is clear, therefore, that what is distinctive and of value is dynamic; it is affected by the interplay between state and voluntary sectors, and subject to pressure from the ideologies of successive governments. New Labour's interest in recognising certain qualities that distinguished the VS no longer holds for the coalition government. Boundaries between sectors appear purposely obfuscated and little overt distinction is made between service providers from different sectors and the values they represent, while market competition and corporate practices are accorded greater legitimacy. This realignment of emphasis highlights new distinctions: between financial reputation, and service expertise and knowledge; between efficiency and localism; and between service contractors and voluntary action.

Independence as a feature of distinctiveness is sidelined, since the continued retreat of the state from public service responsibility locates business and markets as components of an independent civil society.

However, as the state withdraws from responsibility for services, factors that distinguish independent players related to social or for-profit motives are honed, despite being ostensibly underplayed. In some domains, VS expertise is apparently recognised as important, in community-level organising and in voluntary action; but differences between wider civil society and formally constituted VSOs are ambiguous in government rhetoric, in the nebulous vocabulary around the Big Society and citizenship. In the localism agenda, unspecified groups, whose motives may be as much about enterprise and profit motives in running a local facility, such as a shop, have been banded together with engagement in more recognisable community development work.

As pressures on VS resources increase, deeper fractures are appearing between VSOs drawn into contracts and identifying themselves as entrepreneurial, and those withdrawing or resisting. Chapter Seven documented government promises to include VSOs in the Work Programme and how few have subsequently been awarded contracts, even lower in the supply chain. With hindsight, these are unsurprising by-products of marketisation and procurement, based largely on financial criteria, rather than local service knowledge, in which for-profit motivation and cost-cutting are dominant in decisions and operations. Predictably also in times of austerity, examples of rationing activities, short-cuts in assuring quality and gaming in reporting outcomes have emerged (BBC, 2012), reflecting discussion in Chapter Five.

It is clear that distinguishing the VS with special expertise is no longer a useful political strategy for a government predisposed to favour the private sector. This shift in VS–state relations should not mean disregarding VSO concerns about loss of independence. On the contrary, as Murray (2012, p 62) argues, it presents other threats: being assimilated as a subcontractor into privatised public services may mean 'becoming a pawn in the dismantling of the welfare state'. Thus, the dilemma may no longer be whether VSOs can operate *in and against* the state but how they can survive without contributing further to the demise of publicly valued services.

Identifying VS value, not only within community settings, but also VSOs' beneficial contribution to service provision, may be crucial in sustaining a space and habitus for the sector that is not endlessly fragmented. However, this demands a narrative to replace the currently waning discourse of distinctiveness. A problem here is that distinctive value necessarily implies that some entities or actions are more worthy than others – and the value that governments have accorded the VS previously has been based on ideological utility rather than research on what the VS does better. There is a strong argument for more research that compares services delivered by different sectors and also a need for greater clarity on the longer-term impacts that society values and wants from services and projects.

The VS has benefited from asserting distinctiveness, which has been closely allied with independence, but paradoxically, over the New Labour years, with increased financial dependence. There has been beneficial growth and influence but also detrimental outcomes, with pressure for VSOs to shed features and approaches for which they were initially sought and valued. In an environment where these attributes no longer attract special value, there is a need to reassess how the VS and its independence are understood, rather than leaving this to be redefined or fragmented by the ideological influence and actions of other sectors.

Reconstructing or deconstructing the narrative of distinctiveness?

Much of the preceding discussion highlights the dynamic and contested nature of definitions and boundaries both within and between sectors; and what is within or without certain *fields* (Bourdieu, 1992) is both temporal and conditional. That VS commentators are expressing anxieties about erosion of the distinctive role enjoyed by VSOs over the last decade (Butler, 2011) suggests changes resulting from both internal and external factors. Earlier VS research and more recent debates (Alcock, 2010a; Billis, 2010) have been concerned with sector boundaries, also identifying permeability and boundary-crossing at the margins. Boundaries are important constructs that help to define and structure social phenomena and groupings (Abbott, 1995), rationalising social connections and creating order within which ambiguities can be contained. They allow processes of categorisation that support sense making and perceptions of stability.

Inevitably, definitions are problematic and accentuate similarities, and concepts of VS distinctiveness can be understood as social constructs that may well minimise differences. Where sectors and organisations position themselves and where boundaries are drawn around shared cultures and activities are contested fields, and the strong communities of practice identified as distinguishing some VSOs in earlier chapters are both organisational and sector strengths but also align insiders and outsiders. These inclusions and exclusions highlight the exercise of power, competition and splits within the VS and at its boundaries, where differential power also underpins the features required to cross boundaries into other fields or sectors.

Distinctiveness associated with ideas of the VS has been important because it implies advantages over those lacking these distinct features. Therefore, maintaining claims for distinctiveness may continue to be viewed as advantageous to retain appearances of 'strategic unity' among VSOs (Alcock, 2010a), despite the increasing evidence of disparate interests. However, a relational understanding of the VS illustrates the dangers of assuming that its distinctive features are inherent or permanent fixtures; and a key thread running through earlier chapters has been the ways in which autonomy and features attributed to VSOs have been undermined, and could be constructed differently.

While there has been a powerful external realignment of how the VS is positioned, VS workers, their values and the activities they choose to engage in also carry weight in sustaining organisational and sector narratives and how these are situated in relation to the state and private sector. Earlier chapters focused both on damage to VS autonomy and on how some VSOs have relinquished alternative models in favour of maximising competitive advantage in a changing service environment. If distinctive value is more fragile and internal VS divisions have increased, threats to autonomy and the potential for external definition are greater. This highlights conflicting strategies for addressing current difficulties and prompts questions about the kind of VS narrative that is needed. To what extent is it important or even possible to maintain the concept of VS distinctiveness based on notions of broadly shared values and features, which has offered a valuable alliance up until recently? And to what extent are emergent features, such as social enterprise and community-based voluntary action, more strategically useful to emphasise in representing the contemporary VS?

A stronger reconstruction of VS identity is important for underpinning meaning for VSOs and their workers and to provide a counter-hegemonic message to governmental and business influences. This needs to take better account of the value of the sector's diverse components and make space for ideas of legitimacy that are not merely those allowed by others. As Macmillan and McLaren (2012) argue, VSOs are now facing unparalleled changes, and the current discourse of distinctiveness is insufficient to counter the dual pressures from government and business both shaping and fragmenting their roles. The creation of a new and more powerful VS narrative is therefore a pressing task: a narrative in which the changing role of the public sphere and new relationships with private public service providers are better understood.

The VS needs to identify and reconstruct the stories of what it does well; and what and who it represents; and underline its strengths, differences and valuable features, rather than continuing to defend familiar ground or seeking to compete on corporate territory. Many positive features may well be located in difference and present challenges to recent arrangements. They may also be regarded as problematic by some parts of the VS, in particular larger organisations wanting to utilise credentials gained to date to maximise opportunities for survival. This undoubtedly deepens divisions in the recent hard times; but some cases explored in earlier chapters contradict Pfeffer's (2003) resource dependency theory, which argues that organisations necessarily assume features to enhance their competitive advantages in accessing resources and growth. Many VSOs studied present more complex features and behaviours, some combining enterprise with adherence to social values; others, elements of compromise and resistance. Any reconstruction or assertion of organisational narratives, as Chapter Seven illustrates, requires clarity and sense making in organisational purposes, and now highlights dilemmas around the extent to which VSOs identify themselves as allied with the state or the market. It may, however, be time to acknowledge that being both within and outside state arrangements – combining independence and incorporation and using insider tactics against the state – is no longer possible, or possible only with significant challenges.

Reconstructing a VS narrative does, however, assume either the continuance or different formations of a VS, distinct from state and market, and has to explore insights into ways that earlier autonomy and differences have been eroded; ways that power is exercised; and ways that competition and performance frameworks operate – themes from earlier chapters. It also means assessing what choices VSOs have made, who has benefited and their value to service users. Reviewing the value and impact on wider society of VS interventions developed during the New Labour era provides a foundation for identifying potential VS strengths for the future, despite the change in conditions. It is extracting and weighing up some of this information and placing it alongside the social values that differentiate VSOs from for-profit organisations and the wider accountabilities carried by the state, which will help to construct a future narrative. This new narrative needs to be more purposeful in addressing a wider public and drawing on broader alliances. Governmental audiences appear less receptive.

The integral role of the state

So what of the state's role in VS changes? Much of the preceding discussion has focused on perceived VS value to the state, and as Chapter Two described, the state has played a key part in shaping the VS's role in social welfare over time. For several hundred years, the balance between state and VS welfare has been significant in the form and emphasis of VS activities. In the 1960s and 1970s, as the state took greater responsibility for welfare provision, campaigning groups, community development work and small VSOs of all kinds proliferated, advancing a critique of public services and wider social injustices. For some 25 years, relationships with the state have been instrumental in defining many VS activities, in outsourcing, community projects, partnerships and new forms of governance, also channelling the focus of considerable research. As the power and scope of local government are restricted, and corporations increase their share of 'public' service delivery, the business sector is gaining power in shaping conditions for service activities, suggesting the need to research these relationships more closely. Even outside the context of service contracts, funding reductions have prompted a shift in thinking about the potential for VS alliances with business. Such moves are influenced by discourses around corporate social responsibility and mutually beneficial partnerships (Harris, 2012), which can add value through the exchange of finance, goods, time and expertise.

However, shifting the focus of investigation entirely disregards the integral role of the state in engineering the environment encompassing each sector, and plays into government ideology, which understates its role in placing the onus on 'communities' to fill gaps in services that state withdrawal and business-led contracts open up. It is flawed, therefore, to regard VS terrain as becoming independent of the influence and powers of the state, despite its shift away from funding dependency: it is a question of degree. As Chapter Six demonstrated, even partnerships and collaborative ventures, which theoretically facilitate open governance, are free neither from competitive interest nor state interventions; and the hierarchical power that new governance networks were intended to shed habitually reasserts itself (Davies, 2011). By opening up public services and through explicit policy around nudging social behaviours, the state is strengthening its centralised control and extending its governable terrain, not only to formally organised VSOs, as New Labour achieved, but also to wider civil society. The public message, however, is the reverse.

Earlier, I questioned the possibilities of VSOs continuing to work both in and against the state, and retain elements of a distinctive role. This question is significant, not least because local government powers, now in decline, have been the sites of frequent VS interventions. Previous chapters have identified the diverse approaches and actions of different VSOs, illustrating ways in which they have been drawn to serve state agendas and also ways that they have challenged this potential incorporation. The three Ms —markets, managerialism and excessive monitoring demands – have been integral to these isomorphic pressures and in generating resistances.

New Labour was initially criticised for short-termism and projectitis but subsequently the mainstreaming of procurement created an increasingly complex outsourcing environment in which small VSOs found it hard to operate. Encouragement to grow, to build service capacity and to engage in more enterprising projects as economic recession heralded public sector cuts were integral to the stage directions for the VS during the latter years of New Labour. Resource opportunities for VSOs willing or persuaded to engage accordingly advanced isomorphism, masked in apparently consensual arrangements but also increased interdependency.

However, the effects of welfare contractualism are potentially much more extensive in terms of the quality of services and the attitudes of those removed from frontline delivery. Examples in earlier chapters demonstrate that how services are delivered, their flexibility and the responsiveness of individual workers matter in their effectiveness for service users. Of course, users are more concerned about their experiences of the service, its ethos and approaches than which sector provides it. However, the examples illustrate how service goals and intended approaches can be distorted through funding competition, inappropriate targets and rationing. Contrary to the assertions of successive governments about public choice theory and the service benefits of competition, the damaging consequences of marketisation on welfare services have featured in social policy research since the 1970s (Titmuss, 1974; Hills et al, 2002). Welfare contractualism, as Sage (2012, p 371) argues, has the potential to realign fundamental ideas about the 'nature and purpose of welfare' consolidating negative attitudes towards welfare beneficiaries. The coalition government has promoted these attitudinal shifts alongside increased conditionality in welfare, affecting moral judgements about what is viewed as fair in terms of public support. The consequence is damaging to wider social relations, encouraging societal divisions rather than cohesion. Tackling presumed welfare dependency more forcefully than the previous government, and declaring it as substantially responsible for public debts, has allowed the coalition government to exploit existing social fractures to advance a stronger rhetoric around dismantling the public sector.

Localism and opening public services

Little prepared VSOs for either the rapidity of change or the extent of financial losses experienced during 2011 and 2012, or for the reversal in how public services and associated VS services would be regarded. The effects on provision especially in poorer areas, as the National Coalition for Independent Action (NCIA, 2012) reported, have been disturbing. Whereas New Labour identified VS qualities establishing it as a preferred provider, especially for disadvantaged users, the coalition government's reassurances that VSOs would continue to be important contractors have proved hollow to date, with regional and national advice services and unemployment services among casualties. The opening up of public services, rather than offering more opportunity for local design of services, has, in such contexts, intensified the worst effects of contractualism, associated regulatory frameworks and centrally driven performance targets, discussed in Chapters Four and Five; and there is little indication that forthcoming contracts for work with troubled families or health services will reverse these trends.

While VSOs large enough to navigate this new territory have been encouraged to collaborate with corporate partners, for many, this experience too has proved fruitless, with VSOs reporting experiences of being included simply as 'bid candy' and subsequently relinquished (NCIA, 2012). Unlike previous Conservative leaders, David Cameron, in 2006, committed to support compacts with the VS but it is now evident that corporate and not VS interests are paramount. Complex business and financial criteria – market legitimacy – rather than local service experience and social values have increasingly been privileged in service contracts. As market legitimacy dominates and resources become scarcer, funding opportunities for VSOs diminish. However, VSOs are doubly disadvantaged: the advantages that they previously offered are discounted; and despite Cameron's (2010) targets for a post-bureaucratic world, regulations and specifications have become progressively more complex and intrusive.

This is not just about discounting the value previously given to the VS and ushering in business; although, of course, that is happening. These are ideologically driven arrangements, which are steadily opening up public services and shedding state responsibilities for welfare provision, shifting the balance of 'publicness' in services (Murray, 2012). It is a fundamental change in the state's role and in public understanding and expectations of the state that have endured for over half a century: a dismantling of public infrastructure in ways that will be hard to rebuild either ideologically or practically. The approaches or expertise that VSOs might contribute to services in poor areas or in challenging arenas, such as for the long-term workless if public services shrink, have had limited visibility in government rhetoric. Yet failure to identify the expertise needed for difficult services may be a serious flaw, not only in whether provision is effective, but also in sustaining support for the ideological rationale of opening up most services.

Within this new service framework, the VS is somewhat incidental, encouraged to both contribute services within the new supply chain and concentrate on local 'associational' activities. VS proximity to the previous government and its perceived dependency on state resources may justify its demotion in status. VSOs of most interest within the frame of current government policies, therefore, are those deemed innovative and enterprising, ready to 'seize new opportunities' (OCS, 2010, p 6). The re-engineering of the public sphere could well be slowed if potentially subversive VSOs are welcomed within these new frames. Little surprise, then, that this government report entitled, *Supporting a stronger civil society* constructs a deficit model of existing VSOs as overly dependent on state resources, despite its subtitle: *consultation on improving support for frontline civil society organisations*.

Localism and Big Society

Service providers only represent a fraction of VSOs, and VSOs only one element of civil society. Nevertheless, the concept of the 'Big Society' is also integral to how the state has cast the future role of VSOs. The ideological rationale for the Big Society, which encompasses VSOs within broad local aspirations, is to provide a counterbalance to the amoral and individualistic tendencies of market forces (Blond, 2010). As Taylor (2011a, p 3) observes, 'it is encouraging to see ... recognition of the territory between state and market' and priority given to social as well as economic developments. However, the level of investment has been remarkably small and encourages a critical view of underlying purposes that appear more about nudging social behaviours and expectations in particular directions. Chapter Two explored the reasons for emphasising apparently more compassionate and pragmatic elements of conservatism that offset the dominance of neoliberal ideology and rapidly changing public services.

Initially, the coalition government's Big Society, with its promise of localism and community empowerment, offered encouragement to VSOs, highlighting 'communities first' and a specific role for VSOs in locally based community organising. Rather than the professionalised and target-driven approach, within which VSOs were expected to address social problems under New Labour, the ambiguity of Big Society suggests more power locally to define activities, drawing on community skills and assets. However, just as New Labour hijacked and incorporated the discourse and activities of small community-based organisations, the Big Society rhetoric has also 'rebranded' examples of existing community action, as if these were outcomes of the new community organisers' scheme.

It has become clear that minimal, short-term funding for the community organisers' scheme has been outweighed by losses among experienced community development workers; and while some small VSOs have engaged in developing local community plans, concern has emerged about reduced community support in poorer areas and overstretched and scarce resources (Taylor, 2011b). It is also apparent that the line between services and voluntary or community action is deliberately blurred, with greater emphasis on people doing things for themselves, as closures in facilities from local libraries to youth centres claim attention. This maps a threefold role for VSOs:

- to help provide a safety-net in poor communities where there is insufficient funding to meet growing welfare demands;
- to contribute expertise to community organising towards self-help developments;
- to support a small infrastructure for organising volunteers.

These roles are not new but further domesticate community action, deflecting it from more oppositional campaigns.

However, as earlier chapters discussed, well-funded VSOs and the prevalence of volunteers are sparser in poorer areas; and therefore longer-term reliance on voluntary action and self-help activities is likely to lead to significant geographic inequalities. Small VSOs have considerable expertise in community organising but can hardly replace the broad remit of public services without adequate professional training in diverse fields and a supportive infrastructure. The current erosion of services is a tall order to repair; and even where self-help and new community-based groups can contribute, building up services and facilities from informal groups takes a long time, and inevitably involves differences in priorities and conflicts (Brent, 2009), even without the added pressures of complex service needs and scarce resources.

While encouraging community freedom to create provision in line with local aspirations, localism also risks that the services in an area are the unplanned consequences of the available assets and abilities of local groups – whether VSOs or others. As discussed in the context of advocacy in Chapter Eight, these may not meet the needs of less able, less articulate or minority groups in society. Taking a broader policy perspective in decision making has up to now been the role of the state. Losing the local government role as arbiter among the competing interests of local groups could have both unanticipated and unjust outcomes for those least able to advocate on their own behalf.

Locating power

Concepts of 'power' and 'resistance' (Foucault, 1977), as is evident from earlier discussion, pervade themes in this book and are valuable in exploring this changing inter-organisational terrain. While theories of structural resistance (Giroux, 1983) and coercive institutional isomorphism (DiMaggio and Powell, 1983) provide useful frameworks for examining overall transitions, they offer insufficient explanation for the complexity of patterns visible from examples illustrated in earlier chapters: of organisations concurrently accommodating and resisting dominant forces. Other concepts, including the prevalence of 'risk-averse culture' and 'regulatory controls' and, conversely, the values and strengths of communities of practice (Lave and Wenger, 1991), also offer insights into VS compliance coupled with resistance and how VSOs are addressing the challenges and opportunities that they now face.

A question raised in Chapter Two was the extent to which devolution and decentralisation of public services were constructing a shadow state, with a growing VS increasingly responsible for welfare delivery and community development, undertaking state-promoted projects and agendas. The New Labour model and the shared cultures between public agencies and large VSOs and hybrid organisations such as housing associations did indeed seem to presage a shadow state, as large VSOs also took on local strategy and planning roles in cross-sector bodies. The fragmentation of decision making highlighted above as a problem of localism could equally apply to VSOs assuming functions of the state. VSOs, as identified earlier, were often established to work with specific groups in the population or within specific neighbourhoods; few would claim a broad representative perspective. Some infrastructure bodies convey the views of member organisations in their areas or of segments of the VS nationally but this means that access to a 'shadow state' constructed in this way is unevenly distributed and often partial.

Revisiting this concept while privatisation of public services advances and the VS role becomes less influential leads to the conclusion that the state is taking back power while ostensibly ceding it to 'communities' and corporate contractors. The dispersal and greater fragmentation of roles, as the private sector colonises services previously delivered by VSOs, suggests little intention of moving in the direction of a shadow state. The power of citizens to influence services, except through self-help, is diminished and, while the message is about a shrinking state, the dispersal and redistribution of lines of accountability underline the state's power and integral role in processes of realignment. Arguably, its increasing levels of surveillance could suggest more panoptical aspirations (Foucault, 1988).

The exercise of governmental power was repeatedly illustrated in examples of inter-organisational relationships in earlier chapters. The rituals of verification (Power, 1997), the rules of the game (Clegg, 1989) that legitimise certain information, discourses and modes of operation, and the growing trend towards market legitimacy displacing social values in contract criteria, are all ways in which continuity in the exercise of governmental powers is visible from the previous to the current government. In seeking to suppress conflicting communications and influences, there may be an appearance of consensual governance and masquerade of trust (Hardy et al, 1998) used in strategies to promote or coerce engagement among potential dissenters.

One of the signals given by the coalition government, which argues its aspirations to extend governmental controls more than its rhetoric admits, is the creation of a behavioural unit drawing on nudge theory (Thaler and Sunstein, 2008). Its targets include welfare users and its key purposes reducing welfare use and costs; but concerns about improving amoral market practices are absent from its objectives. As Chapter Two identified, nudge theory, drawing on behavioural economics and cognitive psychology, has informed government strategies both in the United Kingdom (UK) and the US intended to influence individuals' behaviours in their everyday social and physical environments, to achieve positive welfare outcomes. The ethical concerns of imposing social norms of behaviour in a diverse multicultural society are significant, and echo criticisms in Chapter Seven of the normative interpretations given to resilience. The emphasis on individual agency also defies theoretical analysis of the interdependency of structure and agency (Bourdieu, 1992) and therefore the parallel importance of socioeconomic structures and institutions in maintaining barriers to change. Choosing to act differently, however encouraging the nudge, may not be an option.

Over some two decades, isomorphic tendencies affecting VSOs have extended the reach of government into previously autonomous organisations. With the expansion of partnership working, hybrid organisations have also evolved, extending normative isomorphic pressures and the cultures of dominant organisational arrangements. Despite the rhetoric of localism (co-existing with centralising practices), the coalition government's intentions to re-engineer the VS are as visible as interventions in New Labour's modernisation agenda – more so, since it aims to influence individual and group behaviours in welfare. Current government projects that promote community engagement and voluntary action extend governmental reach and influence, not only to organisational life but also to the lives of individuals in wider civil society.

The pragmatism and consensual assumptions embedded in political messages around norms of behaviour are integral to strategies aimed at nudging behaviours in the desired directions, away from the purported social disease of state dependency. Agents of local communities – VSOs and civil society actors – are identified as key components, not only in maintaining but also in strengthening a 'civilising' role – constructed rhetorically as Big Society. However, such roles are not only about consensually driven processes of civilising welfare (Lever, 2011); there are markedly punitive alternatives, in the enforcement of harsher controls for rebels and dissenters. Thus, nudging behaviour may also be construed as state discipline; and punishments the outcome of failures to adapt.

The ways in which hierarchies and powerful cultures have pervaded not only the structured frameworks of contracts and performance monitoring, described in Chapters Four and Five, but also the networks of governance underpinning partnership work, suggest that dispersing state functions is different from the state sharing power. Diffuse and fragmented local power structures effectively reinforce centrally held powers and, as Davies (2011) highlights, these are central to neoliberal projects of economic and political modernisation. New Public Management systems replicated and strengthened hierarchical practices that they were supposed to replace (Hood, 2000) and, as Chapter Six showed, hierarchies have also suffused partnerships and cross-sector networks. Understanding theoretical distinctions between management hierarchies and networked models may be less important than exploring the resulting complexity of dispersed decision making; levels of participation; mechanisms of consent and coercion; and processes of inclusion and exclusion. Together these features reveal the exercise of power and hegemonic arrangements. As Davies (2011, p 151) argues, governmentality as a part of the neoliberal project to enrol and transform civil society invariably dominates attempts to foster a more 'connectionist ethos'; and this underlines the significance of the extension of the governable terrain beyond VSOs to wider civil society, exposing local empowerment as a facade.

However, understanding the rules of the game and ways in which power is enacted and reproduced, as the previous chapter considered in discussing advocacy tactics, can also be used as a form of resistance and, sometimes, to redefine the terms of arrangements. Earlier chapters illustrated VSOs sustaining commitment to sharing power with service users, providing examples of resistance to the pressures of dominant cultures. Nevertheless, as localism and the opening up of public services proceed, complexity and fragmentation are increasing; local and national government agencies are mutating; and the locus of power is shifting. This makes it harder to navigate governmental relationships, weakening the potential for collective resistance among VSOs. A stronger interest-based alliance may be needed so that the potential for VS marginalisation and divisions does not simply lead to the most powerful players determining the outcomes. This means creating alliances not only within the VS but also with neglected partners, such as trades unions and wider social movements. As Taylor (2011a, p 305) argues, the 'invited spaces' for influence may be welcome but 'are not enough'; and this is clear from Chapter Eight, which discussed the need for less compliant advocacy strategies, if an important democratic means of asserting contradictory views is not to be lost. Neither political nor business leaders will have much interest in sharing power, resources or privileges (De Filippis et al, 2009); and resistance and constructive changes for poorer communities will need to be pursued by those who have an interest in challenging this growing hegemony.

Change, challenge and hard times

At the outset of much of the empirical research discussed in this book, the VS role in addressing social welfare problems was prominent in government policies, and VSOs anticipated increased funding and a higher profile for their work, alongside expectations of sharing positive practice. Although what followed offered opportunities for multiple and diverse initiatives, funding for core provision declined and state interference grew, often reshaping the emphasis of activities. As formalism, contract specification and regulation increased, trust in the state declined, especially among small VSOs.

More literature concentrates on why public services have failed rather than reasons for VSOs succeeding. Future opportunities for VSOs must encompass better understanding of their strengths and how these can be used and valued within new frameworks. If the current government is to gain from the expansion and extended reach of VSOs since the 1990s to contribute to Big Society priorities, it needs to work more closely with the VS and both acknowledge and understand its strengths. However, without greater recognition of current VS difficulties, VSOs' endeavours in generating alternatives models responsive to the communities they serve may well be permanently damaged, paradoxically, in an era when their 'localism' as service providers and in community organising should place them in a strong position.

Previous sections have highlighted the need to move away from the old narrative of specialism and distinctiveness towards creating stronger interest-based alliances. There is also a pressing need to deconstruct and challenge the growing claims for superiority and efficiency of private sector service contractors, and the bias towards market and financial legitimacy, effectively excluding VSOs from recent tenders. Recent examples cited have shown corporate contractors lacking accountability in providing effective public benefit in services. Equalising access for VSOs through criteria that emphasise relevant service reputation and social values might mitigate the rapidly diminishing trust in current outsourcing arrangements. Current public services legislation proposes the inclusion of social value among criteria for awarding contracts but it remains to be seen how far this will redress criticisms of recent contracting processes. It may provide more opportunity for social enterprises, mutuals and large VSOs to compete successfully when further NHS and local government services are outsourced.

Losing the public sphere and ethos?

Much of the preceding discussion has emphasised the integral role of the state in engineering the organisational environment across different sectors, and has been critical of the governmental means used to steer outcomes in ways that have reduced VS autonomy. However, as the effects of the coalition government's strategies become clearer, with hindsight the aspirations and arrangements of the previous government and the injection of resources into VS developments, acquire a more positive patina. What is currently being eroded is a strong ethos and infrastructure that could underpin VS, community-based and civil society developments, alongside the role of the local democratic state as an arbiter among competing groups and interests and minority concerns. The fragmentation of interests in localist approaches needs negotiation and management through bodies that carry legitimacy. While the state has often been mistrusted, as earlier chapters illustrated, removing understood democratic structures and processes leaves the least powerful members of communities with few avenues for influence, except through recourse to direct action, as seen in English cities in the summer of 2011.

One reason for New Labour devolving many services to VS providers reflected perceptions of VS attributes, including a reputation for commitment to social and public benefits. Trust in the state had declined but outsourcing public services to VSOs served to reassure the public of New Labour's commitment to welfare and associated values, while also acknowledging past public sector failures in tackling social problems. Endorsing ideas of the VS as altruistic promoted public trust in VSOs that they would operate in the interests of service users and local stakeholders, while also offering positive differences to public sector delivery. However, as the state's role moved from provider to regulator, it became divorced from altruistic values traditionally embedded in responsibility for welfare delivery and from closer communication with service users, eroding public trust. As Whitty (2001, p 289) argued of earlier transitions, 'values of community, co-operation, need and equal worth ... [were] replaced by values celebrating individualism, competition and performativity'. Subsequent changes that seemingly professionalised parts of the VS have similarly undermined some of its value to society in supporting responsive, non-competitive forms of organisation.

These transitions are not limited to the UK but have been part of wider global trends, giving rise to social concerns about the erosion of publicness (Newman and Clarke, 2009), the individualisation of risks and promotion of choice and consumerism –all products of dominant market capitalism and trends, which the coalition government has embraced enthusiastically. Mapping these changes in the public sphere, Murray (2012, p 60) argues that the public sector has represented an important moral sphere, embedded in British politics for more than 50 years, and symbolises ways in which society is fair, compassionate and supports the less fortunate, containing risks and 'social anxiety in routine ... ways'. Local provision (including sports, library and rubbish removal services), local government planning and national taxes have all ensured that people could expect to access a minimum level of broadly similar facilities, alongside welfare protection during hard times. The removal or absence of embedded public institutions, together with the potential shadow welfare safety-net constituted through VSOs as more services are privatised and motivated by profit, eliminates that infrastructure and explicit public commitment to a fair society. It also reduces important social and political decisions about service provision to ones based on complex technical procurement criteria and cost-based, utilitarian judgements.

Both New Labour and the coalition government have relied on claims of consensual politics to assert their priorities and strategies, obscuring difference and conflict, which as Chapter Six identified, are often present but suppressed. Among contemporary changes, the coalition government has relinquished the earlier emphasis on partnership governance in favour of a tougher entrepreneurial culture, which not only undermines this moral public sphere but also purposely highlights perceived ills of state provision. Consequently, VSOs are now faced with dilemmas affecting their survival, such as whether they should enter supply chains as subcontractors in privatised services, which may actively contribute to the longer-term demise of *public* welfare (Murray, 2012). If we recognise these changes in the moral sphere and consequent ethical dilemmas, other worrying concerns follow: shifts in ideas of publicness and fairness are fundamental to thinking about the role that states play in promoting wider democracy and enabling representative participation and social justice.

As the invited spaces for challenge and representing alternative views contract, the power of consensual politics also declines, as Chapter Eight identified, and the likelihood of dissent increases. Murray (2012, p 60) similarly identifies that as valued institutions are dismantled, there is 'a sense of starting to grapple with the need for a revitalised civil society'. From a VS perspective, some resistance to new norms and practices is already evident as some VSOs opt out of contractualism. There are also indications of contested spaces emerging within public sector practices around austerity measures, and some continued commitment to community-based providers, despite conflicting pressures. Internationally, governments are also being faced with angry citizens suffering rising unemployment, who are highly critical of the political management of austerity, while they see bail-outs for corporations and banks.

VSOs are not struggling alone, and constructing and articulating a new narrative also has to involve building stronger alliances with other groups within, and connected with, these changing and dissenting spheres: groups who share interests in reconstructing the moral, just and compassionate spaces of society, rather than bowing to competitive interests as inevitable. This may mean alliances with other familiar institutions (trades unions, cooperatives) and across diverse parts of the VS but may also call for engagement with wider social movements, such as around the use of urban and community spaces, health campaigns and environmental developments. It also means a willingness to problematise consent and rethink alternatives in services and voluntary action. Pragmatically, it may mean adaption and accommodation alongside resistance but will almost certainly require VSOs to become less compliant and more actively engage participants in their futures. In VS history, this is quite familiar territory.

Hard times?

This book has considered the effects of changing policy, politics and inter-organisational relationships from the perspectives of VSOs. It has been framed within a number of debates around structural and cultural changes and the exercise of hegemonic power. These changes have been discussed elsewhere at macro levels but less often, as in preceding chapters, applied to understanding the experiences of everyday actors and organisations. Over some 30 years, VSOs have experienced far-reaching changes in their roles, increasingly being drawn into state projects. However, the current transformation of conditions for VSOs and related hardships are unprecedented, especially following some 20 years of growth and community-based initiative funding. The long period of sustained investment and political support for the VS has ended and harder times – reduced income and significantly increased demand on services – have generated casualties, with services and projects in areas of high deprivation being particularly hard hit (*Community Matters*, 2011). Far from benefiting from elements in the Big Society agenda where it has considerable expertise, Slocock's (2012, p 8) audit after two years' of the coalition government shows the VS weakened by a 'major funding gap' – a £3.3 billion reduction in statutory funding to the sector, which cannot realistically be recouped through philanthropic donations or social enterprise.

The impact of these cuts on many projects serves to weaken resistance to the external determination of activities, and reduce the will and enthusiasm to develop the community activities or voluntary services needed. Recent research also confirms that poorer areas and the most disadvantaged communities are faring worst from the effects of recession (Hastings et al, 2012). In such areas, services are in a downward spiral with VSOs reporting significant reductions to incomes even before 2012 budget cuts were implemented and small VSOs often being disproportionately affected by cuts (*Community Matters*, 2011). Among youth projects, for example, cuts of some 75% to VS income were reported across several local government areas (Williams, 2011). Larger VSOs have also suffered, and despite entrepreneurial efforts and growth, have been widely excluded from new contracts, jeopardising their futures and the services they deliver.

A government survey of charities and social enterprises (Cabinet Office, 2010a) highlighted VSOs working with particularly vulnerable user groups as the most reliant on public funding and therefore the most likely to be damaged by losses. As cuts in 2012 take effect and the state distances itself from welfare responsibility, the historical accounts in this book prompt reflections on whether social welfare arrangements are starting to mirror conditions of earlier centuries: with distinctions between the 'deserving' and 'undeserving' poor (Titmuss, 1974); areas increasingly differentiated by unequal resources; and welfare needs dependent on individual and piecemeal philanthropic efforts. The US approach, where there is greater differentiation between state welfare, private services and charity organisations, and more widespread philanthropy (Morris, 2009), may well signal future UK patterns as welfare reforms play out. However, as indicated above, the evidence from the US is that this has produced shortcomings in services and significant inequities in access and distribution.

Whatever outcomes were intended from recent policy changes, reflecting on the landscape left behind is critical for reconstructing ideas and responses. The effects on VSOs have not simply been consequences of austerity measures: loss of funding and growing demands both from vulnerable service users and from rationing other public provision and facilities, although these have had a significant impact. The withdrawal of political support has also signalled a public devaluing of practice that user groups and community stakeholders have recognised as effective and locally responsive service provision and community projects – practice to which VSOs have contributed for several decades.

Basing community work on a few hundred, short-term community organisers and ad-hoc voluntary action, at a time when complex needs are multiplying, is hardly an adequate welfare strategy; nor is replacing longstanding, professionally organised public facilities, such as libraries, with loosely conceived groups of amateur and self-help associations. These may be populist strategies and appeal to some as casting off the negative aura of state dependency but they are inadequate to compensate for shortcomings as parts of core public services are privatised. The Big Society rhetoric recommends local action to address the problems of a purportedly broken and overly welfare-dependent society. However, as preceding discussion highlights, achieving significant social improvements without a clear infrastructure and the resources previously located with public agencies and community-based VSOs could generate chaotic and socially unjust outcomes, if locally accountable public bodies have no role in brokering decisions (Ishkanian and Szreter, 2012). Ball (1990) has highlighted the irrationality of policy making in complex societies such as Britain, and therefore safeguarding social institutions against the flawed or damaging outcomes wrought by unpredictable social policy experiments is vital in protecting fragile developments and less privileged groups in society.

The combined withdrawal of political support and dismantling of many welfare projects underline the challenges facing VSOs and the effort and skills that may be needed to survive in this new landscape, which are certainly beyond the scope of support offered in the shape of web-based toolkits. With a decline in infrastructure bodies providing support and advice, there is limited help for VSOs through these turbulent times. Earlier chapters examined unrealistic demands placed on small under-resourced VSOs, and conditions have since worsened. It is disturbing if organisations that represent an important welfare safety-net fail to survive because of unmanageable expectations and valuable alternatives addressing intractable welfare problems are allowed to disappear. Such VSOs represent a significant loss to locally based experience, damaging and fragmenting the ecology of community support networks.

Different opportunities?

Survival stories from Chapter Seven offer insights into ways that VSOs can foster different opportunities despite the pessimistic outlook outlined above. Making sense of recent changes helps to retain clarity and awareness of VSOs' goals and strengths, and of ways that they can feasibly adapt or develop. This may entail both resistance and accommodation: resisting coercion and automatic compliance; and accommodating changes in ways that make sense of survival needs within their ethos and purposes. As Chapter Seven argued, strong communities of practice and clarity about organisational goals will help individual VSOs to survive. There is also a collective level at which analysis and sense making across the VS is important in constructing a stronger narrative for the present: a narrative that takes account of VS diversity and the fragmentation following the coalition government's new map for VSOs.

Many examples in preceding chapters have concerned ways that VSOs have been subject to more powerful agency cultures, which have constrained their activities. The prospect of local empowerment and greater legitimacy gained by locally designed projects, cooperative and mutual provision of services, is therefore to be welcomed; and there are significant advantages in decoupling from state funding. In particular, shedding the ties of government funding regimes and their excessive regulation and monitoring restores considerable autonomy and offers the chance to develop more creatively, free of constraining performance targets. Hope lies in this reassertion of independence, and there is already some indication that VSOs have engaged positively in local community planning.

VSOs are in a strong position to contribute to Big Society and localism projects, to help construct a clearer direction among nebulous strategies for community empowerment and social action, but if this is to become a positive reality, the government needs to acknowledge some of the current barriers and ambiguities. Policy makers need to develop a better understanding of the diverse strengths that VSOs can contribute and construct a more evenly shared onus for change, rather than simply expecting VSOs to adapt. This requires redressing the deficit model of the VS implicit in recent policies and the prominence given to enterprise; and demands greater recognition of voluntary effort and community-based activities that have underpinned neighbourhood action over time.

A closer understanding of the complex ways in which the VS can and does contribute to society also needs to be coupled with investment in frontline and community-based activities, which require VS infrastructure and not attrition. For all the negative undercurrents this book has highlighted around closer government–VS relationships, there is currently little shared understanding around Big Society; and there is a need for local governments and VSOs to work jointly to underpin (without controlling) developments. VS expertise in poor areas and VSOs' contribution to services for vulnerable groups in society need political recognition and support; and, similarly, any progressive view of social justice has to address the inequities emerging as resources are lost and facilities in an area become more reliant on ad-hoc, voluntary provision. If we are not to condone these growing, area-based and social inequalities, then poorer areas need prioritisation in community interventions and the current bias evident in service commissioning processes, discounting service experience and social values, has to be redressed. Otherwise, we are effectively discounting local VS knowledge and expertise built up over several decades and declaring that only costs and financial reputation matter, belying the ideas embedded in local empowerment.

There are, of course, tensions in the aims of community empowerment and social action, highlighted in earlier chapters, such as in contradictions between service delivery and advocacy roles being both *in and against* the state. As community-based groups assess their futures, they may well question how the state has conceived their role, and its shaping of wider political and social arrangements that impinge on their lives. Chapter Eight considered VSOs working with different community groups to share skills that would enable stronger participation and self-advocacy. If diverse groups exercise greater power over their circumstances, this inevitably provokes questions about perceived injustices, challenging the basis for state-led changes, including the loss of services and facilities. While democratic and participatory action may operate through use of insider tactics, if the space for democratic lobby and action becomes more restricted, as Chapter Eight argued, social action is likely to emerge in different forms of protest: challenges against the state and corporate interests.

While different kinds of VSOs need to reconstruct their own narratives, progressive change has to encompass alliances with others that share interests in social change towards the public good and a fairer society than is currently emerging. This means that defining sector identity and strengthening bonds within the VS may no longer be as significant as building other bridges, not least since sector-based identities have been divisive, as well as cohesive. The common political and campaigning interests that VSOs share locally with public sector workers and trades unions, such as in not finding themselves bound into a 'new ... technocracy managed by a handful of private ... companies' (Murray, 2012, p 60), may be important parts of building new identities within and across sectors.

The ways in which competition has eroded cooperation and learning from others in inter-organisational transactions are visible in examples from earlier chapters, with both personal and inter-organisational consequences in the erosion of trust relationships. In analysing the corrosive and individualising nature of recent capitalism, Sennett (2012) argues that working and living with differences in society, and building cooperation with others, are pressing issues. If we are to solve some of the challenging problems emerging from poverty, austerity and cultural divides, the emphasis has to shift away from discourses of winning and losing, of simply maximising material resources and seeking competitive advantage. As Chapter Five argued, this means reassessing the value of trust-based relationships, in which care about effective services; the values of providers; sharing meaningful communication about service problems; and achieving goals of social equity and cohesion, can be more prominent. In the current economic and political environment, competition and conflict over resources cannot feasibly be removed from state–VS–business relationships but the unpredictable and unjust outcomes generated through the dominance of these competitive regimes need wider recognition. The consequences of restoring trust are significant for developing user-led services and for any renewed emphasis on wider social participation.

Surviving into the future?

This chapter has highlighted a future in hard times. It would be difficult for readers not to share at least some of the frustrations, which participants from many VSOs in my studies have reported. Through these studies I became increasingly aware of how systemic organisational cultures, national policies and different local government practices have combined to generate often damaging pressures for change on small community-based VSOs, jeopardising organisational survival and flexible activities for service users and undermining voluntary efforts. While cases, circumstances, organisations and actors differ, my conclusions overall that recent policy and organisational changes have generated a particularly precarious environment for small VSOs are hard to contradict.

History demonstrates that a longstanding VS in the UK has survived diverse and adverse conditions. VSOs have multiplied, been eroded, endured and adapted, interacting with diverse political, policy and organisational arrangements. The perceived failures of both the state and market at different times have sustained the case for the VS's continued inclusion in an increasingly mixed economy of UK welfare over the last 30 years, a trend also reflected in other European countries, where growing budgetary pressures have promoted growing interest in voluntary activity and the social economy. Flexibility, adaptability and a range of perceived strengths, in particular expertise in reaching and engaging marginalised groups who often mistrust both state and private providers, have, until recently, secured the VS's continued presence.

The prognosis for VSOs that have historically survived many earlier crises should be good. However, the rate of casualties is growing and the costs in human effort for VSOs and those they work with are increasing, with high turnover of trustees, managers and volunteers. Multiple dilemmas beleaguer VSOs daily, in particular around the conditions and politics of survival. Is it better to survive and continue services, even if it means substituting volunteers for hitherto paid work? How far are compromises acceptable and workable without conceding independent purposes and ways that VSO actors find meanings in their activities?

This book has to close but its stories continue, and players are reappraising their moves as the rules of the game shift. For a state intent on modernising and diversifying services, ostensibly to improve their effectiveness, stripping resources and disempowering the agencies struggling with growing social problems at the front line are strange ways to treat rhetorically valued providers. The limited respect displayed is even more perverse given the role ascribed to VSOs and community groups in community engagement and local developments. When some of the VSOs illustrated in preceding chapters are among a handful of VSOs in poor areas to have succeeded in reaching and engaging some of the hardest-to-reach groups in society, what value can be gained, beyond a short-term budget fix, from making it harder for them to survive at the margins of our welfare institutions?

Risks are clearly increasing and VS resilience depends on creating a much stronger narrative and broader alliances of interest for present times. This is likely to involve challenging the apparently depoliticised 'civilising' roles that the sector has been ascribed by recent governments, and reasserting contested spaces. It remains to be seen whether freedom from the strings attached to state resources will allow different opportunities despite the harsh new stage-set, and whether unfunded Cinderella services can meet the requirements of the new court in providing welfare safety-nets and creative community action, without the help of a fairy godmother. It is to be hoped that any sequel to this book will celebrate VS survival and innovation and will not become an elegy for better times and things past, as the VS, in the form that we currently know and value it, becomes needlessly eroded.

References

6, P. (1991) *Defining the voluntary and non-profit sectors*, London: National Council for Voluntary Organisations.

6, P. and Kendall, J. (1997) *The contract culture in public services: Studies from Britain, Europe and the USA*, Aldershot: Arena.

Abbott, A. (1995) 'Things of boundaries', *Social Research*, vol 62, no 4, pp 857-83.

Acheson, N. (2010) 'Welfare state reform, compacts and restructuring relations between the state and the voluntary sector: reflections on Northern Ireland's experience', *Voluntary Sector Review*, vol 1, no 2, pp 175-92.

Adger, W. (2000) 'Social and ecological resilience: are they related?', *Progress in Human Geography*, vol 24, no 3, pp 347-64.

Aiken, M. (2010) 'Taking the long view: conceptualising the challenges facing UK third sector organizations in the social welfare field', in A. Evers and A. Zimmer (eds) *Third sector organizations in turbulent times: Sports, cultural and social services in five European countries*, Baden Baden: Nomos, pp 295-315.

Alcock, P. (2005) '"Maximum feasible understanding": lessons from previous wars against poverty', *Social Policy and Society*, vol 4, no 3, pp 321-9.

Alcock, P. (2010a) 'A strategic unity: defining the third sector in the UK', *Voluntary Sector Review*, vol 1, no 1, pp 5-24.

Alcock, P. (2010b) 'Building the Big Society: A New Policy Environment for the Third Sector in England', *Voluntary Sector Review*, vol 1, no 3, pp 379-389.

Alcock, P. and Kendall, J. (2011) 'Constituting the third sector: processes of decontestation and contention under the UK Labour government in England', *Voluntas*, vol 22, no 3, pp 450-69.

Andalo, D. (2010) 'Challenges *facing voluntary organisations*', *Society Guardian*, 7 April, p 7.

Andersson, F. (2011) 'Organisational capacity and entrepreneurial behaviour in nonprofit organisations: an empirical exploration', *Voluntary Sector Review*, vol 2, no 1, pp 43-56.

Anheier, H. and Kendall, J. (2002) *Third sector policy at the crossroads*, London: Routledge.

Argyris, C. (1999) *On organizational learning*, Oxford: Blackwell.

Armistead, N. (1974) *Reconstructing social psychology*, Harmondsworth: Penguin.

Audit Commission. (2007) *Hearts and minds: Commissioning from the voluntary sector*, London: Audit Commission.

Bachmann, R. (2001) 'Trust, power and control in trans-organizational relations', *Organization Studies*, vol 22, no 2, pp 337-65.

Back, L. (2004) 'Writing in and against time', in M. Bulmer and J. Solomos (eds), London: Routledge, pp 203-13.

Backus, P. and Clifford, D. (2010) *Are big charities becoming increasingly dominant?*, Paper 38, Birmingham: Third Sector Research Centre, University of Birmingham, www.tsrc.ac.uk/Research/QuantitativeAnalysis/Arebigcharitiesbecomingincreasinglydominant/tabid/679/Default.aspx

Bailey, N. (2012) 'Work programme contract is putting providers out of business', *The Guardian*, 14 January, p 9.

Baines, S., Hardill, I. and Wilson, R. (2011) 'Introduction: remixing the economy of welfare? Changing roles and relationships between the state and the voluntary and community sector', *Social Policy and Society*, vol 10, no 3, pp 337-9.

Baker, L., Cairns, B., Harris, J., Hutchinson, R. and Moran, R. (2010) *Thinking about merger*, London: Institute for Voluntary Action Research.

Baker, L., Garforth, H., Aiken, M. and Heady, L. (2011) *Assessing the impact of multi-purpose research community organisations*, London: Institute for Voluntary Action Research with new Philanthropy Capital.

Ball, S. (1990) *Politics and policy making in education: Explorations in policy sociology*, London: Routledge.

Ball, S. (1997) 'Policy sociology and critical social research: a personal review of recent education policy and policy research', *British Educational Research Journal*, vol 23, no 3, pp 257-74.

Baring Foundation (2012) *Protecting independence: The voluntary sector in 2012*, London: Baring Foundation and Civil Exchange.

Barnes, M. and Morris, K. (2008) 'Strategies for the prevention of social exclusion: an analysis of the Children's Fund', *Journal of Social Policy*, vol 37, no 2, pp 251-70.

Barnes, M. and Prior, D. (2009) *Subversive citizens: Power, agency and resistance in public services*, Bristol: Policy Press.

Barnes, M., Gell, C. and Thomas, P. (2010) 'Participation and social justice', *Social Policy Review*, vol 22, part 3, pp 253-74.

Barnes, M., Newman, J. and Sullivan, H. (2007) *Power, participation and political renewal*, Bristol: Policy Press.

Bass, G. (2007) *Seen but not heard: Strengthening non-profit advocacy*, Washington, DC: Aspen Institute.

bassac (2009) *The past, the passion and the potential for change*, London: bassac.

BBC (British Broadcasting Corporation) (2012) *A4e: Department for Work and Pensions probes fraud claims*, BBC News Online, 9 March, www.bbc.co.uk/news/uk-17310557

Beck, U. (1992) *Risk society: Towards a new modernity*, London: Sage Publications.

Benjamin, A. (2011) 'Work programme is a wasted opportunity for charities: fallout from the government's Work Programme', *Guardian Society*, 22 June, p 1.

Bennett, H. (2011) 'Exploring social and market legitimacy in the UK welfare to work industry: a case study of a third sector provider', paper presented to the 7th International Critical Management Studies Conference, Naples, 11-13 July.

Bennett, R. (2008) 'Marketing voluntary organizations as contract providers of national and local government welfare services in the UK', *Voluntas,* vol 19, no 3, pp 268-295.

Benson, A. (2010) 'Hackney Advice Forum: taking back the power', *Voluntary Sector Review*, vol 1, no 2, pp 233-8.

Berger, P. and Luckmann, T. (1971) *The social construction of reality*, Harmondsworth: Penguin.

Berry, J. and Arons, D. (2003) *A voice for non-profits*, Washington, DC: Brookings Press.

Beveridge, W. (1948) *Voluntary action*, London: George Allen & Unwin.

Billis, D. (1989) *The theory of the voluntary sector: Implications for policy and practice*, London: London School of Economics and Political Science.

Billis, D. (2010) *Hybrid organizations and the third sector*, London: Palgrave Macmillan.

Billis, D. and Glennerster, H. (1998) 'Human services and the voluntary sector: towards a theory of comparative advantage', *Journal of Social Policy*, vol 27, no 1, pp 79-98.

Billis, D. and Harris, M. (1996) *Voluntary agencies*, Basingstoke: Macmillan.

Blackmore, A. (2006) *How voluntary and community organisations can help transform public services*, London: National Council for Voluntary Organisations.

Blau, J. (2011) 'Book review: understanding theories and concepts in social policy', *Journal of Social Policy*, vol 40, no 3, pp 632-3.

Blond, P. (2010) *Red Tory*, London: Faber and Faber.

Bode, I. (2006) 'Disorganised welfare mixes: voluntary agencies and new governance regimes in Western Europe', *Journal of European Social Policy*, vol 16, no 4, pp 346-59.

Boffey, D., Holm, T. and Hughes, S. (2012) 'Welfare boss Emma Harrison made a pile renting out her stately home to A4e', *Guardian/Observer*, 25 February, www.guardian.co.uk/politics/2012/feb/25/a4e-welfare-emma-harrison-properties

Booth, C. (1892) *Life and labour of people in London*, London: Macmillan.

Boris, E. (2006) 'Nonprofit organizations in a democracy: varied roles and responsibilities', in E. Boris and C. Steuerle (eds) *Nonprofits and government: Collaboration and conflict*, Washington, DC: Urban Institute Press, pp 1–36.

Bourdieu, P. (1977) *Outline of a Theory of Practice*, Cambridge: Cambridge University Press.

Bourdieu, P. (1992) *The logic of practice*, Cambridge: Polity Press.

Bourdieu, P. (1999) *The weight of the world: Social suffering in contemporary society*, Cambridge: Polity Press.

Boyne, G. (1998) 'Competitive tendering in local government: a review of theory and evidence', *Public Administration*, vol 76, no 4, pp 695–712.

Brandsen, T., van de Donka, W. and Puttersa, K. (2005) 'Griffins or chameleons? Hybridity as a permanent and inevitable characteristic of the third sector', *International Journal of Public Administration*, vol 58, no 9, pp 749–65.

Breeze, B. (2010) *How donors choose charities*, London: Alliance Publishing Trust.

Brent, J. (2004) 'The desire for community: illusion, confusion and paradox', *Community Development Journal*, vol 39, no 3, pp 213–23.

Brent, J. (2009) *Searching for community: Representation, power and action on an urban estate*, Bristol: Policy Press.

Brenton, M. (1985) *The voluntary sector in British social services*, Harlow: Longman.

Brown, P. (1997) 'Cultural capital and social exclusion: some observations on recent trends in education, employment and the labour market', in A. Halsey, H. Lauder, P. Brown and A.S. Wells (eds) *Education, culture, economy and society*, Oxford: Oxford University Press.

Brown, P. and Calnan, M. (2010) 'The risks of managing uncertainty: the limitations of governance and choice, and the potential for trust', *Social Policy and Society*, vol 9, no 1, pp 13–24.

Bryman, A. (2001) *Social research methods*, Oxford: Oxford University Press.

Buckingham, H. (2009) 'Competition and contracts in the voluntary sector: exploring the implications for homelessness service providers in Southampton', *Policy & Politics*, vol 37, no 2, pp 235–54.

Buckingham, H. (2011) 'Hybridity, diversity and the division of labour in the third sector: what can we learn from homelessness organisations in the UK?', *Voluntary Sector Review*, vol 2, no 2, pp 157-75.

Bunge, M. (1996) *Finding philosophy in social science*, New Haven, CT: Yale University Press.

Burnley, C., Matthews, C. and McKenzie, S. (2005) 'Devolution of services to children and families: the experience of NPOs in Nanaimo, BC, Canada', *Voluntas*, vol 16, no 1, pp 69-87.

Butcher, H., Banks, S., Henderson, P. and Robertson, J. (2007) *Critical community practice*, Bristol: Policy Press.

Butcher, T. (1995) *Delivering welfare services*, Buckingham: Open University Press.

Butler, P. (2011) 'There is little charity in the work programme', *Society Guardian*, 11 October, www.guardian.co.uk/society/joepublic/2011/oct/11/work-programme-charities-losing-out?INTCMP=SRCH

Cabinet Office (2007) *Governance of Britain*, London: The Stationery Office.

Cabinet Office (2009) *Real help for communities: Volunteers, charities and social enterprises*, London: Cabinet Office.

Cabinet Office (2010a) *National Survey of Charities and Social Enterprises*, London: Cabinet Office.

Cabinet Office (2010b) *Building the Big Society*, London: Cabinet Office.

Cabinet Office (2010c) *The coalition: Our programme for government*, London: Cabinet Office.

Cabinet Office (2011) *Open public services White Paper*, London: The Stationery Office.

Cairns, B. (2009) 'The independence of the voluntary sector from government in England', in M. Smerdon (ed) *The first principle of voluntary action: Essays on the independence of the voluntary sector from government*, London: Baring Foundation, pp 35-50.

Cairns, B., Harris, M. and Hutchinson, R. (2006) 'Servants of the Community or Agents of Government? The Role of Community-Based Organisations and Their Contribution to Public Services Delivery and Civil Renewal', London: Institute of Voluntary Action Research.

Cairns, B., Harris, M. and Hutchison, R. (2007) 'Sharing God's love or meeting government goals? Local churches and public policy implementation', *Policy & Politics*, vol 25, no 3, pp 413-32.

Cairns, B., Hutchinson, R. and Aiken, M. (2010a) '"It's not what we do, it's how we do it": managing the tension between service delivery and advocacy', *Voluntary Sector Review*, vol 1, no 2, pp 193-208.

Cairns, B., M. Harris and R. Hutchison (2010b) *Collaboration in the voluntary sector: a meta-analysis*, London: Institute of Voluntary Action Research, June 2010.

Cameron, D. (2010) 'From central power to people power', speech, 22 February.

Campbell, D. (2008) 'Getting to yes ... or no: non-profit decision making and interorganisational restructuring', *Nonprofit Management and Leadership*, vol 19, no 2, pp 221-41.

Carmel, E. and Harlock, J. (2008) 'Instituting the "third sector" as a governable terrain: partnership, procurement and performance in the UK', *Policy & Politics*, vol 36, no 2, pp 155-71.

Carnegie Trust (2010) *Making good society*, London: Carnegie Trust.

Carr, H. (2009) 'Tracking the impact of the economic downturn: a view from the Charity Commission', paper presented to the VSSN/NCVO 'Research in the Voluntary Sector' conference, 7-8 September, Warwick University, www.ncvo-vol.org.uk/uploadedFiles/NCVO/What_we_do/Research/Research_Events/Carr_Brennan.pdf

Casey, J., Dalton, B., Melville, R. and Onyx, J. (2010) 'Strengthening government-non-profit relations: international experiences with compacts', *Voluntary Sector Review*, vol 1, no 1, pp 59-76.

Challis, L., Fuller, S., Henwood, M., Klein, R., Plowden, W., Webb, A., Whittingham, P. and Wistow, G. (1988) *Joint approaches to social policy*, Cambridge: Cambridge University Press.

Chambers, R. (1997) *Whose reality counts? Putting the first last*, London: Intermediate Technology Publications.

Charmaz, K. (2000) 'Grounded theory: objectivist and constructivist methods', in N. Denzin and Y. Lincoln (eds) *Handbook of qualitative research*, Thousand Oaks, CA: Sage Publications.

Chaves, M., Stephens, L. and Galaskiewicz, J. (2004) 'Does government funding suppress nonprofits' political activity?', *American Sociological Review*, vol 69, no 2, pp 292-316.

Christians, C. (2000) 'Ethics and politics in qualitative research', in N. Denzin and Y. Lincoln (eds) *Handbook of qualitative research*, Thousand Oaks, CA: Sage Publications.

Ciborra, C. (2002) *Information labyrinths: Limits to the wisdom of systems*, Oxford: Oxford University Press.

Clarke, J. and Newman, J. (1997) *The managerial state*, London: Sage Publications.

Clarke, J., Gewirtz, S. and McLaughlin, E. (2000a) 'New Managerialism New Welfare?' London: Sage Publications.

Clarke, J., Gewirtz, S. and McLaughlin, E. (2000b) 'Reinventing the welfare state', in J. Clarke, S. Gewirtz and E. McLaughlin (eds) *New managerialism, new welfare?*, London: Sage Publications, pp 1-26.

Clegg, S. (1989) *Frameworks of power*, London: Sage Publications.

Clegg, S.R., Kornberger, M. and Rhodes, C. (2005) 'Learning/becoming/organizing', *Organization*, vol 12, no 2, pp 147-67.

Clifford, D. (2011) 'Voluntary sector organisations working at the neighbourhood level in England: patterns by local area deprivation', *Third Sector Research Centre*, Working Paper 65, Birmingham: Third Sector Research Centre, University of Birmingham.

Cochrane, A. (2000) 'Local government: managerialism and modernization', in J. Clarke, S. Gewirtz and E. McLaughlin (eds) *New managerialism, new welfare?*, London: Sage Publications, pp 122-36.

Colley, H., Boetzelen, P., Hoskins, B. and Parveva, T. (2007) *Social inclusion for young people: Breaking down the barriers*, Strasbourg: Council of Europe Publishing.

Community Matters (2011) *Community Matters members' survey*, London: Community Matters.

Compact Voice (2009) *They are the champions: the role and impact of local compact champions*, London: Compact Voice and Commissioner for the Compact, July 2009.

Cooper, A. (2001) 'The state of mind we're in: social anxiety, governance and the audit society', *Psychoanalytic Studies*, vol 3, nos 3-4, pp 349-63.

Coote, A. (2011) 'Big Society and the new austerity', in M. Stott (ed) *The Big Society challenge*, Cardiff: Keystone Development Trust, pp 82-94.

Coutu, D. (2002) 'How resilience works', *Harvard Business Review*, vol 80, no 5, pp 46-55.

Craig, G., Taylor, M., Carlton, N. Garbitt, R., Kimberlee, R., Lepine, E. and Syed, A. (2005) *The paradox of compacts: Monitoring the impacts*, Report 02/05, London: Home Office.

Crawley, J. and Watkin, R. (2011) *Crisis and contradiction*, Bath: South West Foundation, www.the-foundation.org.uk/Megs%20Documents/crisis%20and%20contradiction%20Final2.pdf

CSSAS (Campaign for State Supported Alternative Schools) (1978) *Campaign for State Supported Alternative Schools*, bulletin first issued in 1978, continued as CSSAS until 1982.

Cummings, G. (2008) 'French NGOs in the global era: professionalization "without borders"?', *Voluntas*, vol 19, pp 372-94.

Cunningham, I. and James, P. (2009) 'The outsourcing of social care in Britain: what does it mean for voluntary sector workers?', *Work, Employment & Society*, vol 23, no 2, pp 363-75.

Cushman, M. and McLean, R. (2008) 'Exclusion, inclusion and changing the face of information systems research', *Information Technology & People*, vol 21, no 3, pp 213-21.

Dalrymple, J. (2004) 'Developing the concept of professional advocacy: an examination of the role of child and youth advocates in England and Wales', *Journal of Social Work*, vol 4, no 2, pp 179-97.

Danson, M. and Whittam, G. (2011) 'Scotland's civic society v. England's Big Society? Diverging roles of the VCS in public service delivery', *Social Policy and Society*, vol 10, no 3, pp 353-64.

Davies, J.S. (2011) *Challenging governance theory: From networks to hegemony*, Bristol: Policy Press.

Davis Smith, J. (1995) 'The voluntary tradition: philanthropy and self-help in Britain 1500-1945', in J. Davis Smith, C. Rochester and R. Hedley (eds) *An introduction to the voluntary sector*, London: Routledge.

Davis Smith, J., Rochester, C. and Hedley, R. (1995) *An introduction to the voluntary sector*, London: Routledge.

DCLG (Department for Communities and Local Government) (2006a) *Supporting effective citizenship at local authority level: Background research for good practice guidelines, 'Promoting Effective citizenship and community empowerment'*, Cardiff: DCLG, www.communities.gov.uk/index. asp?id

DCLG (2006b) *Strong and prosperous communities*, London: DCLG.

DCLG (2009) *Strengthening local democracy: Consultation*, London: DCLG, www.communities.gov.uk/publications/localgovernment/ localdemocracyconsultation

DCSF (Department for Children, Schools and Families) (2008) *Aiming High for Young People: A ten year strategy for positive activities (implementation plan)*, London: DCSF.

De Filippis, J., Fisher, R. and Shragge, E. (2009) 'What's left in the community? Oppositional politics in contemporary practice', *Community Development Journal*, vol 44, no 1, pp 38-52.

de Man, A.P. and Roijakkers, N. (2009) 'Alliance governance: balancing control and trust in dealing with risk', *Long Range Planning*, vol 42, no 1, pp 75-95.

Deakin, N. (1994) *The politics of welfare: Continuities and change*, Hemel Hempstead: Harvester Wheatsheaf.

Deakin, N. (1996) *Deakin Commission on the Future of the Voluntary Sector, Meeting the Challenge of Change: Voluntary Action in the 21st Century*, London: National Council for Voluntary Organisations with Esmee Fairbarin and Joseph Rowntree.

Deakin, N. (2001) 'Public policy, social policy and voluntary organisations', in M. Harris and C. Rochester (eds) *Voluntary organisations and social policy in Britain*, Basingstoke: Palgrave, pp 21-36.

Denzin, N. and Lincoln, Y. (2000) 'The discipline and practice of qualitative research', in N. Denzin and Y. Lincoln (eds) *Handbook of qualitative research*, Thousand Oaks, CA: Sage Publications.

DETR (Department of the Environment, Transport and the Regions) (1999) *Modernising Local Government: Guidance for the Local Government Act 1999, Best Value,* Circular 10/99, London: DETR.

DETR (2000) *Ward level indices of deprivation*, London: DETR.

DfES (Department for Education and Skills) (2004) *Working with the voluntary and community sector in learning and skills: Developing a strategic approach*, London: DfES.

DfES (2006) *Youth matters: Next steps*, Nottingham: DfES.

DfES (2007) *Aiming High for Young People: A ten year strategy for positive activities*, London: DfES and HM Treasury.

DiMaggio, P. and Powell, W. (1983) 'The Iron Cage revisited: institutional isomorphism and collective rationality in organisational fields', *American Sociological Review*, vol 48, pp 147-60.

DiMaggio, P. and Powell, M. (1991) *The new institutionalism in organizational analysis*, Chicago, IL: University of Chicago Press.

Donaldson, L. (2007) 'Advocacy by nonprofit human service agencies', *Journal of Community Practice*, vol 15, no 3, pp 139-58.

DSS (Department of Social Security) (1998) *New ambitions for our country: A new contract for welfare*, London: DSS.

DWP (Department for Work and Pensions) (2010) *Framework for the provision of employment related support services: Specification for the commercial requirement*, London: DWP.

DWP (2011) *Massive boost for the Big Society as almost 300 voluntary sector organisations named as part of the Work Programme*, London: DWP, www.dwp.gov.uk/newsroom/press-releases/2011/apr-2011/dwp037-11.shtml

Edwards, A. (2007) 'Working collaboratively to build resilience: a CHAT approach', *Social Policy and Society*, vol 6, no 2, pp 255-64.

Eikenberry, A. (2009) 'Refusing the market: a democratic discourse for voluntary and non-profit organisations', *Nonprofit and Voluntary Sector Quarterly*, vol 38, no 4, pp 582-96.

Ellis, J. (2009) *Monitoring and evaluation in the third sector: Meeting accountability and learning needs*, London: Charities Evaluation Services.

Ellison, N. (2011) 'The Conservative Party and the "Big Society"', in C. Holden, M. Kilkey and G. Ramia (eds) *Social policy review 23*, Bristol: Policy Press, pp 45-62.

Ellison, N. and Ellison, S. (2006) 'Creating "opportunity for all?" New Labour, new localism and the opportunity society', *Social Policy and Society*, vol 5, no 3, pp 337-48.

Etzioni, A. (1995) *Rights and the common good: The communitarian perspective*, New York, NY: St Martin's Press.

Evers, A. (2010) 'Observations on incivility: blind spots in third sector research and policy', *Voluntary Sector Review*, vol 1, no 1, pp 113-18.

Evers, A. and Laville, J.-L. (eds) (2004) *The third sector in Europe*, Cheltenham: Edward Elgar.

Evers, A. and Zimmer, A. (2010) *Third sector organizations in turbulent times: Sports, cultural and social services in five European countries*, Baden Baden: Nomos.

Fairbanks, R. (2007) 'The political-economic gradient and the organization of urban space', in R. Cnaan and C. Milofsky (eds) *Handbook of community movements and local organizations*, New York, NY: Springer, pp 102-17.

Fergusson, R. (2000) 'Modernizing managerialism in education', in J. Clarke, S. Gewirtz and E. McLaughlin (eds) *New managerialism new welfare?*, London: Sage Publications, pp 202-21.

Ferlie, E., Pettigrew, A., Ashburner, L. and Pettigrew, A. (1996) *The New Public Management in action*, Oxford: Oxford University Press.

Fine, M., Weis, L., Wesen, S. and Wong, L. (2000) 'For whom? Qualitative research, representations and social responsibilities', in N. Denzin and Y. Lincoln (eds) *Handbook of qualitative research*, Thousand Oaks, CA: Sage Publications.

Finlayson, A. (2003) *Making sense of New Labour*, London: Lawrence and Wishart.

Flick, U. (1998) *An introduction to qualitative research: Theory, method and applications*, London: Sage Publications.

Foucault, M. (1977) 'Truth and power', in C. Gordon (ed) *Power/ knowledge: Selected interviews and other writings 1972-1977*, New York, NY: Pantheon.

Foucault, M. (1988) *Discipline and punish: The birth of the prison*, New York, NY: Vintage.

Frost, N. and Stein, M. (2009) 'Editorial: outcomes of integrated working with children and young people', *Children and Society*, vol 23, no 5, pp 315-19.

Gamarnikow, E. and Green, A. (2000) 'Citizenship, education and social capital', in J. Cairns and R. Gardner (eds) *Education for citizenship*, London: Continuum.

Geddes, M., Newman, I., Root, A., Woods, R. and Thomas, D. (2000) *Mainstream services, best value and social inclusion*, London: Local Government Information Unit with Warwick Business School.

Gewirtz, S., Ball, S. and Bowe, R. (1995) *Markets, choice and equity in education*, Buckingham: Open University Press.

Ghoshal, S. and Moran, P. (1996) 'Bad for practice: a critique of the transaction cost theory', *Academy of Management Review*, vol 21, no 1, pp 13-47.

Giddens, A. (1998) *The Third Way: The renewal of social democracy*, Cambridge: Polity Press.

Giddens A. (1999) *Runaway world: How globalisation is reshaping our lives*, London: Profile.

Gilligan, C. (1983) 'Do the social sciences have an adequate theory of moral development?', in N. Haan, R. Bellah, P. Rabinow and Sullivan, W. (eds) *Social science as moral inquiry*, New York, NY: Columbia University Press.

Giroux, H. (1983) *Theory and resistance in education: A pedagogy for the opposition*, South Hadley, MA: Bergin & Garvey.

Glaister, A. and Glaister, B. (2005) *Inter-agency collaboration: Providing for children*, Edinburgh: Dunedin Academic Press.

Glasby, J. and Dickinson, H. (2008) *Partnership working in health and social care*, Bristol: Policy Press.

Glaser, B. (1992) *Basics of grounded theory analysis: Emergence versus forcing*, Mill Valley, CA: Sociology Press.

Glaser, B. and Strauss, A. (1967) *The discovery of grounded theory: Strategies for qualitative research*, Chicago, IL: Aldine.

Glendenning, C., Powell, M. and Rummery, K. (2002) *Partnerships, New Labour and the governance of welfare*, Bristol: Policy Press.

Glennerster, H. (1995) *British social policy since 1945*, Oxford: Blackwell.

Glennerster, H. (1997) *Paying for welfare: Towards 2000*, Hemel Hempstead: Prentice-Hall/Harvester Wheatsheaf.

Glennerster, H. (2003) *Understanding the finance of welfare*, Bristol: Policy Press.

Goldberg, S. and Griffiths, P. (1977) 'Double talk', *Teaching London Kids*, vol 9, pp 5-6.

Gordon, D., Adelman, L., Ashworth, K., Bradshaw, J., Levitas, R., Middleton, S., Pantazis, C., Patsios, D., Payne, S., Townsend, P. and Williams, J. (2000) *Poverty and social exclusion in Britain*, York: Joseph Rowntree Foundation.

Gramsci, A. (1971) *Selections from the Prison Notebooks of Antonio Gramsci*, edited and translated by Q. Hoare and G. Nowell-Smith, London: Lawrence and Wishart.

Grey, C. and Garsten, C. (2001) 'Trust, control and post-bureaucracy', *Organization Studies*, vol 22, no 2, pp 229-50.

Habermas, J. (1990) *Moral consciousness and communicative action*, Cambridge, MA: MIT Press.

Halfpenny, P. and Reid, M. (2002) 'Research on the voluntary sector: an overview', *Policy & Politics*, vol 30, no 4, pp 533-50.

Hammersley, M. (1992) *What's wrong with ethnography*, London: Routledge.

Hammersley, M. (1998) *Reading Ethnographic Research: A Critical Guide*, Harlow: Longman.

Hardy, C., Phillips, P. and Lawrence, T. (1998) 'Distinguishing trust and power in interorganizational relations: forms and facades of trust', in C. Lane and R. Bachmann (eds) *Trust within and between organizations*, Oxford: Oxford University Press, pp 65-87.

Harries, J., Gordon, P., Plamping, D. and Fischer, M. (1998) *Projectitis*, London: King's Fund.

Harris, B. (2010) 'Voluntary action and the state in historical perspective', *Voluntary Sector Review*, vol 1, no 1, pp 25-40.

Harris, M. (2001a) 'Voluntary organisations in a changing social policy environment', in M. Harris and C. Rochester (eds) *Voluntary organisations and social policy in Britain*, Basingstoke: Palgrave, pp 213-28.

Harris, M. (2001b) 'Boards: just subsidiaries of the state?', in M. Harris and C. Rochester (eds) *Voluntary organisations and social policy in Britain*, Basingstoke: Palgrave, pp 171-84.

Harris, M. (2010) 'Third sector organizations in a contradictory policy environment', in D. Billis (ed) *Hybrid organizations and the third sector*, London: Palgrave Macmillan, pp 25-45.

Harris, M. (2012) 'Nonprofits and business: toward a subfield of nonprofit studies', *Nonprofit and Voluntary Sector Quarterly*, vol 41, no 5, pp 892-902.

Harris, M. and Rochester, C. (2001) *Voluntary organisations and social policy in Britain*, Basingstoke: Palgrave.

Harris, M. and Schlappa, H. (2008) 'Hoovering up the money? Delivering government-funded capacity-building programmes to voluntary and community organisations', *Social Policy and Society*, vol 7, no 2, pp 135-46.

Harris, M. and Young, P. (2010) 'Building bridges: the third sector responding locally to diversity', *Voluntary Sector Review*, vol 1, no 1, pp 41-58.

Harris, M., Rochester, C. and Halfpenny, P. (2001) 'Twenty years of change', in M. Harris and C. Rochester (eds) *Voluntary organisations and social policy in Britain*, Basingstoke: Palgrave, pp 1-20.

Harrison, B. (1987) 'Historical perspectives', in NCVO (National Council for Voluntary Organisations) (ed) *Voluntary organisations and democracy*, London: NCVO.

Harvey, L. (1990) *Critical social research*, London: Allen & Unwin.

Hastings, A., Bramley, G., Bailey, N. and Watkins, D. (2012) *Serving deprived communities in a recession*, York: Joseph Rowntree Foundation.

Higham, J. and Yeomans, D. (2010) 'Working together? Partnership approaches to 14–19 education in England', *British Education Research Journal*, vol 36, no 3, pp 379–402.

Hills, J., Le Grand, J. and Piachaud, D. (2002) *Understanding social exclusion*, Oxford: Oxford University Press.

Hills, J., Le Grand, J. and Piachaud, D. (2007) *Making social policy work*, Bristol: Policy Press.

HM Treasury (2005) *Exploring the role of the third sector in public service delivery and reform: A discussion document*, London: HM Treasury.

HM Treasury (2006) *Improving financial relationships with the third sector: Guidance to funders and purchasers*, London: HM Treasury.

HM Treasury and Cabinet Office (2007) *The future role of the third sector in social and economic regeneration: Final report*, London: Office of the Third Sector.

Hodkinson, P. and Hodkinson, H. (2002) *Case study research: Strengths and limitations*, Learning and Skills Research, LSDA, volumes 5 and 6, Leeds: University of Leeds.

Hofstede, G. (1980) 'Motivation, leadership, and organization – do American theories apply abroad', *Organizational Dynamics*, vol 9, no 1, pp 42–63.

Hogg, E. and Baines, S. (2011) 'Changing responsibilities and roles of the voluntary and community sector in the welfare mix: a review', *Social Policy and Society*, vol 10, no 3, pp 341–52.

Hoggett, P. (2004) 'Overcoming the desire for misunderstanding through dialogue', in S. Snape and P. Taylor (eds) *Partnerships between health and local government*, London: Frank Cass, pp 118–26.

Hoggett, P., Mayo, M. and Miller, C. (2009) *The dilemmas of development work: Ethical challenges in regeneration*, Bristol: Policy Press.

Holloway, J. (2005) *Change the world without taking power* (2nd edition), London: Pluto Press.

Home Office (1998) *Getting it right together: Compact on relations between government and the voluntary and community sector in England*, London: The Stationery Office.

Home Office (2004) *ChangeUp: Capacity building and infrastructure framework for the voluntary and community sector*, London: Active Communities.

Hood, C. (2000) 'Paradoxes of public sector managerialism, old public management and public service bargains', *International Public Management Journal*, vol 3, no 1, pp 1-22.

Hopkins, N. (2012) 'London 2012: the secret security guard', *The Guardian*, 24 July, p 6.

House of Commons Education Committee (2011) *Services for young people*, London: The Stationery Office.

Howard, J. and Taylor, M. (2010) 'Hybridity in partnership working: managing tensions and opportunities', in D. Billis (ed) *Hybrid organizations and the third sector*, London: Palgrave Macmillan.

Hudson, B. (2006) 'User outcomes and children's services reform: ambiguity and conflict in the policy implementation process', *Social Policy and Society*, vol 5, no 2, pp 227-36.

Huxham, C. (1996) *Creating collaborative advantage*, London: Sage Publications.

Huxham, C. and Vangen, S. (2004) *Managing to collaborate*, London: Routledge.

IDeA (Improvement and Development Agency) (2008) *Evaluation of the national programme for third sector commissioning: Baseline report*, London: IDeA.

IDeA (2009) Evaluation of the national programme for third sector commissioning: Final report, London: Shared Intelligence and IDeA.

Ishkanian, A. and Szreter, S. (2012) *The Big Society debate: A new agenda for social welfare?*, Cheltenham: Edward Elgar.

IVAR (Institute for Voluntary Action Research) (2008) *What makes a successful local compact*, Birmingham: IVAR/Commission for the Compact.

IVAR (2011) *Thinking about collaboration*, London: IVAR.

IVAR (2012) *Recession watch: Interim report*, London: IVAR

Jäger, U. and Beyes, T. (2010) 'Strategizing in NPOs: a case study on the practice of organizational change between social mission and economic rationale', *Voluntas*, vol 21, no 1, pp 82-100.

Jenkins, C. (2006) 'Nonprofit organizations and political advocacy', in W. Powell (ed) *The nonprofit sector: A research handbook*, New Haven, CT: Yale Univeristy Press, pp 307-32.

Jones, K., Brown, J. and Bradshaw, J. (1983) *Issues in social policy*, London: Routledge & Kegan Paul.

Kane, D. and Allen, J. (2011) *Counting the cuts: The impact of spending cuts on the UK voluntary and community sector*, London: National Council for Voluntary and Community Organisations.

Kendall, J. (2000) 'The mainstreaming of the third sector into public policy in England in the late 1990s: whys and wherefores', *Policy & Politics*, vol 28, no 4, pp 541-62.

Kendall, J. (2003) *The voluntary sector: Comparative perspectives in the UK*, London: Routledge.

Kendall, J. (2010) 'Bringing the ideology back in: the erosion of political innocence in English third sector policy', *Journal of Political Ideologies*, vol 15, no 3, pp 241-58.

Kendall, J. and Knapp, M. (1994) 'Government and the voluntary sector in the United Kingdom', in S. Saxon-Harold and J. Kendall (eds) *Researching the voluntary sector, vol 2*, Tonbridge: Charities Aid Foundation.

Kendall, J. and Knapp, M. (1995) 'A loose and baggy monster: boundaries, definitions and typologies', in J.D. Smith, C. Rochester and R. Hedley (eds) *An introduction to the voluntary sector*, London: Routledge.

Kendall, J. and Knapp, M. (1996) *The voluntary sector in the UK*, Manchester: Manchester University Press.

Kendall, J. and Knapp, M. (2001) 'Providers of care for older people: the experience of community care', in M. Harris and C. Rochester (eds) *Voluntary organisations and social policy in Britain*, Basingstoke: Palgrave.

Kimberlee, R. (2001) 'Chasing the money: the common and local problems facing partnerships involved in short-term funded projects for young people in areas of urban deprivation', *International Conference of Multi-Organisational Partnerships and Co-operative Strategy*, Bristol, 12-14 July.

Kimberlee, R. (2002) 'Chasing the money: barriers to partnership working on short-term funded projects', in M. Stewart and D. Purdue (eds) *Understanding collaboration: International perspectives on theory, method and practice*, Bristol: Faculty of the Built Environment, UWE, pp 179-86.

Kincheloe, J. and McLaren, P. (2000) 'Rethinking critical theory and qualitative research', in N. Denzin and Y. Lincoln (eds) *Handbook of qualitative research*, Thousand Oaks, CA: Sage Publications.

Knight, B. (1993) *Voluntary action*, London: Centris.

Kumar, S. (1997) *Accountability in the contract state: The relationship between voluntary organisations, users and local authority purchasers*, York: York Publishing Services.

Lave, J. and Wenger, E. (1991) *Situated learning*, Cambridge: Cambridge University Press.

Le Grand, J. (1998) 'The Third Way Begins with Cora', *New Statesman*, 6 March, p 24.

Le Grand, J. (2003) *Motivation, agency and public policy: Of knights and knaves, pawns and queens*, Oxford: Oxford University Press.

Leat, D. (1995) 'Funding matters', in J. Davis Smith, C. Rochester and R. Hedley (eds) *An introduction to the voluntary sector*, London: Routledge.

Lever, J. (2011) 'Urban regeneration partnerships: a figurational critique of governmentality theory', *Sociology*, vol 45, no 1, pp 86–101.

Lewis, D. (2008) 'Using life histories in social policy research: the case of third sector/public sector boundary crossing', *Journal of Social Policy*, Vol 37, No 4, pp 559–578.

Lewis, D. (2010) 'Encountering hybridity: lessons from individual experiences', in D. Billis (ed) *Hybrid organisations and the third sector*, Basingstoke: Palgrave Macmillan, pp 219–39.

Lewis, J. (1996) 'What does contracting do to voluntary agencies ?', in D. Billis and M. Harris (eds) *Voluntary agencies*, Basingstoke: Macmillan.

Lewis, J. (2005) 'New Labour's approach to the voluntary sector: independence and the meaning of partnership', *Social Policy and Society*, vol 4, no 2, pp 121–31.

Lipsky, M. (1980) *Street-level bureaucracy: The dilemmas of the individual in public services*, New York, NY: Russell Sage Foundation.

Lister, M.R. (2007) 'From object to subject: including marginalised citizens in policy making', *Policy & Politics*, vol 35, no 3, pp 437–55.

Lister, R. (2010) *Understanding theories and concepts in social policy*, Bristol: Policy Press.

Locke, M., Robson, P. and Howlett, S. (2001) 'Users: at the centre or the sidelines?' in M. Harris and C. Rochester (eds) *Voluntary Organisations and Social Policy in Britain*, Basingstoke: Palgrave, pp 213–228.

Locke, M. (2008) *Who gives time now? Patterns of participation in volunteering*, London Institute for Volunteering Research.

Lofland, J. (1996) *Social movement organizations: Guide to research on insurgent realities*, New York, NY: Aldine De Gruyter.

Long, J. (2012) '£46m payout for A4e despite missing Work Programme targets', *Channel 4 news*, social affairs reports, 24 October, www.channel4.com/news/46m-payout-for-a44e-despite-missing-work-programme-targets

Lukes, S. (1974) *Power: A radical view*, London: Macmillan.

Luthar, S., Cichetti, D. and Becker, B. (2000) 'The construct of resilience: a critical evaluation', *Child Development*, vol 71, no 3, pp 543–62.

Mabbott, J. (1993) *Local authority funding for voluntary organisations: Survey report 1993*, London: National Council for Voluntary Organisations.

McAdam, D., Sampson, R., Weffer, S. and McIndoe, H. (2005) '"There will be fighting in the streets": the distorting lens of social movement theory', *Mobilization: An Internal Journal*, vol 10, no 1, pp 17–34.

McCabe, A. and Phillimore, J. (2009) *Exploring below the radar: Issues of theme and focus*, TSRC Working Paper, Birmingham: Third Sector Research Centre, University of Birmingham.

McCall, B. (2011) 'Big Society and the devolution of power', in M. Stott (ed) *The Big Society challenge*, Cardiff: Keystone Development Trust, pp 65-74.

McKnight, D.H., Cummings, L.L and Chervany, N.L. (1998) 'Initial trust formation in new organizational relationships', *Academy of Management Review*, vol 23, no 3, pp 473-90.

Macmillan, R. (2010) *The third sector delivering public services: An evidence review*, TSRC Working Paper 20, Birmingham: Third Sector Research Centre, University of Birmingham, www.tsrc.ac.uk/LinkClick.aspx?fileticket=l9qruXn%2fBN8%3d&tabid=500

Macmillan, R. (2011a) *Seeing things differently? The promise of qualitative longitudinal research on the third sector*, TSRC Working Paper 56, Birmingham: Third Sector Research Centre, University of Birmingham.

Macmillan, R. (2011b) '"Supporting" the voluntary sector in an age of austerity: the UK coalition government's consultation on improving support for frontline civil society organisations in England', *Voluntary Sector Review*, vol 2, no 1, pp 115-24.

Macmillan, R. and McLaren, V. (2012) *Third sector leadership: The power of narrative*, TSRC Working Paper 76, Birmingham: Third Sector Research Centre, University of Birmingham, pp 1-15.

Maguire, M. and Ball, S. (1994) 'Discourses of educational reform in the UK and USA and the work of teachers', *British Journal of In-service Education*, vol 20, no 1, pp 5-16.

Maier, F. and Meyer, M. (2011) 'Managerialism and beyond: discourses of civil society organization and their governance implications', *Voluntas*, vol 22, no 4, pp 731-56.

Marsden, S. (2011) *Pushed to the edge*, London: Locality.

Marsh, D., O'Toole, T. and Jones, S. (2007) *Young people and politics in the UK: Apathy or alienation?*, Basingstoke: Palgrave.

Martikke, S. (2008) *Commissioning: Possible Greater Manchester VCS organisations' experiences in public sector commissioning*, Manchester: Greater Manchester Centre for Voluntary Organisation.

Marwell, N. (2007) *Bargaining for Brooklyn: Community organizations in the entrepreneurial city*, Chicago, IL: Chicago University Press.

Maude, F. (2010) 'Leading your way through a time of change', Speech to Action Planning Conference on 'Leading your charity through a time of change', Westminster, London, June.

Mayer, R.C., Davis, J.H. and Schoorman, F.D. (1995) 'An integrative model of organizational trust', *Academy of Management Review*, vol 20, no 3, pp 709-34.

Mayo, M. (1975) 'Community development: a radical alternative?', in R. Bailey and M. Brake (eds) *Radical social work*, London: Edward Arnold.

Midgley, J. (1995) *Social development*, London: Sage Publications.

Milbourne, L. (2002a) 'Unspoken exclusion: experiences of continued marginalisation from education among "hard to reach" groups of adults and children', *British Journal of Sociology of Education*, vol 23, no 2, pp 287-305.

Milbourne, L. (2002b) 'Life at the margin: education of young people, social policy and the meanings of social exclusion', *International Journal of Inclusive Education*, vol 6, no 4, pp 325-43.

Milbourne, L. (2005) 'Children, families and inter-agency work: experiences of partnership work in primary education settings', *British Education Research Journal*, vol 31, no 6, pp 681-701.

Milbourne, L. (2009a) 'Remodelling the third sector: advancing collaboration or competition in community based initiatives?', *Journal of Social Policy*, vol 38, no 2, pp 277-97.

Milbourne, L. (2009b) 'Valuing difference or securing compliance? Working to involve young people in community settings', *Children and Society*, vol 23, no 5, pp 347–63.

Milbourne, L. (2012) 'Valuing youth in UK policies: instrumental construction or improved spaces for young people's participation?', in S. Pickard, C. Nativel and F. Portier-LeCoqc (eds) *Les Politiques de Jeunesse au Royaume-uni et en France: Désaffection, répression et accompagnement á la citoyenneté*, Paris: Presses de la Sorbonne Nouvelle, pp 201-19.

Milbourne, L. and Cushman, M. (2010) 'Challenges to trust in a changing third sector', European Management Studies Workshop on Trust, Madrid, January.

Milbourne, L. and Cushman, M. (2012) 'From the third sector to the Big Society: how changing UK government policies have eroded third sector trust', *Voluntas*, online first, 19 June.

Milbourne, L. and Murray, U. (2011) 'Negotiating interactions in state–voluntary sector relationships: competitive and collaborative agency in an experiential workshop', *Voluntas*, vol 22, no 1, pp 70-92.

Milbourne, L., Macrae, S. and Maguire, M. (2003) 'Collaborative solutions or new policy problems: exploring multi-agency partnerships in education and health work', *Journal of Education Policy*, vol 18, no 1, pp 19-35.

Mills, H. (2009) *Policy, purpose and pragmatism: Dilemmas for voluntary and community organisations working with black young people affected by crime*, London: Centre for Crime and Justice Studies, King's College London.

Mohan, J. (2011) *Mapping the Big Society: Perspectives from the Third Sector Research Centre*, TSRC Working Paper 62, Birmingham: Third Sector Research Centre, University of Birmingham.

Mohaupt, S. (2009) 'Review article: resilience and social exclusion', *Social Policy and Society*, vol 8, no 1, pp 63-71.

Montagné-Villette, S., Hardill, I. and Lebeau, B. (2011) 'Faith-based voluntary action: a case study of a French charity', *Social Policy and Society*, vol 10, no 3, pp 405-16.

Moran, R., Hutchison, R. and Cairns, B. (2009) '"Assuming the spirit of the whole": small and large organisations engaged in merger', paper presented to the 15th NCVO/VSSN Researching the Voluntary Sector Conference, University of Warwick, September, www.ivar.org. uk/publications/conference-papers/assuming-spirit-whole-small-and-large-organisations-engaged-merger

Morgan, G. (1988) *Images of organization*, London: Sage Publications.

Morris, A. (2009) *The limits of voluntarism: Charity and welfare from the New Deal through the great society*, Cambridge: Cambridge University Press.

Mosley, J. (2011) 'Institutionalization, privatization and political opportunity: what tactical choices reveal about the policy advocacy of human service nonprofits', *Voluntas*, vol 40, no 3, pp 435-57.

Moustakas, C. (1990) *Heuristic research: Design, methodology and applications*, London: Sage Publications.

Moxham, C. and Boaden, R. (2007) 'The impact of performance measurement in the voluntary sector: identification of contextual and processual factors', *International Journal of Operations and Production Management*, vol 27, no 8, pp 826-45.

Muehlberger, U. (2007) 'Hierarchical forms of outsourcing and the creation of dependency', *Organization Studies*, vol 28, no 5, pp 709-27.

Mulgan, G. (1998) 'Social exclusion: joined up solutions to joined up problems', in C. Oppenheim (ed) *An inclusive society*, London: Institute for Public Policy Research.

Mullins, D. (1999) 'Managing ambiguity: merger activity in non-profit housing', *Journal of Non-profit and Voluntary Sector Marketing*, vol 4, no 4, pp 349-64.

Mullins, D. (2010) *Housing scoping paper: Housing associations*, TSRC Working Paper 16, Birmingham: Third Sector Research Centre, University of Birmingham.

Mullins, D. and Riseborough, M. (2001) 'Non-profit housing agencies: "reading" and shaping the policy agenda', in M. Harris and C. Rochester (eds) *Voluntary organisations and social policy in Britain*, Basingstoke: Palgrave.

Muncie, J. (2009) *Youth and crime* (3rd edition), London: Sage Publications.

Murray, U. (2012) 'Local government and the meaning of publicness', in J. Manson (ed) *Public service on the brink*, Exeter: Imprint Academic, pp 41-66.

NAO (National Audit Office) (2007) *Local Area Agreements and the third sector: Public service delivery*, London: NAO.

NCIA (National Coalition for Independent Action) (2011) *Reports from NCIA assemblies*, www.independentaction.net/about-2/the-coalition-assembly/ncia-assembly-meeting-community-action/?utm_

NCIA (2012) 'Is dissent becoming de rigeur?', *National Coalition Independent Action, Newsletter 27*, May, www.independentaction.net/2012/05/24/outbreak-of-dissent-may-newsletter-out-now/

NCVO (National Council for Voluntary Organisations) (1997) *Consultation and report on contractual arrangements between local authorities and voluntary organisations as service providers: The experience of voluntary organisations nationally*, London: NCVO.

NCVO (2010) *UK civil society almanac 2009*, London: NCVO.

nef (new economics foundation) (2009) *Seven principles for measuring what matters*, London: nef.

Nevile, A. (2010) 'Drifting or holding firm? Public funding and the values of third sector organisations', *Policy & Politics*, vol 38, no 4, pp 531-46.

Newburn, T. (2012) 'Counterblast: young people and the August 2011 riots', *The Howard Journal of Criminal Justice*, vol 51, no 3, pp 331-5.

Newman, J. (2000) 'Beyond New Public Management? Modernizing public services', in J. Clarke, S. Gewirtz and E. McLaughlin (eds) *New managerialism, new welfare?*, London: Sage Publications.

Newman, J. and Clarke, J. (2009) *Publics, politics and power*, London: Sage Publications.

NYA (National Youth Agency) (2011) 'National Youth Agency response to Comprehensive Spending Review', *Children and Young People Now*, 10 September.

O'Brien, M. (2006) '"Promises, promises": the experience of the voluntary and community sector within the Liverpool Children's Fund', *Public Policy & Administration*, vol 21, no 4, pp 82-98.

Obholzer, A. (1994) 'Authority, power and leadership: contributions from group relations training', in A. Obholzer and V.Z. Roberts (eds) *The unconscious at work*, London: Routledge.

OCS (Office for Civil Society) (2010) *Supporting a stronger civil society: An Office for Civil Society consultation on improving support for frontline civil society organisations*, London: OCS, Cabinet Office.

OCVA (Oxford Community and Voluntary Action) (2008) *The tender subject of tendering: Research into the effects of competitive tendering of the service delivery voluntary sector in Oxfordshire*, Oxford: OCVA.

ONS (Office for National Statistics) (2009) *Understanding patterns of deprivation*, London: ONS with Department for Communities and Local Government.

Onyx, J., Armitage, L., Dalton, B., Melville, R., Casey, J. and Banks, J. (2010) 'Advocacy with gloves on: the "manners" of strategy used by some third sector organizations undertaking advocacy in NSW and Queensland', *Voluntas*, vol 21, no 1, pp 41-61.

OTS (Office of the Third Sector) (2006) *The future role of the third sector in social and economic regeneration: Interim report*, London: OTS, Cabinet Office.

OTS (2007) *The future role of the third sector in social and economic regeneration*, London: OTS, Cabinet Office, www.cabinetoffice.gov. uk/thirdsector

Owen, D. (1964) *English philanthropy 1660-1960*, Cambridge, MA: Harvard University Press.

Packwood, D. (2007) *Commissioning, contracting and service delivery of children's services in the voluntary and community sector*, London: VCS Engage.

Paton, R. (2009) '(Towards) a sedimentary theory of the third sector', paper presented to the NCVO/VSSN research conference, Warwick University, September.

Peters, T. (1993) *Liberation management*, New York, NY: Knopf.

Pfeffer, J. (2003) *The external control of organizations*, Stanford, CA: Stanford University Press.

Phillips, R. (2006) 'The role of nonprofit advocacy organizations in Australian democracy and policy governance', *Voluntas*, vol 17, no 1, pp 59-75.

Piachaud, D. (2002) *Capital and the determinants of poverty and social exclusion*, CASEpaper 60, London: Centre for Analysis of Social Exclusion.

Plummer, J. (2010) 'Our independence is under threat, claim Age Concerns', *Third Sector online*, vol 30, April, www.thirdsector. co.uk/news/archive/1000669/independence-threat-claim-Age-Concerns/?DCMP=ILC-SEARCH

Pollitt, C. (1993) *Managerialism and the public services*, Oxford: Blackwell.

Powell, M. and Dowling, B. (2006) 'New Labour's partnerships: comparing conceptual models with existing forms', *Social Policy and Society*, vol 5, no 2, pp 305-14.

Power, M. (1994) *The audit explosion*, London: Demos.

Power, M. (1997) *The audit society: Rituals of verification*, Oxford: Clarendon Press.

Power, M. (1999) *The audit society*, Oxford: Oxford University Press.

Prasad, R. (2011) 'Window of opportunity', *Society Guardian*, 4 May, p 5.

Price Waterhouse (2005) *Mapping local authority estates using the Index of Local Conditions*, London: Department of the Environment.

Prochaska, F. (1988) *The Voluntary Impulse,* London: Faber and Faber

Proulx, J.-B .and Denis-Savard, S. (2007) 'The government–third sector interface in Quebec', *Voluntas*, vol 18, no 3, pp 293-307.

Punch, M. (1994) 'Politics and ethics in qualitative research', in N. Denzin and Y. Lincoln (eds) *Handbook of qualitative research*, Thousand Oaks, CA: Sage Publications.

Richardson, L. (2008) *DIY community action: Neighbourhood problems and community self-help*, Bristol: Policy Press.

Rochester, C. (2001) 'Regulation: the impact on local voluntary action', in M. Harris and C. Rochester (eds) *Voluntary organisations and social policy in Britain*, Basingstoke: Palgrave, pp 171-84.

Rochester, C. and Torry, M. (2010) 'Faith-based organizations and hybridity: a special case?', in D. Billis (ed) *Hybrid organizations and the third sector*, London: Palgrave Macmillan, pp 114-33.

Rochester, C., Ellis-Paine, A. and Howlett, S. (2010) *Volunteering in the 21st century*, Basingstoke: Palgrave Macmillan.

Root, M. (1993) *Philosophy of social science: The methods, ideals and politics of social inquiry*, Oxford: Blackwell.

Rose, N. (1999) *Powers of freedom, reframing political thought*, Cambridge: Cambridge University Press.

Rowntree, J. (1901) *Poverty: A Study of Town Life,* (1922 ed.), London: Longmans

Rummery, K. (2006) 'Introduction: themed section: partnerships, governance and citizenship', *Social Policy and Society*, vol 5, no 2, pp 223-5.

Rustin, M. (2004) 'Rethinking audit and inspection', *Soundings*, March, pp 86-107.

Sage, D. (2012) 'Fair conditions and fair consequences? Exploring New Labour, welfare contractualism and social attitudes', *Social Policy and Society*, vol 11, no 3, pp 359-73.

Salamon, L. (2003) *The resilient sector: The state of nonprofit America*, Washington, DC: Brookings Press.

Salamon, L. and Anheier, H. (1997) *Defining the non profit sector: A cross-national analysis*, Manchester: Manchester University Press.

Sanders, M. (2012) 'Getting rich on the NHS', *Dispatches*, Channel 4 report, 29 October, www.channel4.com/programmes/dispatches/articles/getting-rich-on-the-nhs-reporter-feature

Schwabenland, C. (2006) *Stories, visions and values in voluntary organisations*, Farnham: Ashgate.

Scott, D. and Russell, L. (2001) 'Contracting: the experience of service delivery agencies', in M. Harris and C. Rochester (eds) *Voluntary organisations and social policy in Britain*, Basingstoke: Palgrave, pp 49-63.

Scott, D., Alcock, P., Russell, L. and Macmillan, R. (2000) *Moving pictures: Realities of voluntary action*, Bristol and York: Policy Press and Joseph Rowntree Foundation

Scott, M. (2009) *CSC response to TSRC paper: Exploring below the radar*, Working Paper, Community Sector Coalition.

Seale, C. (2004) *Researching society and culture*, London: Sage Publications.

Seccombe, K. (2002) '"Beating the odds" versus "changing the odds": poverty, resilience and family policy', *Journal of Marriage and Family*, vol 64, no 2, pp 384-94.

Sennett, R. (2005) *The culture of the new capitalism*, New Haven, CT: Yale University Press.

Sennett, R. (2012) *Together: The rituals, pleasures and politics of cooperation*, New Haven, CT : Yale University Press.

SEU (Social Exclusion Unit) (1999) *Bridging the Gap: New Opportunities for 16-18 Year Olds Not in Education, Employment or Training*, Cm 4405, London: SEU.

SEU (Social Exclusion Unit) (2001) *Preventing social exclusion*, London: SEU.

Shaw, S. and Allen, J.B. (2006) '"We actually trust the community": examining the dynamics of a non-profit funding relationship in New Zealand', *Voluntas*, vol 17, no 2, pp 211-20.

Shotton, J. (1993) *No master high or low*, Bristol: Libertarian Education.

Simmons, L. (2008) *Contracts, cuts and closures: An uncertain future for SW social purpose organisations*, Exeter: SW Forum.

Skocpol, T. (2003) *Diminished democracy: From membership to management in American civic life*, Norman, OK: University of Oklahoma Press.

Slocock C. (2012) *The Big Society audit 2012*, London: Civil Exchange.

Small, S. and Memmo, S. (2004) 'Contemporary models of youth development and problem prevention', *Family Relations*, vol 53, no 1, pp 3-11.

Smerdon, M. (2009) *The first principle of voluntary action: Essays on the independence of the voluntary sector from government*, London: Baring Foundation.

Smith, J. and Deemer, D. (2000) 'The problem of criteria in the age of relativism', in N. Denzin and Y. Lincoln (eds) *Handbook of qualitative research*, Thousand Oaks, CA: Sage Publications.

Smith, S.R. and Pekkanen, R. (2012) 'Revisiting advocacy by non-profit organisations', *Voluntary Sector Review*, vol 3, no 1, pp 35-50.

Snape, S. and Taylor, P. (2004) *Partnerships between health and local government*, London: Frank Cass.

Sobeck, J., Agius, E. and Mayers, V. (2007) 'Supporting and sustaining grassroots youth organizations: the case of New Detroit', *Voluntas*, vol 18, no 1, pp 17-33.

Sparkes, A. (1989) 'Paradigmatic confusions and the evasion of critical issues in naturalistic research', *Journal of Teaching in Physical Education*, vol 8, pp 131-51.

Stacey, R. and Griffin, D. (2005) *A complexity perspective on researching organisations*, London: Routledge.

Stake, R. (2000) 'Case studies', in N. Denzin and Y. Lincoln (eds) *Handbook of qualitative research*, Thousand Oaks, CA: Sage Publications.

Strauss, A. and Corbin, J. (1990) *Basics of qualitative research: Grounded theory techniques and procedures*, Thousand Oaks, CA: Sage Publications.

Strauss, A. and Corbin, J. (1998) *Basics of qualitative research: Techniques and procedures for developing grounded theory*, Thousand Oaks, CA: Sage Publications.

Suchman, M. (1995) 'Managing legitimacy: strategic and institutional approaches', *The Academy of management Review*, vol 20, no 3, pp 571-610.

Swanepoel, H. and Beer, F. (1995) 'Training of racially mixed groups in South Africa', *Community Development Journal*, vol 30, no 3, pp 296-303.

Tanner, S. (2007) *Common themes on commissioning the VCS in selected local authorities in Greater London*, London: London Councils Association.

Taylor, M. (1995) 'Voluntary action and the state', in D. Gladstone (ed) *British social welfare: Past, present and future*, London: UCL Press.

Taylor, M. (2001) 'Partnership: insiders and outsiders', in M. Harris and C. Rochester (eds) *Voluntary organisations and social policy in Britain*, Basingstoke: Palgrave.

Taylor, M. (2006) 'Communities in partnership: developing a strategic voice', *Social Policy and Society*, vol 5, no 2, pp 269-79.

Taylor, M. (2011a) *Public policy in the community* (2nd edition), Basingstoke: Palgrave Macmillan.

Taylor, M. (2011b) 'Community organising and the Big Society: is Saul Alinsky turning in his grave?', *Voluntary Sector Review*, vol 2, no 2, pp 257-65.

Taylor, M. and Kendall, J. (1996) 'History of the voluntary sector', in J. Kendall and M. Knapp (eds) *The voluntary sector in the UK*, Manchester: Manchester University Press, pp 28-60.

Taylor, M. and Lansley, J. (1992) 'Ideology and welfare in the UK: the implications for the voluntary sector', *Voluntas*, vol 3, no 2, pp 153-74.

Thaler, R. and Sunstein, C. (2008) *Nudge: Improving decisions about health, wealth and happiness*, London: Yale University Press.

Thompson, E.P. (1980) *The making of the English working class*, London: Penguin (first printed 1936).

Thompson, G.F. (2003) *Between hierarchies and markets: The logic and limits of network forms of organization*, Oxford: Oxford University Press.

Tisdall, K., Davis, J.M., Hill, M. and Prout, A. (2006) *Children, young people and social inclusion: Participation for what?*, Bristol: Policy Press.

Titmuss, R. (1974) *Social policy: An introduction*, London: Allen & Unwin.

Tomlinson, F. and Schwabenland, C. (2011) 'Enacting diversity in the third sector: a model of socially responsible organising?', paper presented to the Seventh International Critical Management Studies Conference, Naples, July.

Toynbee, P. (2011) 'Big society isn't new but the Tories are purging the past', *Society Guardian*, 23 May, p 5.

Toynbee, P. (2012) 'Anna's charity was bid candy: now it's bankrupt', *The Guardian*, 19 July, p 38.

Ungar, M. (2004) 'A constructionist discourse on resilience', *Youth and Society*, vol 35, no 3, pp 341-65.

UNISON (2000) *Best value and equalities*, London: UNISON.

Von Krogh, G., Roos, J. and Slocum, K. (1994) 'An essay on corporate epistemology', *Strategic Management Journal*, vol 15, pp 53-71.

Walgenbach, P. (2001) 'The production of distrust by means of producing trust', *Organization Studies*, vol 22, no 4, pp 693-714.

Walker, A. and Walker, C. (1997) *Britain divided: The growth of social exclusion in the 1980s and 1990s*, London: Child Poverty Action Group.

Weeks, M.R. and Feeny, D.F (2008) 'Outsourcing: from cost management to innovation and business value', *California Management Review*, vol 50, no 4, pp 127-46.

Weick, K. (1995) *Sensemaking in organizations*, Thousand Oaks, CA: Sage Publications.

Weick, K.E. (1993) 'The collapse of sensemaking in organizations: the Mann Gulch disaster', *Administrative Science Quarterly*, vol 38, no 4, pp 628-52.

Weisbrod,B. (1987) *The non-profit economy*, Cambridge, MA: Harvard University Press.

Wenger, E. (1999) *Communities of practice: Learning, meaning and identity*, Cambridge: Cambridge University Press.

Whitty, G. (2001) 'Education, social class and social exclusion', *Journal of Education Policy*, vol 16, no 4, pp 287-95.

Whyte, W.F. (1991) *Participatory action research*, Newbury Park, CA: Sage Publications.

Wilding, K. (2010) *Summary analysis of UK civil society almanac*, London: National Council for Voluntary Organisations.

Willcocks, L.P. and Craig, A.S. (2009) *Step-change: Collaborating to innovate*, Reading: Logica and London School of Economics and Political Science.

Willetts, D. (2008) *Renewing civic conservatism*, The Oakeshott Lecture, London: London School of Economics and Political Science.

Williams, N., Lindsey, E., Kurtz, P. and Jarvis, S. (2001) 'From trauma to resiliency: lessons from former runaway and homeless youth', *Journal of Youth Studies*, vol 4, no 2, pp 233-53.

Williams, R. (2011) 'Teens are left to their own devices as council axes all youth services', *Society Guardian*, 24 August, p 36.

Wolch, J. (1990) *The shadow state: Government and voluntary sector in transition*, New York, NY: The Foundation Center.

Wolcott, H. (1994) *Transforming qualitative data: Description, analysis and interpretation*, Thousand Oaks, CA: Sage Publications.

Wolfenden, J. (1978) *The future of voluntary organisations: Report of the Wolfenden Committee*, London: Croom Helm.

Wright, N. (1989) *Assessing radical education*, Milton Keynes: Open University Press.

Wynne, A. (2008) *Support for success: Commissioning and contracting in Greater Manchester*, Manchester: GMVSS Consortium.

Yanow, D. (2003) 'Accessing local knowledge', in M. Hajer and H. Wagenaar (eds) *Deliberative policy analysis: Understanding governance in the network society*, Cambridge: Cambridge University Press, pp 228-46.

Yin, R. (1994) *Case study research: Design and methods*, Thousand Oaks, CA: Sage Publications.

Yong, E., Liu, G. and Sekhon, Y. (2010) 'Institutional perspective on alliance partners and knowledge exchange among non-profit organizations: a road to commercialisation', paper presented to the 5th Workshop on Trust within and between Organizations, Madrid, January.

Zimmeck, M. (2010) 'The compact 10 years on: government's approach to partnership with the voluntary and community sector in England', *Voluntary Sector Review*, vol 1, no 1, pp 125-33.

Index